The Illusion of Control

The Illusion of Control

Why Financial Crises
Happen, and What We Can
(and Can't) Do about It

Jón Daníelsson

Yale UNIVERSITY PRESS
New Haven & London

Published with assistance from the Louis Stern Memorial Fund.

Yale University Press books may be purchased in quantity for educational, business, or promotional use. For information, please e-mail sales.press@yale .edu (U.S. office) or sales@yaleup.co.uk (U.K. office).

Set in Galliard type by Newgen North America.
Printed in the United States of America.

Library of Congress Control Number: 2021948855
ISBN 978-0-300-23481-7 (hardcover : alk. paper)

A catalogue record for this book is available from the British Library.

This paper meets the requirements of ANSI/NISO Z39.48-1992 (Permanence of Paper).

10 9 8 7 6 5 4 3 2 1

Contents

Acknowledgments   vii

1 Riding the Tiger   1

2 Systemic Risk   6

3 Groundhog Day   26

4 The Risk Panopticon   51

5 The Myth of the Riskometer   72

6 Ideas Matter: Risk and Uncertainty   94

7 Endogenous Risk   109

8 If You Can't Take the Risk, Change Riskometers   128

9 The Goldilocks Challenge   147

10 The Risk Theater   168

11 The Uniformity, Efficiency, and Stability Trilemma   189

12 All about BoB: Robots and the Future of Risk   205

13 The Path Not to Take   223

14 What to Do?   240

Notes   255

Bibliography   259

Index   267

Acknowledgments

Several friends and colleagues made invaluable contributions to the book. I borrowed many arguments from joint work with Charles Goodhart, Kevin James, Robert Macrae, Andreas Uthemann, Marcela Valenzuela, Ilknur Zer, and Jean-Pierre Zigrand.

I had the privilege of consulting several experts, including Peter Andrews, formerly of the FCA, Jon Frost at the Bank for International Settlements, risk system expert Rupert Goodwin, fund manager Jacqueline Li, Eric Morrison from the FCA, physicist Donal O'Connell, and three lawyers: Gestur Jonsson, Hafliði Kristján Lárusson, and Eva Micheler.

I was fortunate to employ several excellent London School of Economics (LSE) students to assist me on background research for the book: Sophia Chang, Jia Rong Fan, and Morgane Fouche. Our manager at the Systemic Risk Centre, Ann Law, was very helpful in getting the book under way. The many drawings in the book were made by two excellent artists, Lukas Bischoff and Ricardo Galvao.

Without all of these people, this book would not have seen the light of day.

I am grateful to the Economic and Social Research Council (UK), grant number: ES/K002309/1 and ES/R009724/1, and the Engineering and Physical Sciences Research Council (UK), grant number EP/P031730/1, for their support.

The Illusion of Control

1

Riding the Tiger

The man who didn't trust the models saved the world.

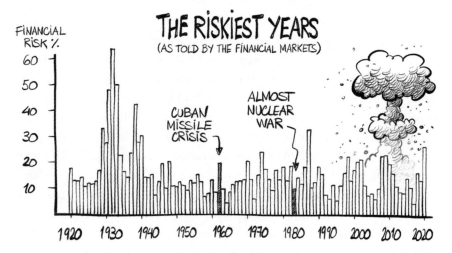

Figure 1. Credit: Copyright © Ricardo Galvão.

Almost every economic outcome we care about is long term. Pensions, the environment, crises, real estate, education, you name it, what matters is what happens years and decades hence. Day-to-day fluctuations don't matter to most of us—the short run isn't very important. So it stands to reason that the way we manage our financial lives should emphasize the long run. But by and large, it doesn't. We are good at managing today's risk but at the expense of ignoring the promises and threats of the future. That is the illusion of control.

A quick test. What do you think are the riskiest years of the past century? Covid in 2020? The global crisis in 2008? The Great Depression in the 1930s? Let's ask the financial markets and their go-to measurement of risk, volatility. The accompanying drawing depicts the annual stock market risk in the United States, and it confirms the usual suspects (Figure 1).

But these are not the riskiest years by a long shot. In 1962 and 1983 we were almost hit by the ultimate tail event, even though the financial markets remained calm. The Cuban missile crisis nearly brought the United States and the Soviet Union to blows in 1962, only for the Soviets to back down at the last minute. Even more interesting is 1983 because that is when we almost got into a nuclear war, even if we didn't know that until much later.

What happened was that the premier of the Soviet Union, Yuri Andropov, got it in his head that the United States was planning to launch a preemptive nuclear strike. He instructed his spies to find evidence supporting his suspicion, and KGB agents everywhere went into overdrive, looking for that evidence. Careers depended on it. If you have a choice of a juicy posting in Washington or being literally sent to Siberia (as the KGB rep in Novosibirsk) of course you find proof. A prime example of confirmation bias. We believe something terrible will happen and find grounds to support that, even if there is no truth to it. In 1983 the early warning models of the Soviet Union detected a nuclear attack. The man on watch that night, Stanislav Petrov, didn't trust the signal and decided unilaterally not to launch a counterattack. The man who didn't trust the models saved the world. The Soviet investigators subsequently confirmed he was right. The false alarm came about because of a rare alignment of sunlight on high-altitude clouds above North Dakota and the Molniya orbits of the detection satellites. Colonel Petrov died in 2017, by that time globally recognized for having saved humanity.

The way we measure financial risk today, with what I call the riskometer, has much in common with Andropov's early warning systems. Both rely on imperfect models and inaccurate measurements to make crucial decisions. While high-altitude clouds bedeviled the Soviet's models, the problem for today's riskometer arises from its emphasis on the recent past and short-term risk. The reason is simple. That is the easiest risk to measure, as the modelers have plenty of data.

The problem is that short-term risk isn't all that important, not for investors and especially not for the financial authorities. For them, what matters is systemic risk, the chance of spectacular financial crises, like the one we suffered in 2008. Long-term threats, like systemic crises or our retirement not being as comfortable as hoped for, are easy to under-stand, at least conceptually. Take crises. Banks have too much money and can't find productive investments, so they start lending to increasingly low-quality borrowers, often in real estate. In the beginning it looks like magic. Money flows in, developers build houses, and everybody feels rich, encouraging more lending and more building in a happy, virtuous cycle. Then it all comes crashing down.

What are we to do? Regulation, of course, using the Panopticon. An idea dating to the eighteenth-century English philosopher Jeremy Bentham, who proposed regulating society by setting up posts to observe human activity. Does it work? In traffic certainly. If no police or cameras monitor speeding, I suspect many will be tempted to drive too fast. The chance of getting caught keeps the roads relatively safe. Surely we can also employ the Panopticon to regulate finance and so prevent crises and all the horrible losses. We do use it, but it doesn't work all that well. The reason has to do with the interplay of two complex topics, the difficulty of measuring risk and human ingenuity.

Unlike temperature or prices, risk cannot be directly observed. Instead, it has to be inferred by how prices have moved in the past. That requires a model. And as the statistician George Box had it, "All models are wrong, but some are useful."[1] There are many models for measuring risk, they all disagree with each other, and there is no obvious way to tell which is the most accurate. Even then, all the riskometers capture is the short term because that is where the data is.

And then we have human behavior. Hyman Minsky observed forty years ago that stability is destabilizing. If we think the world is safe, we want to take on more risk, which eventually creates its own instability. And since the time between decisions and bad things happening can be years or decades, it is hard to control risk. As my coauthor Charles Good-hart put it, "Any observed statistical regularity will tend to collapse once pressure is placed upon it for control purposes."[2] What Goodhart's law tells us is that when the risk managers start controlling risk, we tend to react in a way that makes the risk measurements incorrect.

I have been working on the human dimension to risk for some time and, along with coauthors, have come up with a helpful classification scheme: exogenous and endogenous risk. Endogenous risk captures what results from the interactions of the human beings that make up the financial system. The opposite of endogenous is exogenous. When an asteroid hit the Gulf of Mexico sixty-five million years ago, wiping out the dinosaurs, that was an exogenous shock. The dinosaurs certainly did nothing to cause their demise.

By viewing the financial system through the lens of endogenous risk we learn quite a bit about what works and what doesn't, often in surprising ways. At the root of many a financial crisis and large losses is a vicious feedback between well-meaning rules and the self-preservation instincts of market participants. But as such forces of fragility only show themselves at the worst possible moment, we don't know how dangerous they are until it's too late. It is difficult, to the point of impossible, to measure endogenous risk. Why? Because all the riskometers can capture is the less important exogenous risk. And that, in turn, explains why it is so easy to manipulate risk measurements. Suppose my job is to manage the risk of some portfolio. One day my boss calls me into her office: "Jón, risk is too high, and you have to make it lower. However, our traders are doing a fantastic job, and I want to keep the nice returns. Now go and play with your computers and make it happen. And ~~don't get caught~~ make sure you comply with all regulations." Easy. The UBS bank went bankrupt in 2008 because it deliberately chose to measure risk incorrectly, a common problem in that crisis. The banks are good at manipulating the riskometers, thinking they are fooling the regulators, but, at the end of the day, they're just deceiving themselves.

Endogenous risk is at the heart of the Goldilocks challenge facing the financial authorities. We want financial regulations to be just right. Not too strict, so all economic activity is strangled. Not so relaxed that we get too many crises and lose all our money. We need a balance, and that is not easy. The regulators focus on what went wrong last time around, while the next crisis will happen in a completely different place. Precisely what happened in the years before 2008 when the central banks were concerned only with inflation, missing all the warning signs of the pending crisis. And the reaction to Covid-19 in 2020 was shaped by the lessons of 2008. Incorrectly, as the financial impact of the virus was very different. Regulation by the rearview mirror.

There are broader lessons from the dichotomy between exogenous and endogenous risk, and one is a particular fallacy of composition. The financial authorities aim to get the best out of the financial system by making all the financial institutions prudent, like Volvos, the world's safest car. Nobody makes crazy investments, and everybody follows the rules. Surely, then, investors will enjoy stable returns, banks won't fail, and financial crises will not happen. Will turning the banks into Volvos make us safe? No. It perversely makes crises even more likely, since it reduces the shock-absorbing capacity of the system.

Is artificial intelligence, AI, the proper response to the challenges of endogenous risk? It depends. AI will increase efficiency, allowing us to eliminate a lot of tedious risk management and compliance jobs. Financial services will become cheaper and more reliable, and regulations will be better enforced. So what can go wrong? Imagine the Bank of England bot—BoB—is put in charge of financial stability. He talks to his counterparts in regulated banks, passing on information and enforcing compliance. It sounds like the perfect way to control the financial system. Except we have to trust BoB to make the right decisions. And, unlike humans, we don't know how he reasons and decides. So what will happen when BoB runs into some problem he has never seen before? A human being can draw on their accumulated experience and the canon of human knowledge. AI will not be able to do that. Meanwhile, it is pretty easy for hostile agents to take advantage of BoB. He has to look everywhere. A hostile agent—some trader or terrorist or nation state or criminal—only has to find one weakness to exploit. And they can do that in complete secrecy until it is too late for BoB to do anything about it. BoB cannot win regardless of the state of technology.

These observations all sound a bit pessimistic, but that is not the impression I want to leave. The financial system is highly resilient and by and large does a good job—most public comments to the contrary. However, the way we deal with the system today takes us in the wrong direction. So, what to do? Embrace diversity, the most potent force of financial stability and good investment performance. The more different the financial institutions that make up the system are and the more the authorities embrace that very diversity, the more stable the system becomes and the better it performs. To the benefit of us all. What gets in the way is self-interest and politics. The decision makers are antidiversity, preferring uniform ways of doing business to protect their profits and jobs. All that is needed is political will.

2

Systemic Risk

The financial crisis was a pest epidemic, spreading with raging speed from house to house.
—*Stephan Skalweit*

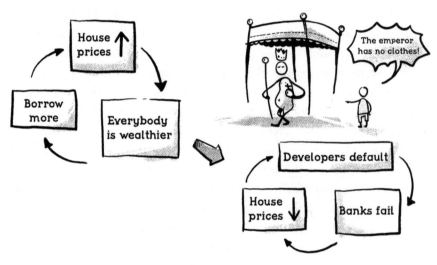

Figure 2. Credit: Lukas Bischoff/IllustrationX.

Leendert Pieter de Neufville was only twenty-one in 1751 when he founded his Amsterdam bank, De Neufville Brothers. His big chance came a few years later with the Seven Years' War, what Americans call the French and Indian War. Amsterdam was then the most sophisticated financial center in the world, leading in financial innovation and having the most creative bankers and the highest amount of speculative capital. The Dutch guilder was the US dollar of its day, the reserve currency that facilitated trade throughout Europe and beyond. Leendert took full advantage, building up one of the world's wealthiest and most prestigious banks by financing the Prussian side of the war. He lived well, furnishing his house only with the finest-quality objects and owning an excellent collection of paintings—but not a single book.

The way he made his money was thoroughly modern: rapid, irresponsible financial innovation in the form of acceptance loans, not all that different from the financial instruments so damaging in the 2008 crisis. Cheap short-term borrowing was used to make long-term loans at high interest rates, involving long chains of obligations, spanning multiple banks and countries.

The key to all the profit was borrowed money. For every twenty-three guilders he lent to Prussia, De Neufville supplied one and borrowed twenty-two, secured by commodities. Highly profitable in good times, but it didn't take much for things to go wrong, as they did, spectacularly, when the war ended in 1763, culminating in the first modern financial crisis.[1] Commodity prices crashed when the war ended because the farmers could now finally start producing again, making all the commodity-based collateral behind De Neufville's acceptance loans worth little. Investors got spooked and decided not to roll over these short-term loans—they all went on strike, just like their successors in 2007. As De Neufville didn't have enough ready cash to repay his creditors and keep his bank alive, he had to sell his vast holdings of commodities. However, that only caused prices to fall further, a process known as a fire sale. Falling prices induce speculators to sell, and when they sell, prices fall further, in a vicious loop. It did not take long for De Neufville to default.

Thus was born the first global systemic crisis, described at the time as a pest epidemic. It spread with raging speed from house to house. The city of Hamburg was hit hard, and on 4 August its mayor wrote to the mayor of Amsterdam asking him to bail out De Neufville. Amsterdam refused. Fortunately, the crisis turned out to be relatively short-lived, and Amsterdam, Hamburg, and the other major centers recovered quickly. Berlin suffered badly because of how its emperor, Friedrich II, reacted. He imposed a payment standstill and bailouts, violating the contracts that allowed funds to flow from Amsterdam to Berlin and causing the bankers to mistrust the Prussian authorities. The money stopped flowing, and a severe recession ensued. Not the only time a government's response to a crisis made things worse.

The 1763 crisis is what might now be classified as a V-shaped crisis, except for Berlin, which suffered a U crisis. In a V crisis we see a sharp temporary drop in economic activity, but as nothing fundamental is destroyed the recovery is similarly quick. The Asian crisis in 1998 was also of the V variety while the Great Depression and the 2008 crises, given their sharp crash and slow recovery, were U shaped. What about Covid-19? The jury is still out, but it seems closer to K, quick winners and losers.

De Neufville's creditors tried to claw their money back but with limited success. He was forced to auction off some of his paintings in 1765, including *The Milkmaid* by Johannes Vermeer for 560 guilders, now one of the finest attractions of the Rijksmuseum in Amsterdam. Leendert managed to retain most of his houses, including one at Herengracht 70–72 in Amsterdam, a very desirable address then as now.

What happened in 1763 was a systemic financial crisis, and the chance of that happening is systemic financial risk. For the remainder of the book I will omit the word "financial" and just call it systemic risk. Seventeen sixty-three was the first modern global financial crisis because it was not a crisis caused by war or crop failure but rather by shadow banking and the extensive use of sophisticated financial instruments allowing risk to hide and spread by efficient and interconnected financial centers. We have experienced many systemic crises since, and it is remarkable how similar they all are. Even though the world in 1763 was very different from that in 2008, the crisis dynamics were eerily similar: shadow banking creating deep vulnerabilities that became visible only when it was too late. Crises are all fundamentally the same. They differ only in details.

My definition of systemic risk is the chance that the financial system will fail spectacularly in doing what it is supposed to. The global authorities, in the form of the International Monetary Fund, the Bank for International Settlements, and the Financial Stability Board, prefer a narrower definition: "The disruption to the flow of financial services that is (i) caused by an impairment of all or parts of the financial system; and (ii) has the potential to have serious negative consequences for the real economy."[2] The key here is the two words "financial system." It has to be either the root cause or the amplifier for a crisis to be called systemic. Since the financial system is so fundamental to the economy, most economic crises are also systemic crises. What about Covid-19? It certainly hit the economy, shaving 10 percent to 20 percent off most countries' GDP in the second quarter of 2020. But the financial system was a bystander, not the cause, and it made things neither better nor worse. The Covid-19 crisis was not systemic.

The focus of systemic risk is not on any individual financial institution; instead, it is on the financial system in its entirety and how it affects the real economy. The failure of a bank, or even a banking crisis, is not necessarily systemic. We need a connection between the financial system and the real economy.

Systemic crises are costly, easily 10 percent of GDP or more, so for the United States in the trillions of dollars. Fortunately, they are not frequent, and I think most people can expect to suffer such a crisis at most once in their lifetime. If one takes the relatively loose definition used in the IMF crises database, then maintained by Luc Laeven and Fabián Valencia, we find that the typical OECD country suffers a systemic crisis once in forty-three years on average. While the one in forty-three years is the historical average, it is hotly debated whether the future will be as tranquil. A lot of commentators maintain that increased complexity and interconnectedness make financial crises more frequent. The United States, and especially the United Kingdom, are more crisis prone, the UK enduring a systemic crisis once every seventeen years. The last one was in 2008, so 2025 is the due date for the next one if it arrives on schedule. If anything, the once-in-forty-three-years figure is an overestimate, as the database includes relatively nonextreme events like Black Monday in October 1987 and the Long Term Capital Management crisis in 1998. If we exclude all the mildest crises, we get about one systemic crisis per typical lifetime.

The reason for the once-in-a-lifetime frequency is that the most severe crises happen only after we forget the last one. Crises change behavior, and those who come of age during one will be affected by it for the rest of their lives. We had to wait for the twenty-year-olds of 1929 to retire in the 1970s for the seeds of the next crisis to be sown. It then took a quarter-century for the seeds to bear fruit, culminating in the events of autumn 2008. Politics and lobbying push toward a high-risk, high-return financial system, and when memories of the previous crisis fade there is little pushback.

Considering the once-in-a-lifetime frequency of systemic crises, the term "systemic crisis" is as overused today as it was underused before 2008. Most of this usage is imprecise and contradictory, and one often gets the impression that commentators are talking only about the last crisis or financial scandal when they use the phrase "systemic crisis."

The financial system is vulnerable to many types of shocks, some coming from outside the financial system, like Covid-19, and others generated by the system itself. Some shocks are idiosyncratic, affecting only a single institution or asset, while others impact the financial system as a whole plus the real economy. The small shocks often arrive from outside the system; all the large ones are created by the interaction of the human beings who make up the financial system. There may be an outside trigger, but the real damage is caused by the system turning on itself.

If I had to describe a textbook financial crisis, it would go something like this: Financial institutions have too much money to lend. When they run out of high-quality borrowers, they start making increasingly low-quality loans, often in real estate. In the beginning it all looks ingenious. Developers borrow money to build new houses, which stimulates prosperity and demand for homes. Property prices go up. Everybody feels wealthier and more optimistic, thereby encouraging more lending and more building in a happy, virtuous cycle. This caused many a crisis, like the savings-and-loan debacle in the United States in the 1980s and the Spanish crisis in 2010.

Eventually, when the little boy yells, "The Emperor has no clothes!" people realize that all the prosperity was built on sand (Figure 2).[3] There is no strong underlying economy, and it all comes crashing to the ground; the virtuous feedback loop becomes vicious. Prices fall, developers fail, the banks lose money, the economy contracts, prices fall more—the same fire sale process De Neufville endured. The precrisis rise in prices is much slower than the fall: prices go up the escalator and down the lift (or elevator if in America).

Most crises follow the textbook. The one in 1914 was atypical, which is why it is my favorite. It was triggered by the assassination of Archduke Franz Ferdinand of Austria on 28 June 1914, leading to posturing among the great powers of Europe amid raised expectations of an impending war. This anticipation created worries that financial institutions would experience difficulties in having cross-border loans repaid—after all, if two countries are at war enforcing contracts across borders would naturally be difficult. Surprisingly, even after the war started, remittance between the Central Powers and the Allies continued via neutral countries, notably Switzerland, which helped propel it into the ranks of major financial centers.

The immediate consequence of the assassination of the archduke was difficulty in clearing trades. When one buys and sells stocks, it takes time for ownership to be transferred to the buyer and money to the seller, a process called clearing. In 1914 clearing took two or three weeks, and if one was buying stocks across borders, the securities were sent one way and the money the other way by post. Given all the modern databases and fast computers today, one might think clearing nowadays is instantaneous. But even now clearing can take days and even weeks. Slow clearing was at the heart of the Gamestop and Robinhood crisis and conspiracy theories in January 2021.

Any disruption to the clearing process is costly. Suppose you sell Google stock. You are legally required to deliver the Google stock and you have a legal right to receive cash at the same time, that is, the trade clears. If all you are doing is selling Google, a short-term disruption to the trading process might not be that problematic. However, most people have plans for the money they received from the sale. Perhaps you want to use it to buy Microsoft, and to pay for it you need the money from selling Google. If, for some reason, you don't receive that money, you may default on the obligation to pay for Microsoft, even if you acted prudently and in good faith.

The 1914 crisis first affected the stock exchanges in Berlin, Paris, and Vienna. To protect their local banks the authorities in those cities decided to suspend the clearing process, giving the dust time to settle. If everybody is trading locally that should not be a huge problem; at least nobody defaults because they cannot deliver cash. However, it is problematic if London remains open when Paris is closed. London-based banks send cash and securities to banks in Paris, but the reciprocate does not happen. One might think this is an issue only for the sophisticated London banks doing business with the continent. Not so. The interconnectedness of the financial system meant that everybody was vulnerable. Even banks that thought they were sensible, like conservative rural banks trading only with major London banks and judiciously avoiding taking on too much risk, were nevertheless immediately affected.

First, those dealing with the continent got into difficulty, as they had to deliver to the continental trading partners but did not receive cash from their European counterparts. Then their business partners got into trouble, and in short order those dealing with them faced difficulty. In the financial system everybody is exposed to everybody, whether they like it or not. We might think we are prudent by not doing business with those who like a lot of risk. However, if the people we are dealing with are exposed to risk, so are we.

A good example of the network effect, why financial crises are often said to be like a contagious disease, is as follows. Patient Zero infects the people around her, who in turn infect the people around them, and in short order everybody is sick. Similarly, the vulnerability quickly spreads from Bank Zero to all the other banks. The financial system is vulnerable not only because of risk but also—and even more so—because of how everybody is connected to everybody else.

London was at the center of the network in 1914, a place it had by then already occupied for a century and a half, after eclipsing Amsterdam. Made in 1774, a drawing shows the network system of the European financial system, with London in the center (Figure 3). We have been making network diagrams ever since, and after the crisis in 2008 the creation of network diagrams became a veritable industry. Such diagrams never made much sense to me, as all they show is that everybody is connected to everybody else, which we know anyway. The players change, but the network is always there, the source of simultaneous danger and prosperity. The network makes the economy efficient, creating wealth, good jobs, and ample cheap goods, but it also transmits crises, both financial and medical. The plague in the 1300s was transmitted by trading networks, just as Covid-19 was in 2020.

If the 1914 crisis had been purely financial, nobody would really have cared besides a handful of people involved with the financial system. But it never is. The financial system directs resources for the real economy, and if it is not doing its job companies can't borrow and invest. They can't

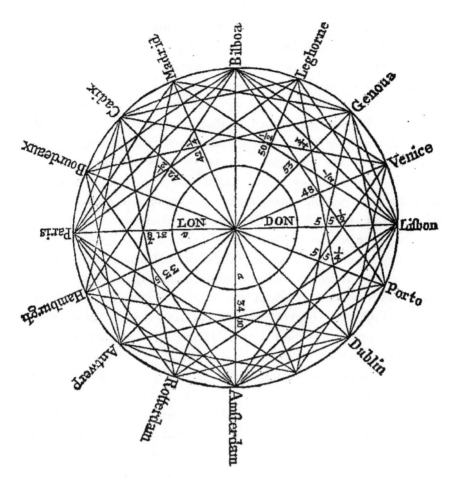

Figure 3. The financial system network in 1774. Source: M. Postlethwayt, *The Universal Dictionary of Trade and Commerce,* 4th ed. (London, 1774), vol 1. Arbitrage.

pay suppliers and salaries, the very essence of a systemic crisis. Economic activity grinds to a halt, and everybody suffers. That is the reason finance is so heavily scrutinized and regulated, and why the banks always get these obnoxious bailouts when they misbehave.

Once under way, the 1914 crisis followed predictable patterns. Market participants became very cautious, wanting the safest asset: gold. Banks deposited their excess funds to the safety of the Bank of England instead of lending them out, so that the crisis quickly spread from the City of

London to the real economy as commercial credit evaporated. In the beginning the Bank of England and the leading financial institutions in the City of London tried to sort it out by themselves. However, things got worse, and it ultimately became the Treasury that made the most critical decisions. It is always like that. A serious crisis response needs the legitimacy of the political leadership, something an institution like the Bank of England, led by nonelected bureaucrats, simply cannot deliver.

Finally, both London's and New York's stock exchanges closed on 31 July and remained closed until January 1915. Why would one want to close the stock exchange? To prevent a vicious mark-to-market feedback loop. A company is solvent if the value of its assets exceeds the value of its debt. If the price of its assets falls, the company may find itself in difficulty or even insolvency because debt does not fall along with the value of the assets. To protect itself, the company may then sell its holdings. That, however, makes prices fall even more, putting even more companies into difficulty, who will then also sell, and a vicious mark-to-market feedback loop is born. Soon everybody seems to be moving in lockstep, doing exactly the same thing, all selling and all buying the same assets. The resulting extreme volatility is the outward manifestation of a crisis in the making.

When the stock exchange closed, prices froze and the feedback loop was halted. Provided confidence has recovered by the time the market reopens, a crisis is averted. The same thinking is behind the circuit breakers on modern exchanges, which, if prices fall too much, halt trading to give market participants time to make sense of what is happening. The Chinese wanted to prevent the worst when they closed the Shanghai market on 24 January 2020 for six trading days when its Covid-19 crisis broke out. The closing might have prevented the appearance of excessive volatility, but the market still opened down 8 percent.

The 1914 crisis showed that it does not take all that much for panic to happen when confidence evaporates. The very same efficiency that was so beneficial before a shock is a curse after it amplifies the initial shock into something much worse. Even rumors that a large institution might fail could cause panic. In 1914 it was clear that some banks were heavily exposed to cross-border lending and would fail in case of war. That was enough to trigger the crisis. People did not need the actual event of a war to make this happen; the mere expectation of one was sufficient.

The financial authorities in 1914 did the right thing, effecting a massive intervention, saving the City of London from the worst and, along with it, the real economy. By comparison, events in the 2008 and Covid-19 crises were quite mild. However, the ultimate consequence for the City of London was severe. It was the most important financial center in the world in 1914, but by 1918 was eclipsed by New York, which still retains the crown.

There are two main ingredients in the typical crisis story: excessive leverage and an interconnected financial system; in other words, too much risk and a dangerous network structure. But we don't need extreme risk-taking for a crisis to happen. The 1914 crisis did not happen because of too much risk. No, instead, the forces of instability preyed on the very sophisticated financial system we depend on to give us efficient financial intermediation and leverage, helping the economy grow—but only in good times. That fantastic financial system also acts as the catalyst for financial crises. And that means it is all about politics.

It's the Politics, Stupid

When Bill Clinton was running for president in 1992, his campaign's unofficial theme was "It's the economy, stupid."[4] Indeed, the main reason he defeated George Bush Sr. was the economic recession of the previous year. Today, it is the other way around—when explaining the market, one might say, "It's the politics, stupid." Today's primary source of financial risk is not excessive risk-taking; it is quantitative easing and low interest rates, Brexit and Donald Trump and the South China Sea, Russia, Ukraine, Qatar, and Italy. The most severe financial crisis of the world today, that in Venezuela, is caused by politics. Politics strongly shape the reactions to Covid-19.

Government policies drive the financial markets. The financial markets react to central banks' interest rate decisions and quantitative easing. When Covid-19 hit in early 2020 and the financial markets came under stress, the central banks were expected to step up to the plate and save the market. Not surprisingly, many commentators question why we simultaneously permit all the excesses in the financial system and also allow it to exercise the Greenspan put every time something bad happens. The moniker "Greenspan put" is named after the former chairman of the Federal Reserve, Alan Greenspan, because every time the financial markets got the hiccups, the Federal Reserve was ready with a liquidity injection. If the Fed bails us out there is no reason to behave reasonably: profits are private, while losses are socialized. The consequence was that almost everybody was blind to the hidden risk being created before 2008; those times were even labeled the Great Moderation. The socialization of losses and privatization of profits continue to anger activists on the left and the right and is one of the main drivers of populism.

Governments can be a direct trigger of systemic risk, as in 1914. The leading cause of the European sovereign debt crisis in the 2010s was not bank misbehavior but government profligacy. The subprime mortgages that were so instrumental in the 2008 crisis were created because successive US governments wanted to encourage homeownership for its poorest and riskiest citizens. However, the link between today's politics and the instability of tomorrow is not clear except to a handful of people who closely monitor the relationship between the two. The very government policies that culminated in instability may have been launched with the best intentions, and their impact on systemic risk is often indirect and counterintuitive.

As a consequence, some commentators have made robust remarks on the origins of systemic risk. The late Fischer Black, of Black-Scholes[5] fame, stated, "When you hear the government talking about systemic risk, hold on to your wallet! It means that they want you to pay more taxes for more regulations, which are likely to create systemic risk by interfering with private contracting. . . . In sum, when you think about systemic risks, you'll be close to the truth if you think of the government as causing them rather than protecting us from them."[6]

Do the policy makers recognize that governments also cause systemic risk? No. A few years ago I was at a large central bank conference in a European capital discussing how the European authorities should respond to the European sovereign debt crisis, then raging. In the closing panel, leading policy makers debated what should be measured, controlled, and eliminated, all the standard things like excessive risk-taking, opaque financial instruments, and perverse incentives. In the Q&A session I asked the panel whether it was possible that the governments also caused systemic risk. The chairman of the panel shouted at me, "No, the governments are the solution, not the problem."

Systemic crises are serious. Hundreds of millions of people suffered in the Great Depression, driving the politics that caused World War II. People lost their jobs, their savings, and even their lives. Populism thrived. No wonder we would like to prevent them. The first lecture of my LSE course Global Financial Systems is about systemic risk. About twenty minutes into it I ask the students the following question: "Those of you who would want to live in a country without any systemic crises, please raise your hands." In a typical year about eighty out of one hundred students will do so. If I reverse the question and ask them if they want to live in a country with systemic crises, nobody raises their hands. If we were to ask most politicians, journalists, regulators, and pundits the same question, I suspect most would agree with the students.

It is straightforward to prevent systemic crises: both Cuba and North Korea manage it quite well. Get rid of the financial system, and voilà, no more systemic crises. Easy, but the costs are unacceptable. Who wants to live in Cuba or North Korea? We need the financial system to take risk. With risk comes failure, an essential part of a healthy economy; an economy without failures does not take enough risk and does not grow fast enough. While it is easy to regulate risk out of the financial system, it is not easy to do so without killing economic growth at the same time.

On the other hand, too many bankruptcies and crises are also a sign that something is wrong. The financial system could be too unstable, with excessive risk, perhaps too much corruption, or money channeled to unproductive uses for political reasons. There is a balance between having too many and too few crises. We need to encourage the financial industry to take enough risk so the economy grows while also preventing too much risk from causing systemic crises. A classic risk–return trade-off, and one that is not trivial.

Economic crises afflict poor, less developed countries more frequently and severely than their rich and more developed counterparts, not least because developing countries are more likely to suffer from bad economic management and volatile politics. They depend on a small number of exports, often commodities, and are hence vulnerable to the whims of the global markets. It is hard to raise money in these countries, as the wealthy export their capital, forcing governments and other borrowers to raise funds in foreign currency from global financial centers. No surprise that sovereign debt, foreign exchange, and general economic crises are endemic in less-developed countries.

It is not so with systemic risk: the very lack of development protects them. Countries with underdeveloped financial systems, where credit cards and bank accounts are rare and everybody uses cash, are mostly safe from systemic risk. If the banks in such a country fail, most people can shrug it off. If my bank in London fails today, my debit card stops working, so I can no longer buy lunch. All my money is tied up in my bank accounts, and if I no longer have access to them there is nothing I can buy. Not only will I starve to death, but all the vendors selling to me will also not get any business. In developed countries the safety of the banks is of primary importance. The more sophisticated the financial system becomes, the more vulnerable it is to disruptions. Systemic risk is the disease of the affluent.

We Had Forgotten History by 2008

Everybody thought we had solved the problem of crises by 2007. Why? Two reasons. The first is that systemic crises are quite rare, so nobody was worried. If you haven't experienced one in your lifetime, you will not expect one to be around the corner either. The second reason is hubris. The experts had come to believe that modern risk management systems and regulations were sophisticated and robust. Policy makers and academics and practitioners all thought crises were associated with less-developed economies, countries with Weak financial regulations, and plenty of corruption and abuse. The developed Western economies had found the magical way of preventing crises by combining efficient financial regulations and atomistic risk management. Hubris.

Atomistic risk management means that if we use sophisticated risk management techniques to manage all the small risks, they will not grow into big risks—voilà, crises are eliminated. That logic is fatally flawed. It is true that the whole of the financial system is made up of everything that's going on within it, all the way down to individual transactions. We can know all about the atoms that make up the human body and be experts in biology, but all that knowledge tells us nothing about what makes a person tick. It's the same in finance. We simply don't know how to add up all the individual micro risks to get the risk in a portfolio, bank, or the system. If we think we do, all we end up with is a false sense of safety.

We thought risk had magically disappeared by 2007 because all the micro risks were under control. What we missed was that all the sophisticated risk management techniques accomplished was to increase systemic risk. The reason is simple. The financial system is, for all practical purposes, infinitely complex, so no matter how intensively we study the system and how hard we try to control it, we still can focus only on a tiny part of it—systemic risk emerges precisely where we are not looking. Paradoxically, the sophisticated risk management techniques increased the complexity of the financial system, thereby creating new avenues for crises to emerge.

Take US subprime mortgages, an important contributor to the 2008 crisis. The value of American subprime mortgages was about $1.3 trillion in March 2007. In normal conditions only a fraction of those borrowers were likely to default. In a disaster scenario, if half the borrowers default and only half of the creditors' money were recovered, total losses would be $325 billion. While that figure sounds like a lot, it is quite small compared to the overall size of the American financial market. Right before the crisis in 2007 the outstanding volume of bonds in the United States was $32 trillion, or twice the GDP, while the total value of the stock market was $20 trillion, so a $325 billion loss is about 1.6 percent of the stock market. A loss of that magnitude on the US Standard and Poor's 500 index has happened on 1,274 days since 1929, or 5.5 percent of the time. The actual subprime losses turned out to be much smaller.

How can a worst-case potential subprime loss of $325 billion cause so much damage when the stock market can suffer losses of $325 billion multiple times without batting an eye? The reason is that stock market losses are visible and expected. The mortgage losses were opaque; the risk was hidden, and it caught almost everybody by surprise. I say almost because some did anticipate it, like the heroes of Michael Lewis's book *The Big Short*.

Two thousand eight was not the first time a financial crisis played out this way. Financial crises tend to be quite similar to each other, and the crises of 1763 and 1914 have plenty in common with 2008. Why then did 2008 happen? Hubris and forgotten history. While the policy makers of a hundred years ago were alive to the danger of systemic risk, their twenty-first-century counterparts assumed the problem away. I recall being in central bank conferences in the early 2000s and hearing most speakers argue that the central banks should focus only on inflation. Financial stability was not something the central banks should be concerned with because it is impure, sullying the pristine reputation of monetary policy, so crucial for price stability. Precisely why the financial authorities were caught by complete surprise in 2008. The Bank of England, deciding in the early 2000s that all that mattered to it was monetary policy, proceeded to close down divisions focusing on financial stability and regulations, so when the crisis in 2008 started it was desperately short of expertise. The then governor of the Bank of England, Mervyn King, said in August 2007 after the crisis was already under way and Northern Rock was failing, "Our banking system is much more resilient than in the past. . . . The growth of securitization has reduced that fragility significantly." It wasn't only the central banks. Just about the only academic institution concerned with systemic risk was the London School of Economics. Credit goes to Charles Goodhart, who constantly reminded us that systemic risk was important and worth studying. Still, it was not good from a career perspective. I recall getting a referee report from a top journal on one of my papers on crises in 2003, rejected as "irrelevant because the problem of crises has been solved."

The reaction to the Covid virus has its origins in the fumbling response to the crisis in 2008. Having been caught short in 2008, the policy authorities in 2020 responded with vigor, aided by strong political support and determined to prevent a repeat of 2008. Policy making is often like that. Underreaction followed by a rearview-mirror-guided overreaction. Unfortunately, though crises are all fundamentally the same, the details differ, and regulations target the details much more than the fundamentals.

Covid-19 offers a fantastic example of the trade-off between safety and growth: Do we lock the economy down to prevent the virus from spreading but at the expense of very significant economic damage, or keep everything open and hope for herd immunity? The answer to that question shows why we need political leadership; the authorities concerned with health tend to prefer lockdown, and the economic authorities to keep things open. It is the job of the prime minister or president to arbitrate and decide on the best course of action. Directing the fight against Covid-19 is not a job that can be delegated to officials.

We have the same debate in the financial system: Do we seek risk and so deregulate the system, hoping for more growth, or do we nail the system down to prevent crises? Both camps have their adherents, and it is the job of the political leadership to decide.

The Covid-19 and 2008 crises have a lot in common. Like most, they comprise a four-step process. Willful dismissal of the threats before the crisis event, followed by a weak initial reaction. When things get so bad they can't be ignored, we get overreaction and eventually, as we gain knowledge and experience, an uneasy balance between safety and growth. But the differences the two crises are more important. When the Covid-19 was under way I wrote a piece with three of my LSE colleagues, Robert Macrae, Dimitri Vayanos, and Jean-Pierre Zigrand, titled "The Coronavirus Crisis Is No 2008," in which we argued that these two crises were quite different. The 2008 crisis originated within the financial system, caused by its willingness to take risk, aided by the willful ignorance of the dangers and excessive complexity. Covid-19 came from nowhere, certainly not the financial system. While the policy authorities reacted strongly to Covid-19, finance was a small part of that, and we haven't seen any financial crisis to come out of Covid-19.

So Covid-19 impacted the financial markets, but it cannot be called systemic in a financial sense. What Covid-19 does do for us is to provide a handy framework for thinking about financial regulations, what works and what doesn't work. I'll return to that theme once I have erected the necessary scaffolding to make the argument. But as a brief preview, recent empirical evidence suggests that how the financial authorities reacted to Covid-19 has sharply increased moral hazard, that is, the financial markets' expectation that the central banks are ready, willing, and able to step in and bail them out. They, as always, will react by taking yet more risk.

Who Is to Blame? Banksters? Politicians? Regulators? Nobody?

When a systemic crisis happens, someone must be to blame. Is it the "banksters" who took too much risk and abused the financial system? Is it the regulators who were asleep on the watch? The politicians who cheered the banks on and protected them from scrutiny? The households that borrowed too much and saved too little? Someone made the decisions that led to the crisis. Should they be put in jail?

Take the example of Spain, going through a huge boom after it joined the euro, fueled by the influx of very cheap money. While some banks were careful, others were not, especially the savings banks, the cajas. The lending boom seemed beyond anyone's control from about 2005, and everybody enjoyed the party. Who is responsible? The designers of the euro? The European Central Bank? The Spanish government that joined the euro? The international banks that lent to Spain? The central bank of Spain? The Spanish commercial banks? The borrowers? If we try hard enough, we can always find someone to blame. As Cardinal Richelieu said, "Give me six lines written by the most honest man, and I will find something there to hang him."[7]

Still, it is not that easy to find someone to blame if we can't use the methods of Cardinal Richelieu. My native country, Iceland, was the country worst hit by the global crisis in the autumn of 2008 and since then has been trying very hard to find someone to blame. The government convened a special court to prosecute the then prime minister for allowing the crisis to happen, eventually convicting him of negligence—to my mind, a miscarriage of justice. Imagine, if we were able to prosecute politicians for incompetence, there wouldn't be many left.

The Icelanders had better luck in going after the bankers, some of whom have spent years in jail. But it took an extraordinary effort, a special prosecution service, and financial police with considerable resources and very strong political backing, all helped by questionable actions like long solitary confinement for those accused but not yet convicted. In the end, the bankers were convicted not for causing the crisis but for minor misconduct relating to individual transactions: just like the US authorities got Al Capone for tax evasion, not for being a mafia boss. The regulators and most of the political leadership got off scot-free, even if they are as much at fault as the bankers. The Central Bank of Iceland, which bore so much blame for allowing the crisis to happen, fired the governors but promoted everybody else. So, ironically, the career bureaucrats who were responsible benefited.

The Icelandic case is an extreme form of what we have seen in other countries. The prosecutors can go after bankers for specific misconduct, some abuse of office, but they cannot convict anyone for causing a crisis. Spain sent its former finance minister and IMF chief Rodrigo Rato to jail for four years and six months for embezzlement. He was not convicted for the failure of his bank (Bankia), rescued at huge expense by the Spanish taxpayer. He was not punished even for the losses suffered by two hundred thousand savers whom he had persuaded to buy subordinated Bankia bonds right before it failed. No, he misused his corporate credit cards. One might wonder what the Spanish regulator was doing all along, not only condoning but also actively encouraging such abuse of unsophisticated investors. Why aren't they prosecuted?

The former CEO of Barclays, John Varley, is the only CEO of a global bank to face charges because of his conduct in the financial crisis. However, that was only because of how he tried to save his bank, not for getting it in trouble in the first place. The United States has sent at least thirty-five bankers to jail for crimes related to the financial crisis, most relating to small amounts of money at small banks for personal gain. One person, known as Fabulous Fab—real name Fabrice Tourre—was convicted of crimes relating to structured credit products while working as a junior employee at Goldman Sachs. He and everybody else convicted in the United States were small-fry.

Even when there is clear abuse we cannot find anyone to blame. The best case is LIBOR, the standard benchmark interest rate used to decide on interest rates charged on mortgages and loans worldwide. It was surprisingly easy to manipulate LIBOR, as it was based on an average of banks' estimates of market interest rates, and the employee making the submission in each bank had some leeway in the number she came up with. Is it 5.25 percent or 5.26 percent? A derivative trader who knows which of these two numbers is to be submitted has more than an even chance of profiting, and it is alleged that employees across banks colluded in their submissions, guaranteeing profits. The banks maintain it was all the fault of rogue junior employees, and nobody higher up had an inkling of the abuse. Still, they didn't question the profits from manipulating LIBOR. Did the regulators know? While strenuously denied, many observers allege that banks deliberately posted excessively low numbers during the 2008 crisis with the acquiescence of the regulators in order to lower funding costs for banks in difficulty.

The manipulation of LIBOR is very costly for lenders and borrowers, and one might think the abuse would be severely punished. Not so. Employees in several banks were found to have been manipulating LIBOR, and some banks have admitted to doing exactly that. Exactly one person has, at the time of writing, been punished: a junior UBS and then Citigroup employee who was sent to jail by the British authorities for eleven years. No senior manager, financial institution, or regulator has been prosecuted or convicted for the LIBOR abuse.

The reason is that it is really difficult to find anyone guilty in a court of law. The prosecutors in the United Kingdom and the United States have tried but mostly failed. The bankers might be responsible for causing a crisis in the court of public opinion, but the Icelandic bankers, like their counterparts in other countries, were careful not to break the law. Stupidity is not a crime. Greed is not a crime. Legally manipulating the rules is not a crime. Recklessness was not a crime in 2008, even though it has become a criminal offense in the United Kingdom since.

The bankers, regulators, and politicians cannot be convicted of a crime that does not exist, and we cannot (or should not) change the law retroactively. When we do a postmortem on financial crises, we see that the bankers excessively expanded their banks, taking on too much risk, not properly scrutinizing lending decisions, and ignoring liquidity risk. The regulators looked the other way, and the politicians cheered the excesses. It may be greedy, incompetent, arrogant, and immoral, but not, so long as the letter of the law is complied with, illegal.

All we have is specific misconduct, and even then it is really hard to prove. It involves complicated financial transactions understood only by a handful of experts and difficult to explain in a court of law to nonexpert judges and juries. Especially since conviction hinges on a fine interpretation of rules, the burden of proof is on the prosecutors, and it is not easy to find people guilty beyond a reasonable doubt.

There is another, more insidious problem in finding banks or bankers guilty, and that is the problem of too big to fail, illustrated by an example from the world's second largest bank, HSBC. In the years before 2010 it failed to monitor transactions involving drug traffickers in its Mexican subsidiary. Because these transactions were in US dollars they were subject to clearing in New York and hence to US law. The US government refused to prosecute HSBC because, as explained by Eric Holder, the US attorney general at the time, "I am concerned that the size of some of these [financial] institutions becomes so large that it does become difficult for us to prosecute them."[8] In other words, if the US government had decided to go after HSBC it might have triggered its failure, and, because HSBC is a systemically important financial institution, such failure might result in a systemic crisis. The largest banks have a get-out-of-jail-free card. What the US authorities ended up doing is to fine the banks, and in the aftermath of the 2008 crisis banks have paid over $320 billion in fines without admitting to any misconduct. The fines have become yet another revenue source for the government, a tax by another name, borne by the banks' clients in the form of higher fees. Other countries haven't even gone that far.

Systemic risk is the chance that the financial system does not do its job, perhaps that a major financial crisis causes an economic recession. It happens because of the typical dilemma ever-present in the financial system. We want economic growth, and that necessitates risk. With risk comes the chance of failure and crisis. It is hard to prevent systemic risk because it emerges in the most obscure parts of the financial system, exploiting unknown vulnerabilities, making the policy makers' job difficult—but certainly not impossible. We know quite a lot about why crises occur and how to prevent them. Yet they are all too familiar.

3

Groundhog Day

To Stop the Duke, go for Gold.
—*Poster from 1832*

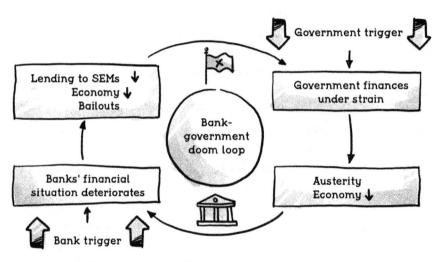

Figure 4. Credit: Lukas Bischoff/IllustrationX.

In the movie *Groundhog Day* a TV weatherman played by Bill Murray is covering the annual Groundhog Day event in Punxsutawney, Pennsylvania. What was meant to be a one-day assignment turns into an infinite loop, the same day being repeated endlessly until he finds a way out. It is the same with banking crises. They happen again and again, and the financial authorities cannot make them go away. I don't think they can either. Even Bill Murray's solution, virtue, will not work.

The inevitability of crises gives me one of my favorite exam questions: "We know what causes banking crises and how to prevent them, and still they happen all the time. Why?" There are many ways to answer. The glib reply is "greed and fear," but perhaps the simplest is that the financial system has the annoying habit of misdirection, telling us it is okay to take more risk when we really should not.

We need banks and all the other parts of the financial system, as without them we wouldn't have anything resembling the modern economy. The problem is that financial institutions like to take on too much risk, and bankruptcies and crises are the inevitable outcome. As so often happens, the very thing that makes the economy grow also can destroy it. We need a balance between stability and growth, and that balance is tough to achieve.

It is hard to defend banks. They are a symbol of greed. Of the privatization of profits and socialization of losses. Bankers are highly paid, arrogant, all too quick to blame the less fortunate for not being as successful as they are, and lacking in empathy. That makes banks an obvious target for political activists, and we have seen many attempts by anticapitalist protesters like Occupy Wall Street to exhort people to go and take their money out of banks for political reasons—a politically motivated bank run, an event in which people queue up to take their money out of a bank.

If the activists were to get enough people to run the banks, they would succeed, and the banks, or even the entire banking system, would collapse. Occupy Wall Street activists, with no luck whatsoever, hope that that would destroy the capitalist system. It is hard to motivate enough people to deliberately cause a bank run. The only case I know of in which such a politically motivated bank run was successful occurred in 1832 when the prime minister of the United Kingdom, the Duke of Wellington, was resisting any changes to how members of Parliament were selected. The so-called rotten boroughs were popular with the political leadership. The problem was that entire regions were effectively disenfranchised, and the demand for reform was strong. Still, the duke resisted until the launching of a successful campaign under the banner "To Stop the Duke, go for Gold," which plastered posters all over the country urging people to take their paper money to the Bank of England and convert it to gold. Since it had only about 40 percent of the gold necessary to cover all outstanding paper money, there was a real chance the Bank of England would run out of gold and, as a consequence, go bankrupt, while the government quite possibly would default also. Enough people queued up, and the government was forced to pass the Reform Act.

Do We Need Banks?

Banks are essential for the economy. They provide financial intermediation—the channeling of funds from one person or entity to another across time and space. Banks reallocate resources, diversify risk, allow us to build up pensions for old age, and enable companies to make multidecade investments. At one end, a large number of savers put small amounts of money into the banks, expecting their money to be safe and available on demand. At the other end, the banks make a small number of large thirty-year loans to companies building factories. Banks are also dangerous and exploitative. They take advantage of their clients, fail, and cause financial crises. The response of society is to enjoy the benefits of the banks while also regulating them heavily.

Easy in theory, hard in practice. If we don't want banks to fail, they can make only safe loans, and that means lending only to risk-free governments—if we can find any. If the banks are too safe, the cost of thirty-year loans would be too high while interest on bank deposits would be too low, so people would not save and companies would not borrow. The factories would not get built and the economy would not grow. We could not borrow money to buy a car or a house, nor save for old age. The argument is reminiscent of that made by the Peruvian economist Hernando de Soto in his book *The Mystery of Capital,* that a system of property rights and enforceable legal contracts is a necessary condition for economic prosperity.

The result is one of the dilemmas we find so often in the financial system. If we make the banks too safe, we throttle economic growth. If we are too eager and unshackle them, the banks fail. Thus we are continually debating the trade-off between safety and growth. After the Great Depression we heavily regulated the banks, then deregulated them after the Bretton Woods system collapsed in 1973, and turned back to regulations after the 2008 crisis. There are early indications that the regulatory pendulum has now started to swing back, with banking regulations to be relaxed yet again. That process was already under way when Covid-19 hit in 2020, accelerating the process.

There is nothing unique about the safety or growth debate in the banking system. It applies to most areas of the public domain, like speed limits, and today it is most strongly manifested in the debate over how to respond to Covid-19. Do we lock everything down to halt the virus but at the expense of killing the economy?

Banks are inherently fragile, but it is hard to address that fragility. Suppose a chocolate maker is in difficulty. If the business's debts exceed its assets, it is insolvent and will be shut down. Most likely, someone else will buy the factories and continue production. And if not, competitors will happily step in. The disruption to society is minimal; shareholders and perhaps employees lose out but not many others.

Banks are different. They can fail even when prudently run and, conversely, remain solvent so long as they are trusted. If I believe my bank is well managed and properly regulated, I will keep my money in a bank so it can continue operating. If, however, I lose faith in the bank and take my money out, that, by itself, can cause the bank to fail, even if it is prudently run and solvent.

A bank run can happen at a bank even if there is nothing wrong with it. All we need is for depositors to get worried, then a bank run becomes a self-fulfilling prophecy. I remember seeing a news item on CNN concerning a bank about to be closed down. The journalist made a mistake, using an image of a different bank. That is all it took for the other bank to be hit by a run.

Why are banks fragile? Two main reasons. The first is *bank runs*. If a sufficient number of depositors want their money back, the bank cannot fulfill all those requests because most of its assets are tied up in long-term loans. I can take my money out of the bank anytime I want, but my bank cannot and should not be able to call in its thirty-year loans when it pleases.

My favorite description of a bank run comes from the 1946 movie *It's a Wonderful Life*, featuring James Stewart, who plays a banker faced with a bank run during the Great Depression. In the following scene, he addresses the angry crowd demanding their money back. Though the transcript doesn't do it justice, you can (at the time of writing) find it on YouTube: "No, but you, you . . . you're thinking of this place all wrong. As if I had the money back in a safe. The money's not here. Your money's in Joe's house . . . right next to yours. And in the Kennedy house, and Mrs. Macklin's house, and a hundred others. Why, you're lending them the money to build, and then, they're going to pay it back to you as best they can. Now what are you going to do? Foreclose on them?"[1]

When a bank is hit with a run it may fail. It is not insolvent as it has more assets than liabilities, but it is illiquid—it cannot convert its assets into cash on demand. It is a little like a situation in which I suddenly need a large amount of money, far more than what I have in my bank account. While I own a house in London, it will take time to sell it, and I cannot satisfy an immediate demand for a large amount of cash. If depositors become worried about their bank's solvency—perhaps it has made too many bad loans—depositors will want their money back. If enough depositors agree, they will queue up in front of the bank to get the money—the classical definition of a bank run.

The second bank fragility arises because of how banks create money. Every country in the world uses fiat money: money that is the creation of the central bank as an agent of the government and underpinned by its stability and reputation. Money takes many forms. The central banks create the monetary base, $M0$, consisting of money held on account with the central bank plus the total amount of physical money: notes and coins. That is, however, only a fraction of the overall amount of money in the system, the reason being we have a fractional reserve system where the banking system creates money. Suppose the reserve requirement is 1 percent. If I deposit €100 into a bank account, the bank has to hold on to €1 (reserve requirement) and can lend out €99. I still own my €100 and can spend it whenever I like, but now the borrower has €99, and she can spend it also whenever she likes: together we have €199 ready cash, known as $M1$. If the borrower then leaves the money in her bank account, her bank can lend out 99 percent of that, €98, and that can, in turn, be further lent out, etc., etc. This is the most basic way the banking system creates money. So what are the amounts?

In the eurozone in August 2018 base money was €3.2 trillion, but the amount of physical money in circulation plus demand deposits was M1 (€8.1 trillion), M2 (€11.1 trillion) further adds savings accounts, and M3 (€12.0 trillion) is large amounts of money that are locked for a period of time deposits, institutional money market funds, short-term repurchases, and other, similar assets. Every euro created by the European Central Bank becomes €3.4 when the banks are done with it. Even that captures but a fraction of the money in the system because as we go about our daily economic life we constantly create new money simply by borrowing and lending. Nobody knows how much money is in the system, and certainly nobody controls it. That is why it is so hard to control inflation.

The amount of money has a direct impact on the fortunes of the economy. If the economy is growing rapidly, the supply of money needs to grow with it to prevent deflation. If, however, the supply of money collapses, there is not enough money to maintain economic activity, and the economy goes into recession. Now you see why it is dangerous when banks are clamoring for liquidity in a crisis. They take all the higher forms of money, M1, M2, M3, and beyond and convert them into M0. The supply of money is collapsing, taking the economy down with it.

These two vulnerabilities, bank runs and the nature of money, come together in banking crises. A bank run can lead to cascading failures because depositors might view a single bank's bankruptcy as a symptom of system-wide difficulties. Depositors have limited information about the quality of banks' assets and may feel that if hidden problems have been allowed to fester in one bank, they might also be present in other banks. They see bankers as incompetent and greedy and the regulators as bungling and even corrupt.

The best-known example of bank runs causing a systemic crisis happened during the Great Depression of 1929 to 1933. The United States lost over a third of its banks to bankruptcies, and people preferred to store their money under their mattresses rather than keeping it in banks—the backdrop to *It's a Wonderful Life*. The panic originated in 1931 with the Bank of United States (which specialized in immigrant clients) misleadingly and deliberately implying by its name that it was government-owned. In early 1931 rumors spread that it might be in trouble. Initially, the local authority—the New York Federal Reserve Bank—tried to arrange a rescue package but did not manage to put it together. The failure of the Bank of United States marked a profound change in public sentiment toward banks. A real estate bubble in Chicago collapsed soon after, in May 1931, and thirty Chicago banks defaulted. Depositors, who were unable to tell whether a bank was good or not, began pulling their cash indiscriminately out of all banks, good and bad, triggering multiple bank runs.

Such withdrawals caused the supply of money to collapse. Each M0 dollar in 1928 was amplified into $6.5 by the financial system. By 1933 the corresponding number was $4 and continued to fall for a decade afterward. That meant that while the amount of M0 increased in the Depression, M2 fell, from $46.4 billion to $32.2 billion, with devastating consequences for the real economy. Milton Friedman and Anna Schwartz, in their seminal book *A Monetary History of the United States: 1867–1960* (1963), argued that the collapse in the supply of money was a leading cause of the Great Depression. The reason we got all the liquidity created in the crisis in 2008 is owing to the lesson from the Great Depression and the arguments in Friedman's and Schwartz's book.

A vicious cycle ensued. All banks felt the need to protect themselves, and desperate bankers called in loans, which the borrowers did not have the time or resources to repay. With economic prospects poor, capital investment ceased, and the surviving banks became even more conservative. Servicing debts became harder because prices and incomes fell significantly while debts remained at the same dollar amount. If this all sounds familiar, it is not unlike what happened (but on a smaller scale) in the aftermath of the 2008 crisis.

Fortunately, banking crises are not all that frequent, contrary to what many think. Figure 5 shows the year when every banking crisis in the world starts from 1800.[2] Two thousand eight has the highest number of new banking crises at twenty-two, followed by 1931 with eighteen. Still, since the number of countries in 2008 is much higher now than in 1931, a much higher fraction of countries in the world suffered a banking crisis in the Great Depression. The most dangerous decade is the 1990s, with seventy-four new banking crises.

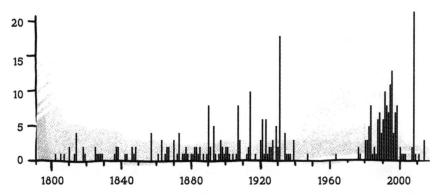

Figure 5. Number of banking crises in each year from 1800 to 2017. Credit: Lukas Bischoff/IllustrationX.

Banking crises are not pleasant. Growth turns negative, bankruptcies abound, unemployment skyrockets, and general misery spreads. While the immediate cause of banking crises is the interplay between bank runs and the fractional reserve banking system, that is only the technical endgame. The fundamental causes are deeper, and the vulnerabilities are created years, even decades, before the actual crises hit the newspaper headlines.

The origin is usually a stable economy that we perceive as having low risk. Since risk is seen as low, everybody thinks borrowing to invest or consume is a fantastic idea. Banks are highly profitable, and all that investment and consumption make the economy grow. As if by magic, we are always right. The investors must be really smart, getting into the market at the right time, and the bankers are brilliant. But eventually the only thing keeping the growth alive is borrowing. As time passes it becomes harder and harder to find productive investments, and in the endgame the money goes to speculative real estate and the like. And that cannot go on forever: a crash is inevitable. Most crises are as simple as that. Suppose instead we had played it safe and not borrowed. Then the economy would not have grown, and we did the right thing, this time by playing it safe. We are right either way, and our choices are self-validating, at least in the short run.

There are exceptions. Some crises, but not many, are caused by corruption and outright theft. I can only think of three, and I keep asking people if they know better examples. Please get in touch if you know of any. Two are from Latin America: Venezuela in 1994 and the Dominican Republic in 2003, in both cases involving banks that were so large as to be systemically important. The banks did not record deposits as liabilities; instead, the insiders (senior management and owners) looted the banks from within by stealing their assets. Because of the banks' systemic importance, the central bank felt it was necessary to compensate depositors. At a high cost: the macroeconomy's destabilization. In Venezuela the rogue bank paid high interest rates, forcing other banks to do the same, thereby weakening the entire banking system. More recently about a billion dollars disappeared over two days from three Moldovan banks that had been taken over by unknown owners in 2012. The money was sent to British- and Hong Kong–based companies with equally opaque ownership. The Moldovan government was forced to bail out the banks at the hefty cost of 15 percent of GDP.

Other crises have been caused by external events like wars, natural disasters, or a change in the political system. Even viruses. Some have their roots in disastrous economic policies, as in Venezuela today. However, these origins of banking crises are uncommon and, since they are caused by outside forces, hard to prevent. Even if the banks are safe, the crisis storm can be so strong that it destroys everything in its wake, leaving little for financial policy to do except to mitigate the worst.

The most common type of banking crisis is caused simply when banks make too many bad loans. There is no reason such a crisis couldn't be prevented—in theory. There are plenty of signs, including excessive buildup of credit, a boom in real estate, relaxed lending standards, and economic well-being that is at odds with the economy's fundamentals. But it is very hard to do something about it.

Banking crises remind me of the old Road Runner cartoons in which Wile E. Coyote is chasing the Road Runner and, on occasion, Coyote runs off a cliff. He keeps running for a few meters until he looks down and sees there is nothing but air beneath him. Bankers do that too (Figure 6). Like Wile E. we believe everything is okay until it is too late, and there's nothing we can do except manage the crisis. The reason was voiced best by the former CEO of Citigroup, Chuck Prince, who, when

Figure 6. Running off a cliff. Credit: Copyright © Ricardo Galvão.

asked before the 2008 crisis why nobody stopped all the excess, said, "As long as the music is playing, you've got to get up and dance."[3]

Booms precede most banking crises. Everybody enjoys the benefits. The economy is growing. Everybody feels richer. The politicians, policy makers, and bankers must be geniuses. The financial system tells us what we want to hear: we are doing the right thing, and we are really, really smart. All agree until it all goes horribly wrong. Some know better. Experts in the central banks, inquisitive journalists, and the bankers who write the crazy loans. But it is not in their interest to issue a warning. If they do, they risk being denounced, losing their income, and even being subjected to prosecution. So nobody speaks out, and the party continues. The former head of the Federal Reserve wrote in the 1950s that the Fed's most important job is "to take away the punch bowl just as the party gets going."[4] It is really hard to do so.

One of the main causes of banking crises is financial liberalization. It can be enormously valuable for a country to become a global financial center. The City of London and Amsterdam were the key to the success of the British and Dutch empires and their prosperity ever since. On the face of it, liberalization can seem like a sensible idea. Enjoy the fruits of a financial system that is open for business, welcoming companies from all over the world. In some countries the attraction is to unshackle lethargic domestic banks and encourage them to invest in the domestic economy, especially the small- and medium-sized enterprises that are the drivers of job creation and economic growth. Elsewhere, the appeal is all the high-paying jobs that come with international finance.

By converting a country into an international financial hub, vast riches await. We only have to look at the wealthiest country in the world, Luxembourg, which got rid of its inefficient mining and industrial base and replaced it with finance, very successfully and with lightning speed, in 1973. Singapore has even gone so far as to give the central bank a mandate to develop the financial sector, which so far has been quite good for Singapore. Except it isn't that easy. Many a country has tried financial liberalization, and most experiments have ended up in tears. Cyprus, Iceland, and Thailand are among the many cautionary tales. The reason is that we face one of those dilemmas we find everywhere in finance: the benefit is the same as the vulnerability.

Some countries can sustain advanced financial systems for centuries. The three cities that were the global financial centers in the sixteenth century have kept their status to this day: Amsterdam, London, and Hamburg (if we allow for Hamburg losing its financial industry to Berlin and eventually to Frankfurt after it joined the German Empire in 1871). Something in these countries' DNA allows them to make a success out of it. They have specialized schools focused on finance, a stable political leadership, a robust legal system that understands finance, government agencies familiar with regulating high finance, and banks with experience operating in lightly regulated environments. It confirms what my sociologist colleagues like to stress: culture matters.

Large financial systems are certainly beneficial to those lucky enough to have them. Dutch merchants' success in the seventeenth century and the British industrialization in the nineteenth century would not have been possible without a robust financial system backing them up. Finance is the source of the highest-paying jobs around and creates a lot of tax revenue. The UK is an example: the House of Commons found in 2017 that the gross value added by the financial system to the UK economy is £124.2 billion a year, 7.2 percent of the total. The financial sector provides 1.1 million jobs. Even better, the UK has a large trade surplus in finance: exports of financial services were £55.5 billion and imports only £11.7 bil-

lion. The financial sector contributed £71.4 billion in the tax take, 11.5 percent of government revenue.

No wonder many countries aspire to do the same. That said, it is not as
easy as it sounds, and the execution has to be just right. A common mistake is to reduce oversight and activity restrictions but maintain implicit
or explicit government guarantees such as deposit insurance. This creates
a nasty moral hazard problem because it can enable financial institutions
to borrow cheaply and use the money for high-risk activities, all implic-
itly or explicitly underwritten by the taxpayer. This is what happened in
many Asian countries, such as Thailand and South Korea, that got into a
crisis in 1998. Their banks borrowed abroad, and because of government
guarantees and lax oversight the banks did not care whom they lent the
money to. Not surprisingly, it did not end well. It is much better to learn
from the one country that made a recent success by becoming a financial
center, Luxembourg. I was once in a panel discussion there, along with
the governor of the central bank and other experts. When the governor
learned I was from Iceland, he snickered and said that Icelanders forgot
the first lesson of creating an offshore financial center: protect the country from financial institutions' failures.

The typical outcome is that following liberalization, banks overexpand,
artificially inflating asset prices, creating positive feedback loops among
bank lending, market prices, and profits. Meanwhile, the banks lack experience in managing risk and are disdainful of risk management, seeing
it as a loss-maker that gets in the way of making money. The regulators
are similarly ill-prepared, focusing on the positive outcomes while missing
the signs of excessive risk because they have never been there before. And
the political leadership always keeps the regulators on a short leash, not
allowing anything to spoil the party. Meanwhile, government policies are
accommodating, interest rates are low, and governments cut taxes and
increase expenditure because the economy is booming.

The financial crises in Iceland and Ireland in 2008 had precisely these
roots. Even countries with a culture of a liberalized, competitive financial
system can make the same mistakes, like the United States in the Savings & Loan (S&L) crisis. Mortgages were the raison d'être of the S&L
banks—banks like that used to be common in many countries, often
under the name of savings banks or something similar. The crisis started

when the sleepy S&Ls found it difficult to cope with all the financial turmoil in the 1970s. Inflation was high and increasing, interest rates did not keep up, and banks that focused on collecting deposits and making mortgages suffered increasingly large losses. The financial authorities decided to deregulate the industry with the view that the S&Ls would grow their way out of trouble; at the time, deregulation was de rigueur in the United States. The intention was to allow the S&Ls to expand into the parts of banking services previously closed to them.

The financial authorities allowed the S&Ls to use lenient accounting rules, eliminated restrictions on the minimum numbers of stockholders, and reduced the level of oversight. However, crucial to the story, the government continued to provide deposit insurance, guaranteeing that depositors would get their money back if the S&Ls went bust. Many S&Ls took advantage, often falling into the hands of rogue bankers. The best known was Charles Keating, who got into the business because "I know the business inside out, and I always felt that an S&L, if they'd relax the rules, was the biggest moneymaker in the world."[5] Initially, his S&L, Lincoln, grew rapidly, but its investments, not least in real estate and junk bonds, turned out not to be as good as he'd hoped for. Eventually, Lincoln was closed down, with the cost to taxpayers exceeding $3 billion. Keating, for his troubles, lost all of his wealth and spent 4½ years in prison. Eventually, the total cost of resolving all the failed S&Ls was $160 billion, including $132 billion from taxpayers.

After the United States lost so many of its banks in the Great Depression, it took Franklin Roosevelt's election as president to change things. He pushed Congress to pass the 1933 Banking Act in June 1933, establishing the Federal Deposit Insurance Corporation (FDIC), which provided insurance coverage for deposits up to $2,500. This proved quite effective, and the bank runs stopped. Europe had its share of bank runs in the Great Depression, not as many as the United States, but, unlike those in the US, the most serious were deliberately caused by the French government. It all started when the German and Austrian governments announced their intention to create a customs union in March 1931. The French did not like that very much and forced their banks to run the Austrian banks—in effect, run Austria. France could do that because it had been deliberately undervaluing its currency for quite some time and, as a consequence, had the biggest gold reserves in the world. The largest bank in Austria,

Credit-Anstalt, consequently defaulted, and the crisis spread to other Austrian banks and soon after to German and Hungarian banks. The European bank failures triggered by the French government were a significant contributor to the subsequent political instability and depression in Europe. While France succeeded in its immediate political objective, that is, preventing the customs union, it paid a heavy price both politically and economically.

So, what to do about bank runs? Deposit insurance as eloquently modeled by Douglas Diamond and Philip Dybvig. Their model concludes that so long as depositors believe they will be protected they will not run their bank; a credible deposit insurance scheme will consequently never actually need to pay out. In the United States today, the FDIC continues to provide deposit insurance to depositors up to a limit, now $250,000, payable on the day a bank is closed. I once saw that in action while visiting a friend in Houston, Texas. He was working for a company whose bank went bust. On the same day the bank was closed, he got a phone call saying he could collect his deposit insurance check. We went to the bank, queued up for half an hour, and got a check for the full amount. Amazingly efficient. This efficiency and the public recognition of it have been very beneficial to the financial stability of the United States. If Europe had such an efficient system, some of the drama in Europe's 2008 crisis would have been averted, and the Northern Rock run would not have embarrassed the Bank of England and the British government.

In the good old days (or at least the textbook version of the good old days) a bank was an institution that collected deposits that were used to make loans. The money came from what is known in the jargon as retail clients, you and I. Banks today are just as likely to borrow from other financial institutions, what is known as wholesale funding. That creates new sorts of vulnerabilities because wholesale lenders are much more likely to be aware of pending difficulties and can be very quick in pulling their money out. This was the root of the last bank run in the United Kingdom, Northern Rock in 2007—thereby embarrassing the British authorities who had forgotten the lessons of their previous bank run (Overend & Gurney in 1866).

The run was caused by the cleverness of Northern Rock management which had captured about a third of the British mortgage market by using an ingenious business model. In the old-school model of banking,

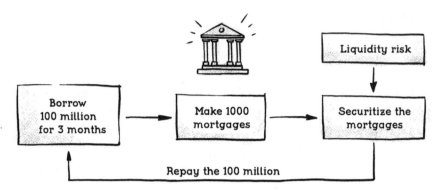

Figure 7. Northern Rock's business model. Credit: Lukas Bischoff/
IllustrationX.

people deposit money in banks that then make mortgages. Not Northern
Rock. It found a new model (Figure 7). Suppose Northern Rock borrowed £100 million for three months from the wholesale markets, using
the money to make one thousand mortgages. It then bundled the mortgages into a structured credit product that it sold to investors and used
the proceeds to repay the three-month £100 million loan. Highly profitable. But there was hidden liquidity risk.

All was fine so long as Northern Rock was able to sell the mortgages—
if it could not, the bank would be forced to default on the initial three-
month loan, which eventually happened in the summer of 2007. It wasn't
Northern Rock's fault when the credit markets worldwide froze; it was
said that investors went on strike, just like their Amsterdam ancestors
back in 1763. Nobody wanted to buy structured credit products, and the
first victim was Northern Rock. It took a few months, but its impending demise was known to everybody in the credit markets except, as it
appears, the bank's regulators: the Financial Services Authority and the
Bank of England. Eventually, the authorities tried to resolve the crisis
behind the scenes.

The Bank of England then made an unfortunate mistake, announcing
in October 2007 that Northern Rock was in difficulty and receiving support from the Bank of England. The Bank's decision makers seem to have
believed that the public would find the announcement reassuring—all is
fine, no reason to panic, we know what we are doing and are here to pro-

tect you. It didn't quite work out that way, and the following day people around the United Kingdom queued up to get their money out of Northern Rock—the first bank run in Britain for a century and a half. The Bank of England should have known better. The same mistakes happened with the Reconstruction Finance Corporation in the Great Depression and many times before and since. We have to trust the banks, regulators, and the government. Unfortunately, by the time the crisis comes along, the trust has long evaporated. Not surprisingly, Northern Rock's retail clients called the bluff.

Northern Rock went through two waves of bank runs, first by the sophisticated wholesale investors in July 2007 and then by unsophisticated retail investors in October. The wholesale run shows that the financial markets had a much better understanding of the bank's problems than either the supervisor or the general public. One reason for the October run was that the British deposit insurance scheme was relatively weak, and depositors felt they had no choice but to queue up and take their money out. After the first £2,000 of deposits, the scheme protected only 90 percent of savings of up to £33,000—guaranteeing a maximum payout of £31,700. Even worse, it would take several months to get the money. This so-called coinsurance was intended to incentivize depositors to monitor the banks. Well, given that the Financial Services Authority missed the problems at Northern Rock, it would be surprising if ordinary depositors with less information could do better. The only sensible strategy for depositors was to run the bank. Contrast this with the American deposit insurance scheme and my friend's experience in Houston. The Northern Rock run would not have happened there.

With the benefit of hindsight, it is clear that Northern Rock's failure was inevitable given time. It remained only solvent so long as it could borrow without limits. Because there were no limits on borrowing, Northern Rock and most other banks in the world behaved in a way that ensured that credit would dry up. The failure of Northern Rock was a self-fulfilling prophecy.

In response, the British authorities overreacted, announcing unlimited deposit insurance to reassure bank clients and prevent contagious runs across the United Kingdom. This demonstrates the problem created when the authorities have inadequate policies in place and then are confronted by a crisis. The United Kingdom went from having a deposit insurance scheme that was too weak to one that was too strong. Underreaction, followed by overreaction, is a common problem in policy making.

The unlimited guarantee soon came to haunt the authorities, aided by the fact that the internet speeds up the bank run process—even worse, making them when the regulators are not at work. In 2007 and 2008 an Icelandic bank (Icesave) facing difficulties borrowing from the capital markets hit on the ingenious idea of opening high-interest accounts in the United Kingdom. By promising interest rates considerably above the prevailing market rates, Icesave saw money flooding in. Because the British government provided unlimited deposit insurance, nobody was too concerned. Eventually, when the crisis hit its maximum intensity at the end of September 2008, depositors did get worried and ran the Icesave bank. Because it was an internet bank, the bank run was not only much faster than the classical ones (in which people have to physically queue up in front of a bank), it also inconveniently took place over a weekend when the supervisors were off duty.

The British authorities were not the only ones who forgot the historical bank run lessons. The Troika—the European Commission, the European Central Bank, and the International Monetary Fund—made the most elementary of mistakes when dealing with the Cypriot crisis in 2013. Most European crisis countries got into trouble for typical reasons: Ireland, Spain, and Iceland from bank overexpansion, Greece and Portugal due to misbehaving governments. Cyprus was different. It was a victim of two unique policy mistakes.

First, the Cypriot banks' business model was unusual, as they didn't borrow from the wholesale markets. It all started when the Cypriots, looking for an industry, realized that becoming an offshore banking center was a marvelous idea. If it works for Singapore, why not Cyprus? They started to collect deposits from wealthy foreign individuals, primarily Russians, becoming an offshore haven inside the European Union. The Cypriot banks then had a quandary: what to do with all the money? In a typical banking model, banks lend to households and companies and the government. But there is only so much lending Cyprus can absorb, so the Cypriot banks decided to invest in the sovereign bonds of the European country next to them, Greece. It seemed like a good idea. The prevailing attitude among the financial markets and the authorities was that European sovereign debt was risk free, that somehow it was all insured by the collective. This rather unfortunate misunderstanding was reinforced by law in a European Union directive stipulating that sovereign debt was, and is, recorded as risk free in banks' accounts. The European Commission told the Cypriot banks that they were to consider Greek government bonds safe on their books, and that is where they put their money. Think about it for a second. Sovereign debt is, in fact, risky, and governments are free to default on it, but the banks buying the debt are obliged to consider the debt entirely safe. Talk about mixed signals.

When the crisis started, 37 percent of the Cypriot banks' deposits belonged to foreigners, 80 percent of whom were Russians. Then the Greek sovereign debt crisis happened, and in the second bailout, in 2011, the owners of Greek sovereign debt were made to suffer a 50 percent haircut. At that moment it became clear that the Cypriot banks were the walking dead, so a slow-running but accelerating bank run ensued. As so often is the case, those in the know took their money out first. It didn't happen quickly: Greece defaulted in early summer 2011, and it wasn't until early spring 2012 that the Cypriot banks finally started to run out of money. The Cypriot government refused to recognize the problem at first, and the Troika did not press the issue. A crisis was clearly about to happen, and nobody did anything. Not the Cypriot government, not the IMF, not the European authorities. Still, that is not the dumbest mistake they made, as a dumber one was to follow.

Now it became really interesting. The typical way to resolve a failing bank is to let junior creditors take the first loss. However, the Cypriot banks didn't have any bondholders—all they had was depositors. That left the government in a quandary. Whom to hit for the money? Under European regulations, depositors with less than €100,000 in a bank are fully insured. In the crisis meeting with the Troika and Ecofin, the Cypriot authorities maintained they did not want to excessively hurt the foreign depositors, so key to the country's business model, one from which the political and regulatory leadership personally profited. Instead, they opted to hit all depositors with a 6.75 percent tax, including insured deposits.

Why would they do such a thing? So that offshore clients would not suffer, as otherwise they might leave and never come back. Why would the European authorities agree? The best explanation is that the emergency meeting was held on 25 March 2013, and by four in the morning, when the decision was made, the policy makers were really tired. When the press release eventually came a few hours later, it was pointed out that insured depositors throughout Europe would no longer think they were fully protected, so everybody would rush to run the banks when the next crisis came along. Not surprisingly, the authorities quickly backtracked. It was perhaps the dumbest policy blunder in the whole crisis. Given that everybody knew for almost a year that the banks were failing and that the importance of confidence in preventing bank runs is well known, it is incomprehensible that no authority, neither Cypriot, European, nor the IMF, prepared for what was an entirely foreseeable and avoidable crisis.

Banks and governments have a symbiotic relationship. Banks are always encouraged (and usually required) to buy government debt. Banks are also the primary source of financing for small and medium-sized companies, the main driver of economic prosperity, and a source of significant tax revenues. In good times this relationship is virtuous. Profitable banking and increasing risk go hand in hand with growth and rising government revenues. This is when governments should pay down their sovereign debt, the one saving grace of the Irish and Icelandic economic policy before their 2008 crisis. If only Britain and the United States had done the same thing.

This virtuous cycle can quickly turn vicious, and it can be the fault of the banks, the governments, or both. A crisis in the banking sector will put government finances under considerable strain: directly because of the cost of providing bailouts and indirectly since banks slow down their financing of the economy. If things get especially bad, a banking crisis can culminate in a sovereign debt crisis, where the government cannot meet its obligations. That is what happened in Ireland and nearly in Spain and Iceland too.

Similarly, a government facing financial difficulties can cause problems for the banking system. It may need to increase taxes or spend less, which then slows down the economy. A more direct channel is when banks own a lot of government debt. If the government's credit rating gets downgraded, the banks' holdings of sovereign debt are immediately and adversely affected, so their riskiness goes up. Governments know this, and most have a law saying that government debt is risk free. However, that has the unfortunate side effect of subsidizing government debt at the expense of lending to productive private sector companies, further slowing growth. If it goes too far and the government defaults, it can take the banks down with it, precisely what happened in Cyprus and is likely to happen in certain European countries, such as Italy.

This process is known as the bank–government doom loop, a major cause of the European crisis in the past few years. While there is no easy way to deal with the bank–government doom loop, it can be mitigated by reducing banks' holdings of their own government debt. Banks need to hold some safe assets, but there is no reason Italian banks should not hold their safe assets in the form of German government bonds, except the Italian government needs someone to buy its own bonds. Therefore, it is unfortunate that the opposite has been happening in Europe; banks are buying more of their government debt, not least because of the way the European Central Bank has to do quantitative easing. When the Bank of England does quantitative easing, it can directly buy gilts, British government bonds. It is the same with the Federal Reserve, the Bank of Japan, and almost every other central bank. It is not so with the European Central Bank. Until recently it was prevented from buying government bonds by its rules, so if it wanted to do quantitative easing it had to give money to other entities, which then bought government bonds. And those entities are the banks. So, Italy's banks were obliged to buy Italian government bonds and use those as collateral to borrow from the European Central Bank.

How serious is this problem? The think tank Bruegel collects bank holdings of sovereign debt for some countries. Only 4 percent of US sovereign debt is held by its banks, while the corresponding numbers for Germany and Italy are 23 percent and 20 percent, respectively. Not a serious problem for Germany because of its low debt, but not so for Italy because of its very high debt levels. A sovereign debt crisis in Italy will most likely trigger its banks' failure in a typical bank–sovereign doom loop.

Crises are costly. The government spends large amounts of money dealing with them, and they affect economic growth. The first type of cost is termed the direct impact and can be more or less accurately identified, while the longer-term economic consequences, the indirect impacts, are much harder to measure. A common way to put a number to it is to

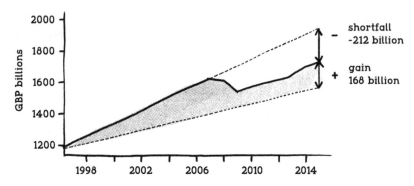

Figure 8. UK cost of crisis scenarios. Credit: Lukas Bischoff/IllustrationX.

estimate output losses by extrapolating from the trend of real GDP before a crisis and calculating the difference between the trend prediction
and actual outcomes. We can see the direct and indirect costs in the IMF
crisis database. The costliest crisis was Indonesia's in 1998, with direct
costs of 57 percent of GDP, and the highest indirect costs happened in
the Finnish 1991 crisis, at 75 percent of GDP. However, while the direct
impacts are fairly accurately measured, the indirect impacts are likely to be
overstated. The reason is that economic growth tends to be abnormally
high in the years before the crisis because of the financial excesses that
culminated in the crisis. That is why many commentators on the 2008
crisis overstate their case. The real GDP in the United Kingdom is presented on the accompanying graph (Figure 8). If one directly extrapolates
from economic growth before the crisis, the indirect cost would be £212
billion. However, if a more prudent policy path would have led to lower
growth, there actually might have been a gain from the combined precrisis excess and postcrisis decline. There is no right way to identify which
outcome is more likely.

The IMF crisis database was initially developed by the World Bank, and
some of the early developers of the database, including Patrick Honohan
and Daniela Klingebiel, published an interesting paper focusing on the
fiscal costs of banking crises and how the various government responses
contribute to the cost or resolution. They find that if countries do not
extend some policies of unlimited deposit guarantees, open-ended liquidity support, repeated recapitalizations, debtor bailouts, and regulatory

forbearance, the fiscal costs of resolution would be around 1 percent of GDP on average, one-tenth of the actual costs. However, if governments employ all of these approaches the fiscal costs will be six times larger. We like to waste money on resolving financial crises. The primary damage to the economy brought on by a crisis may not be caused by the actual crisis event but by inappropriate government responses. It is interesting that Patrick Honohan later became the governor of the Bank of Ireland, facing very high fiscal costs (caused by the sort of mistakes identified in his study) by the Irish authorities before he took office.

It is also hard to estimate the cost of inaction. One of the most controversial decisions in the 2008 crisis was allowing Lehman Brothers to fail. Some commentators maintain that this was a colossal mistake, one that set in motion the subsequent damaging events. Others argue that bailing out Lehman would only have delayed the inevitable. Both arguments have considerable merit (I lean toward the latter). But a silly interpretation of Lehman's failure is often expressed by European politicians who like to blame it for all the ills that came after, including the European crisis and, in particular, the Greek bailout. Lehman haunts us to this day. One reason for all the Covid-19 bailouts is that the consensus in the policy makers' circle is that Lehman's failure is at the root of all the horrors that happened afterward. If only Lehman had been bailed out.

The late 1980s and early 1990s were a time of banking crises. While the most spectacular was the blowup of the Japanese banking system in 1992, the Scandinavian crisis is more interesting. Three Scandinavian countries, Sweden, Norway, and Finland (well, Finland is not Scandinavian if you go by strict geography, but it identifies as such), suffered a severe banking crisis in the early 1990s. The reason for it was that these countries liberalized their financial markets and implemented expansionary macroeconomic policies in the late 1980s, including removing caps on lending and interest rates and encouraging more competition, all while reducing the level of oversight. The result was a huge lending boom in the late 1980s, followed by a crash in the early 1990s. While the chain of events is depressingly familiar, what is interesting is the way the Scandinavians (especially the Swedes) dealt with the crisis.

The ideal way for governments to resolve a banking crisis is the good bank/bad bank method, perfect in theory, hard in practice. Split up a failing bank, separating the dodgy assets into one institution (the bad bank) while keeping most of its operations and solid assets in the good bank. The bad bank becomes an asset management firm; the government aims to sell the good bank but hold on to the bad assets until they expire. If the dodgy assets are valued cheaply during the crisis when the bad bank is established, as they tend to be, the government potentially can make significant profits, an argument often used to justify this approach to taxpayers. However, if the bank was insolvent, the bad bank must, by definition, have a negative value, so a profit for the government is not the expected outcome. Realistically, the taxpayers should expect to lose money, but hopefully the benefits from having a well-functioning bank replacing a failing bank outweigh the expected loss. The Swedes eventually kept their crisis costs to 4.3 percent of GDP, a fraction of what was initially feared.

It is difficult to implement such ruthless efficiency because all the special interests pull it in different directions—everybody wants a bailout. Most governments find it hard to follow the Swedish example, and two factors determine whether they can. The first is how much faith we have in the government's ability to implement sensible policies that benefit us in the long run. Do we trust the government to do the right thing or see it as incompetent or corrupt, its every initiative to be resisted, no matter how sensible they are. Second is the degree of democracy, that is, whether the government has to take the will of the people into account. In democracies where the trust in government is low, like Italy, it is difficult to deal with banking crises, while the Swedish government was able to make difficult decisions in the 1990s because the Swedes trusted their government.

The trade-off can be easily depicted (Figure 9). The financial authorities need to be competent, determined, and given sufficient political cover to deal efficiently with a financial crisis. Muddling through and wishing the problem would go away are more common, the end result often being zombie banks. That is when banks are insolvent, but the governments cannot close them down, like parts of the Italian banking system today. The term "zombie bank" was first used when discussing the S&L crisis in the 1980s, but it became widespread when referring to the Japanese crisis in the 1990s. Instead of shutting down or recapitalizing its failed banks,

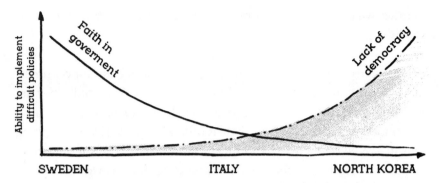

Figure 9. Ability to execute policy. Credit: Lukas Bischoff/IllustrationX.

the Japanese government kept them on life support. Banks were allowed to—even expected to—keep nonperforming loans on their books *as if* they were performing, that is, lending to failed borrowers, just so they could repay old loans: a tactic known as evergreening. This steadily weakened the banks and denied credit to the better-performing parts of the private sector. The Japanese authorities' inability to effectively deal with their banking crisis is one of the main reasons the Japanese economy has been stagnating ever since.

The contrast between the Swedish and the Japanese crises shows what the authorities should do: prevent the emergence of zombie banks at all costs; restructure or shut down failed banks as quickly as possible; and let the banks' creditors and shareholders take the losses. To put it simply, the two main objectives of banking crisis resolution are for the banks to continue serving the real economy and minimize the cost to the taxpayer. That is what the Swedes did better than anybody and that explains why their resolution of the 1992 crisis remains the gold standard.

In the 2008 crisis and the subsequent European crisis, some governments, including those of the United States, Switzerland, and the United Kingdom, actively tried to prevent the emergence of zombie banks. Other European countries, like France, Italy, and Germany, have found that more difficult, lobbying in the G20 for lenient regulations. That reflects their banks' weakness, that is, why they are becoming ever more uncompetitive. Continental European banks are in retreat, American banks in ascendance. The worst problems are in Italy and other Mediterranean countries, which have a large zombie banking sector they find difficult to deal with.

Banking crises are not complicated. They have plagued us for centuries, and we know why they happen and how to prevent them. Still, they are depressingly frequent. Even when there are clear signs of excesses that in all likelihood will lead to a crisis, there is little willingness to do something about it. We enjoy the party too much. What we can do is monitor the banks more closely and force them to measure and manage risk properly. A vast edifice has been created for precisely this purpose. Still, crises happen.

4

The Risk Panopticon

Quis custodiet ipsos custodes?

Figure 10. Credit: Copyright © Ricardo Galvão.

A few years ago, when taking a London black cab, I saw the cabbie reading one of my favorite books on risk, Peter Bernstein's *Against the Gods*. We started chatting, and I mentioned the book I was then writing (what you are now reading). He then told me a great story about why it is difficult to control risk. He had just made a trip to Canary Wharf (the London financial district) and got stopped in a security check. My driver was really surprised when he saw that the only cars being searched were London black cabs. Upon asking the security guard why he got the answer: "Because I have a family." The point is that the most unlikely type of terrorist in London is a driver of a black cab, so if one wants to avoid an unpleasant encounter with a terrorist when tasked with randomly scrutinizing vehicles, the safest choice is indeed black cabs.

This anecdote shows the difficulty facing regulators. While it is easy to identify the bad behavior we want to see modified or stopped, we need human beings to implement the regulations. They will have their own abilities and biases and interests, which, more likely than not, will frustrate the objectives of the regulations. We need oversight—*Quis custodiet ipsos custodes?*[1]—ensuring that the person implementing regulations does what is expected of her, instead of what is easiest or safest or most profitable. If you hire a security guard to randomly check cars entering Canary Wharf, you also need to employ someone to ensure that he does not pick only the safest of cars to investigate. Otherwise, it just ends up being a regulation for peace of mind, for the appearance but not the reality of safety—security theater.

Some regulations work better than others. Take traffic. We drive on the left side of the road in Britain and the right side in France, and we have no problem switching sides when emerging from the Channel Tunnel. We stop at red, hesitate on amber and go on green. We mostly stick to the speed limit, and if we misbehave an army of computers and police keep us in line. It works quite well if we judge it by the rapid fall of traffic accidents. While we complain about getting a ticket, I suspect most people are quite happy that other drivers are kept in check. We mostly agree with and support what the traffic regulators are trying to do. What about financial system? Isn't regulating finance just like regulating traffic? There is plenty of abusive behavior and many crises.

Here I need to distinguish between the acts of regulating and supervising. In common usage, we often use these interchangeably, which is usually perfectly fine, but sometimes it helps to separate the two. Regulations are the rules, supervision the enforcement of them. It is much easier to create good regulations than good supervision. I was once in a car driving on the two-lane motorway between New Delhi and Agra in India. The Indians drive on the left side of the road, as we do in Britain, and most of the traffic laws are quite similar. It is different with supervision. On that motorway I saw people driving in the wrong direction, various animals wandering around, people having a picnic, and the occasional market stall. This is something I have never seen on a British motorway.

Okay, I once played football on the M25 motorway when stuck because of an accident. While many things could account for the difference, I suspect a major one is the intensity of supervision, the enforcement of traffic laws. India and Britain have similar regulations (traffic laws) but different supervision (enforcement of traffic laws). Without efficient enforcement, the regulations become meaningless.

Financial regulations are broadly similar in most countries in the world. They tend to take the lead from G20, the group of the world's largest economies that represents about 90 percent of global GDP; for example, the Basel banking regulations, securities regulations, and insurance regulations. So, regulations are broadly similar. It's different with supervision. Countries interpret the regulations differently, many authorities do a decent job, some are incompetent, others have been captured, and they are often too underfunded to do the job properly. What is really needed for effective supervision is the risk Panopticon.

The intellectual origin of the risk Panopticon is the work of the seventeenth-century English philosopher Jeremy Bentham. It all started when he visited his brother, who was working in Russia. What interested Jeremy was that his brother had come up with an ingenious way to manage his unskilled employees. He set up observation posts in the middle of his workshops, allowing inspectors to monitor the workers without being seen. Jeremy thought this a splendid idea and proposed using it for other human activities such as schools, factories, and even hospitals. It is his proposal for prisons that got the most traction, the Panopticon, from the Greek παν ("all") and οπτικος ("seeing"). If you find yourself in London, you can go see Jeremy Bentham's body, still on display at the University College London.

In the Panopticon the prison cells are located in buildings that surround a central monitoring tower, allowing the prison guards to observe the prisoners without being seen themselves. Because the prisoners never know if they are being observed, they assume they are and thus behave properly, allowing a small number of prison guards to keep watch over many prisoners. Not too different from all the CCTVs installed in our cities. The only remaining job is to prevent the prison guards from abusing the convicts, accomplished by allowing the public to inspect the jails any time they want.

I once saw the power of the Panopticon in action while driving from Spain to Portugal. The traffic laws are the same on both sides of the border, and the speed limit on the motorway was 120km/h. On the Spanish side everybody drove at 120 or below. As soon as they crossed the border, their speed increased to an average of 150. The reason is simple: the Spanish traffic police had unmarked cars checking speed while the Portuguese police did not. The experiment's simplicity rules out any other factors; it involves the same drivers and the same cars. They did not start disregarding their personal safety or acquire better cars upon crossing the border. The only thing that changed their behavior was the chance of getting a ticket on the Spanish side.

The one area where the Panopticon view of regulation has been particularly successful is in public transport. Most bus systems are based on users' contactless cards, so one is left with two options: either buy a ticket and travel legally or commit fraud and hope to get off the bus without being caught. What determines one's choice? Morality and individual attitude to risk. Getting caught can be painful. Just ask Jonathan Burrows, a lapsed fund manager at BlackRock, caught in November 2013 going through a London Underground ticket gate, not having paid the right amount. He admitted to regularly traveling without the right ticket, and the train company estimated the amount of money he had dodged at £43,000. After he was caught he did not inform his employer as he was supposed to. The relevant financial regulator, the Financial Conduct Authority (FCA), took a dim view and declared him "not fit and proper," ending his twenty-year career in finance. He did not need to avoid the £21.50-a-day fee, as, by all accounts, he was well compensated by BlackRock and owned two mansions worth £4 million.

Burrows was just exploiting a loophole. His local station, Stonegate, an hour and twenty-two minutes from his final stop in the City of London, is rural and has no ticket barriers. So he took advantage, tapping his Oyster Card only when arriving. This meant that he paid only the price of the Underground, not the full fare from Stonegate to the London Underground stop. So why would the FCA care about a simple fare fraud? Because Burrows was in a position of trust at BlackRock, so how could he be trusted with other peoples' money if he so casually committed petty fraud? What I find surprising is, why bother? I have my Oyster Card checked a few times a year, and the fine if caught does not seem to be worth the benefit of cheating, not to mention losing a glittering career as a BlackRock fund manager.

Modern financial regulations very much fit into this Benthamite view of the world. Financial institutions release large amounts of information to the public authorities in the full knowledge that the authorities can look only at a small fraction of all that information. But the banks don't know where the authorities are looking, and, even more important, how information released today will be used in future investigations. The regulators can inspect the banks without being seen. The problem is that there can be too much of a good thing, including too much data. So, how well does the panopticon work for the financial supervisors? It depends on the objective. It might help the micro regulators focused on individual banks, protecting individual bank clients. However, what it misses is the risk that arises from market participants' interactions in times of stress—most important, systemic risk.

We Used to Execute Failed Bankers and Still Suffered Crises

Long before we had much in the form of economic regulations, we had banking regulations. They are embedded even in major religions: Christians banned usury until the fifteenth century and Muslims to this date. Financial regulations in many European countries have religious undertones, such as restricting or banning various trading strategies because they might be construed as gambling. There are two reasons banking has always been so regulated. First, banks are a good source of government revenue, so governments like to keep them on a tight leash. Second, efficient and uninterrupted banking services are essential to all economies. Many economic historians will tell you that the establishment of the Bank of England in 1694 was key to the emergence of London as the world's financial center by the eighteenth century, underpinning the United Kingdom's status as the world's greatest economy of the era.

Bank failures impose costs on society far exceeding the private costs of the banks' owners, employees, and counterparties, so it stands to reason banks should be regulated. But it is not an easy job, much harder than regulating other human endeavors, like traffic. We have recently seen plenty of banking crises and abuse, and it is not possible to make a credible case that the banking system, unlike traffic, is better behaved now than it was in the past.

Why is regulating banks so much harder than regulating traffic? The problem is that the financial system is one of the most complex of all human constructs, and the financial entities have strong incentives to misbehave in a way that is undetected. The private incentives of bankers are not well aligned with the interest of society at large. There is little downside for bank employees working with other peoples' money (dismissal, at worst), but they can enjoy a significant upside in terms of high salaries and bonuses. Hence bankers have an incentive to take more risks than desired by either their employers, clients, shareholders, or society. Banks have significant advantages over their clients. They sell sophisticated financial products to people who probably have only a very rudimentary knowledge of finance, perhaps not even understanding basic percentages or present value calculations. An OECD study found that 40 percent of the population does not understand diversification, and only 27 percent are able to both calculate simple interest and recognize the added benefit of compounding over five years.

Given a chance, banks certainly don't hesitate to abuse their clients: witness the Wells Fargo account fraud scandal. The abuse of clients and financial crises happen all too frequently. What can we do? Punish the bankers severely if they misbehave? Claw back their bonuses or even put them in jail? Perhaps even reintroduce the pillory, appropriately on the square in front of the Bank of England. What better place to punish all the failed bankers?

We did try more strict punishments in the olden days. In the thirteenth century one of the major financial centers in Europe was Barcelona, as told by Meir Kohn in his 1999 article "Early Deposit Banking." Banks were tightly regulated. They were forced to have substantial capital and were required to pay cash within twenty-four hours of demand. If banks failed, the owners got into serious trouble, both with the Almighty and the city authorities. Francesch Castello was beheaded in front of his bank in 1360, yet even the threat of decapitation did not stop his fellow bankers from misbehaving.

We aren't going to reintroduce the pillory, not to mention decapitation, and it is not easy to put bankers in jail. What we have is compensation—money. The received wisdom maintains that what motivates bankers is money. Threaten to take the money away, and they will behave prudently. The reality is much more nuanced. I don't think the absolute level of compensation is what matters most to people; relative compensation is much more important. If I get a $1,000 bonus and my buddy gets $500, I am happy, but if I get a million dollars and he gets three million, I'll be sad. It doesn't have to be money; power and authority motivate just as well. We can certainly have abuse and crises without bonuses or excessive compensation, as in the Japanese crisis of 1992.

Might clawbacks work better, in which bankers have to give up compensation that is paid out only in the future? One could ask the senior bankers behind the Wells Fargo phantom account scandal. John Stumpf, the CEO, will give up $69 million, while the person directly responsible, Carrie Tolstedt, the head of community banking, will lose $67 million. This might sound like a lot, but their regular annual compensation (not subject to clawbacks) was in the millions of dollars. I am skeptical that clawbacks will deter many bankers, despite its being a useful outlet for moral outrage.

Punishing the bankers is predicated on actually finding misbehavior, like fraud or abuse. But it's much harder to discipline someone for making a bad investment, even one that leads to a financial crisis. The reason is that someone whose job it is to make investment decisions is, by definition, employed to take risk, and with risk comes the chance of failure. There are two problems with punishing someone for making bad investments. The first is that they most likely will get large bonuses if they succeed, regardless of how dumb the investment was in the first place, while if they fail, at worst they lose their bonus and their job—the upside is much better than the downside. The second reason is that if we hire someone to take risk, we must accept failure, and if we punish them for failed investments, they may end up becoming too risk averse. Not so fast, you may think, we can simply measure the amount of risk they take and reward or punish them accordingly. Well, to do that we have to be able to measure the risk accurately. It is next to impossible to measure financial risk precisely, and it may well be impossible to discriminate between unlucky, incompetent, and corrupt bankers.

Given how the financial system is set up and what drives its cycles, banks can and will end up taking too much risk. Individual bankers take excessive risk again and again, and we will go through repeated boom-to-bust cycles. It is really hard to effectively prevent the worst outcomes with regulations, but there is a right way and the wrong way to regulate banks. Punishing bankers or even executing them as the regulators did to poor Francesch Castello is unlikely to work. We need something else.

Bank Capital

The primary tool for controlling how banks behave is bank capital. Bank capital has two purposes. The first is a buffer so that if a bank gets into difficulty, it has some reserves to draw on before hitting bankruptcy. The main reason for capital is, however, limits to leverage. The more capital a bank has to hold, for the same amount of assets, the less levered it is, and hence safer. The concept of bank capital is quite confusing, especially for those trained in accounting, economics, or the law. The most common usage follows Adam Smith, who defines capital in *The Wealth of Nations* (1776) as "that part of a man's stock which he expects to afford him revenue." To Karl Marx, in *Das Kapital,* capital is more nefarious: wealth that is used to create more wealth, something that exists only because of economic exchange or the circulation of money. Modern usage follows both Smith and Marx and is often quite contradictory. We have concepts like capitalization—the market value of a corporation—and economists talk about capital as one of the two main inputs in production, the other being labor. One can also find capital to be the net market value of a firm after all its debts have been subtracted.

A few years ago the university lecturers' union in the United Kingdom was protesting in front of the main entrance of the London School of Economics against the evils of capitalism. As I walked through the door, crossing the picket line, the protesters asked me if I was a capitalist, as if that were a horrible thing. I answered, "Yes" and added, "So are you." They disliked that and demanded an explanation. I responded by asking them if they belonged to the university pension fund. They said yes. Well, the pension fund owns stock in companies, and the definition of a capitalist, according to Karl Marx, is someone who owns the means of production. Therefore, anyone who owns stock in a company, which every member of our pension fund does, is a capitalist. The protesters did not like that reply.

When thinking about bank capital, especially for those trained in economics or accounting, you should forget everything you know about capital and start anew. Bank capital is an artificial accounting construct and has only a vague relationship with the term's most common usage, as discussed by Smith and Marx. When I lecture on capital to my students, I like to define it as things that the banking regulators have chosen to call capital. Bank capital is composed of two components: common equity, that is, assets minus liabilities and financial instruments that are not quite common equity but help meet the objectives of the regulators—equity-like.

At the end of 2019 the world's largest bank, JP Morgan, had total assets worth $2.7 trillion, while its capital was $169 billion. The ratio of capital to total assets is called leverage ratio, and regulations require the leverage ratio to be at least 3 percent. JP Morgan beats that comfortably at 6.3 percent. Some of the bank's assets, such as loans to governments, are quite safe, but others, like mortgages and loans and medium-sized enterprises (MSEs), are risky, hence regulators have come up with the concept of risk-weighted assets: the higher the risk, the higher the weight. JP Morgan's risk-weighted assets are $1.5 trillion.

The $64,000 question is how much capital a bank should have. One might think it would be a good idea to make capital really high, but there is a downside. The more capital a bank has to hold, the less it can lend and the more expensive those loans are to borrowers. And since banks are a major source of funding to companies, especially the all-important small and medium sized enterprises (SMEs), the end result is less investment and less economic growth. The balance is delicate.

Some observers, like Anat Admati and Martin Hellwig, maintain that capital should be much higher than it is now because the costs from the inevitable bank failures outweigh the benefits a high-risk banking system provides to society. The banks respond by arguing that this underestimates the costs to society because the cost of bank lending will become much higher and interest paid on savings much lower—both borrowers and savers lose out, and economic growth will suffer. Regardless of which is right, this is the proper debate to have because it frames the discussion in terms of what we want from banks, not in a more narrow sense of just wanting banks to be safe.

Before I leave capital, I want to make two points, one technical and one philosophical (if you want more details, you are welcome to download my slides on regulations and capital).[2] The technical point is that capital is made up of multiple parts. At the most basic level, we have common equity. We then have additional bits that are called Tier 2 and Tier 1 capital. Add to that a buffer for banks in case they run into difficulty, called the capital conservation buffer, and another for countries in trouble, the countercyclical capital buffer. Finally, a special buffer for systemically important banks. I used all of this buffer complexity to good effect in my exam in 2020, asking which part of capital requirements would be relaxed to help banks so they could help with the Covid-19 recovery.

The philosophical point is that even though it is often said to be a buffer that protects when things go sour, that is only partially true. The reason is that banks are required to hold minimum capital, which they are unable to reduce in bad times. As noted by Charles Goodhart, a capital buffer that can't be used isn't much of a buffer: "The weary traveler . . . arrives at the railway station late at night, and, to his delight, sees a taxi there who could take him to his distant destination. He hails the taxi, but the taxi driver replies that he cannot take him, since local bylaws require that there must always be one taxi standing ready at the station."[3]

Schrödinger's Bank

Financial regulations used to be something each country set for itself. There were some agreements between countries but not many international standards. This was fine so long as the global financial system remained fragmented or heavily regulated, as it was under the post–World War II Bretton Woods system, when banks were by and large confined to their home countries and not allowed to operate across borders.

This state of affairs changed when the Bretton Woods system collapsed in 1972, bringing a philosophical change in attitudes toward global finance: the Washington Consensus. From then on, national frontiers continued to open up to global finance. Banks could operate across borders, and money moved freely between countries. Financial regulations did not keep up. Even after the borders started opening, regulations were still national, and the regulators didn't talk much to their counterparts in other countries. This arrangement was not sustainable, and a series of crises brought home the need for global coordination.

Failures don't have to be very large to have severe repercussions, as when the bankruptcy of the eightieth-largest bank in Germany, Bankhaus Herstatt, in 1974, caused serious disruption to global financial markets. The Herstatt family has a long history in banking, dating back to Jowan David Herstatt in 1727. After the collapse of the Bretton Woods system, Bankhaus Herstatt was an active player in the foreign exchange market, speculating on the exchange rate between the German mark and the US dollar. It was not all that successful, and losses mounted. Eventually, the bank was forced into liquidation on 26 June 1974.

Interestingly, when Herstatt failed, it was not closed down in every jurisdiction simultaneously. The German authorities closed the domestic operations, but the bank continued operating abroad because the German authorities did not inform their foreign counterparts of the closure. Herstatt was half dead and half alive, like Schrödinger's cat. The day Herstatt failed, it had been buying a large number of German marks, receiving them in Germany, and due to pay dollars for them in New York. It failed after receiving the German marks and before delivering the dollars. The reason was the time zone difference between Frankfurt and New York. It received marks at the end of the German business day and was to pay out dollars at the end of the New York business day, six hours later. The eventual losses to its creditors were $1.3 billion, the single largest being Moscow Norodny at $365 million. While $1.3 billion was undoubtedly a more serious number in 1974 than it is today, it is still a relatively small amount.

It was damaging because of how it occurred. The German regulators kept their foreign counterparts in the dark about the seriousness of Herstatt's risk. They had been intensively monitoring the bank for at least three years before 1974 and knew a collapse was imminent. Why did they keep it a secret? We can only speculate, but I think there are two main reasons. First, their mandate was to protect Germany, its processes, laws, and reputation, which meant mistrusting foreigners. Second, they were embarrassed that a bank on their watch would fail. Whatever the reason, the German financial regulatory system was reformed soon after.

When the German bank Wirecard failed in the summer of 2020, the circumstances were eerily similar to those of Herstatt half a century earlier. The German regulators of Wirecard had been aware of some problems but failed to act. The head German regulator said in a testimony to the German parliament, Bundestag, that the German regulatory system functioned well in normal circumstances but failed in a crisis.

The Herstatt bankruptcy demonstrated a weakness of the settlement system, until then not recognized, and served as a wake-up call to the global financial authorities. They might want to be purely domestic, managing their banks with minimum international coordination, but the banks don't play ball. They are international—and that requires international coordination.

It wasn't really until the case of Banco Ambrosiano eight years later that the case was forcefully made. Ambrosiano was the largest private banking group in Italy, with operations in fifteen countries. At the center of the bank's failure was its chairman, Roberto Calvi, called God's banker by the Italian press due to his close association with the Holy See. Calvi was determined to transform his bank from a relatively small regional bank with strong religious overtones into a major international financial institution. One of his initial steps was to form a holding company in Luxembourg, which was not subject to Italy's banking regulations.

Calvi's problems began in 1978 when the Bank of Italy conducted an extensive audit of his financial empire, noting unorthodox operations involving $1.2 billion in unsecured borrowings. Ambrosiano was buying up its stock by using dollars, an illegal operation according to Italian banking regulations. Ambrosiano collapsed for quite predictable reasons: the Italian lira fell relative to the dollar, so the lira amount of its liabilities sharply increased, while the value of its Italian assets stayed constant in lira terms. Calvi was sentenced to four years in jail but released pending appeal. He fled Italy but was found hanging under the Blackfriars Bridge in London in 1982. To this day, it's not know whether he committed suicide or was killed, a topic that continues to arouse controversy. I cross Blackfriars Bridge on my way to work every day and have frequently spared a thought for poor Calvi. The failure of Banco Ambrosiano left more than two hundred international financial institutions with large losses, threatening the stability of the entire international banking system. Ultimately, this triggered major changes in international regulations.

The Ambrosiano collapse turned out not to be the last chapter in the reform saga, as the failure of the Bank for Commerce and Credit International (BCCI) showed. BCCI was registered in Luxembourg with head offices in Karachi and London and branches throughout the world. It was closed down by the London authorities in July 1991 because of widespread fraud, and it is now believed that BCCI's financial statements had been falsified from its establishment in 1972. BCCI failed to record deposits as liabilities and created fictitious loans that generated substantial profits, using depositors' money to fund their own proprietary trading activities and covering up the resulting losses with more fictitious loans.

One reason BCCI got away with it was that it used a complex structure consisting of a holding company, incorporated in Luxembourg, and two principal subsidiaries in the Cayman Islands and Luxembourg. Even before these problems surfaced in 1990 supervisors and commercial bankers were wary of BCCI because of its rapid growth and opaque corporate structure. Yet while BCCI was sometimes mentioned in the press "chiefly for the mystery that surrounded it," market participants generally saw BCCI as a bank that lost money through incompetence rather than fraud. Concerns about fraud led eventually to discussions between BCCI's then current and previous auditors (Price Waterhouse and Ernst & Young), the banking supervisors, and BCCI's shareholders. After BCCI failed, the liquidators, Deloitte & Touche, filed a lawsuit against the auditors, settling for $175 million in 1998. BCCI creditors also attempted to sue the Bank of England as BCCI's regulators.

I draw two main lessons from the case of BCCI. The first is that it is necessary to ensure that banks are supervised everywhere they operate and that neither the regulators in their home country nor the countries where they operate should be able to avoid regulating them. The second lesson is more interesting because it nicely demonstrates the reputation risk of central banks that conduct banking supervision. The reputation of the Bank of England took a hit, and that was worrying because the bank needs its high reputation to be able to credibly implement monetary policy. The BCCI scandal motivated the separation of banking supervision from the Bank of England in 1997, creating the Financial Services Authority (FSA). And since Britain is generally seen as a leader in regulatory methodology, many countries followed suit.

Was that a good idea? The global crisis in 2008 showed what can happen if the central banks are not in charge of supervision: they lack oversight, don't know what is happening on the ground, don't have the necessary expertise, and can refuse responsibility. The British authorities eventually split the FSA into the independent Financial Conduct Authority (FCA) and the Prudential Regulation Authority (PRA), which was remerged with the Bank of England. Other countries are now following suit. I am curious to see what the British authorities will do after the next crisis. Will the PRA be remerged with the FCA or will the FCA rejoin the Bank of England?

The Rules from Basel

In the years after World War II banks were mostly prevented from operating outside their home countries. As the restrictions were gradually lifted in the 1960s, banks started to operate internationally, and the need for global coordination was recognized. In response, the main financial centers at the time, those making up the G10 group (Belgium, Canada, France, Italy, Japan, Germany, Sweden, the Netherlands, the United Kingdom, and the United States), together with Luxembourg, set up the Basel Committee on Banking Supervision, or Basel committee in short, as a new international organization tasked with designing international banking regulations in 1974. Charles Goodhart wrote a history of the committee.

Each country had two or more members on the committee, typically one from the regulator and one from the central bank. But why Luxembourg? you may ask. It is undoubtedly a financial center but hardly belongs in the G10. The reason is that a Luxembourgish banker, Albert Dondelinger, was instrumental in setting up the committee, and it would have been churlish to exclude him and Luxembourg. However, since Luxembourg did not have a central bank (it used the Belgian franc as currency, so the National Bank of Belgium was its central bank), it got only one seat.

The Basel committee is hosted at but is distinct from the Bank for International Settlements, whose head office is in Basel, Switzerland. It does not possess any formal powers, acting instead as a vehicle for seeking agreement on common standards but leaving implementation to member countries. The Basel committee's limited membership used to be a source of frustration for the rest of the world, as many countries have felt they had no choice but to implement Basel-style regulations without the ability to influence them. This aggravation has now been remedied, as following the 2008 crisis the committee expanded to include twenty-eight jurisdictions.

The Basel committee reports to the G20 group of countries, as do other parts of the international financial architecture. The most important part of the committee's work is the Basel Capital Accords, a set of rules for determining how much capital a bank should have. The first Basel Accord, now referred to as Basel I, was decided in 1988 and implemented in 1992. The successor, Basel II, was proposed in the late 1990s and partially implemented from 2008.

Why did the Basel committee decide to harmonize bank capital rules? It goes back to the early 1980s, when bank capital ratios of major banks in Europe and the United States were perhaps 8 percent to 10 percent, while the Japanese banks operated with much lower capital, around 4 percent, giving them a competitive advantage. The lower the capital ratio, the lower the cost of lending. Not surprisingly, the Japanese banks became a significant presence in the European and American corporate lending markets, elbowing out the local banks. Understandably upset, the European and American banks pushed for their capital ratios to be lowered to match those of the Japanese. The regulators didn't like that very much and instead forced the Japanese to raise their capital standards to the European and American levels.

When I spent a few months at the Bank of Japan in 2000, some of my Japanese colleagues called Basel I the anti-Japanese conspiracy, blaming it for the collapse of the Japanese banking system in the early 1990s and the subsequent recession. There is a lot of truth in that. Having to double the capital ratio within a few years proved quite difficult and certainly contributed to the Japanese banking crisis.

Basel I succeeded in achieving its intended purposes, raising capital levels when they were low and trending down. Still, the accord wasn't perfect, focusing on credit risk with crude risk weights. If a bank lent $1 billion to an AAA-rated firm, like Apple, it had to hold $80 million in capital. If it lent the same amount to an OECD government, like Turkey, Japan, Mexico, or Greece, no capital was needed. It is easy to see why governments liked this arrangement. It made loans to companies and individuals more expensive than loans to governments, subsidizing government borrowing at the private sector's expense. Financial repression, the economists call it.

Long before the 2008 crisis, and anticipating some of the things that would eventually go wrong, the Basel committee embarked on a revision of Basel I in the 1990s, what came to be known as Basel II. It did away with the zero-risk weighting for the OECD government debt, but the European Union didn't like this move very much and passed a directive saying that all member states' sovereign debt was risk free. While subsidizing government borrowing in Europe, the directive also helped Greece to borrow itself into default and was the leading cause of the Cypriot crisis in 2012 (see chapter 3). While Basel II was announced at the turn of the century, the extensive lobbying that followed delayed its implementation until 2008. This meant that Basel II reflected the regulatory concerns and technological developments of the mid-1990s, so it was already out of date by the time of implementation, a common problem in international financial regulations.

I was always of two minds about Basel II. It was a big step toward making risk management and especially financial regulations scientific. But what bothers me most is the belief that risk can be measured and controlled accurately. While that might be a reasonable (or at least acceptable) assumption in the internal management of individual risks, it is a big leap to apply it to risk control for an entire financial institution, not to mention the entire financial system. The Basel II proposals inspired me to write my favorite paper, eventually published in 2002 under the title "The Emperor Has No Clothes: Limits to Risk Modeling," where I argued that risk was not all that well measured.

When Basel II was announced I got together with several LSE colleagues, including Charles Goodhart and Hyun Song Shin, to write an official comment, titled *An Academic Critique to Basel II,* in response to a call for comments on the initial Basel II proposals. We certainly were skeptical: "Heavy reliance on credit rating agencies for the standard approach to credit risk is misguided as they have been shown to provide conflicting and inconsistent forecasts of individual clients' creditworthiness. They are unregulated, and the quality of their risk estimates is largely unobservable." One of the leading causes of the 2008 crisis was structured credit products composed of subprime mortgages that could not have been created without the credit-rating agencies. As it turned out, the ratings were abysmal, demonstrating the folly of relying on the rating agencies for financial regulations: "Statistical models used for forecasting risk have been proven to give inconsistent and biased forecasts. The Basel committee has chosen poor quality measures of risk when better risk measures are available."

When the Basel II regulations were initially proposed in the mid-1990s there was little understanding of the underlying risk-measurement techniques' reliability. By the time the proposals came out, that had changed. The low-quality methods chosen by the Basel committee significantly contributed to the regulators' and the banks' improper appreciation of financial risk before 2007: "The proposed regulations fail to consider the fact that risk is endogenous. Value-at-Risk can destabilize and induce crashes when they would not otherwise occur. Financial regulation is inherently procyclical. Our view is that this set of proposals will, overall, exacerbate this tendency significantly. Insofar as the purpose of financial regulation is to reduce the likelihood of systemic crises, these proposals will actually tend to negate, not promote this useful purpose."

The statement describes exactly what happened in the years before 2008. As banks were implementing Basel II in the early 2000s, the risk management methodologies they were required to implement told them that risk was low and therefore it was perfectly acceptable, even expected, to take more risk. By not recognizing the consequent risk, the Basel II regulations amplified the financial cycle, helping to create the right conditions for the 2008 crisis.

Regulating a Malevolent Entity

The tallest skyscraper in the world was built in Taipei in 2004. While the appropriately named Taipei 101 is no longer the world's tallest, it is the most interesting from the perspective of risk. Every tall building has to contend with the elements—in Taipei 101 earthquakes and typhoons—so risk management is critical to prevent a catastrophe. The devices used to manage the risk are usually hidden, but not in Taipei 101. It uses a 728-ton gold-painted orb that is open to the public as a counterweight that swings like a pendulum at the top of the building. A risk management system that has become a tourist attraction in its own right. The engineers even hired the Sanrio Company, the creators of Hello Kitty, to create the "Damper Babies," cute figurines representing the risk management system.

Taipei 101 was tested in August 2015 when it was hit by Typhoon Soudelor, with winds of 145 mph. The golden orb swung more than a meter from its regular position, but nothing happened to the building, a monument to the engineers' calculations. If structural engineers can create risk management systems that protect tall buildings like Taipei 101, why can't the financial engineers working in the regulatory agencies protect us from financial crises? Because of a crucial difference between the risks in these two disciplines. The reason the job of the civil engineers is relatively straightforward is that they can ignore the human element. If they calculate that a wall one meter thick is expected to collapse every five hundred years, nature couldn't care less. Risk is exogenous.

In finance, nature is not neutral, it is malevolent, and risk is endogenous. The reason is that all rules and regulations change behavior and outcomes. Human beings, being human, don't just naively comply—they change their behavior in response. Immediately after a regulator comes up with rules, perhaps for determining bank capital, the bankers look for a way around the rules. They will try their best to make the capital appear to be very high to the outside world while making it as low as possible in practice. The technical name for this is capital structure arbitrage. Many of the banks that failed in 2008 had some of the highest levels of capital going, but that capital turned out to be illusionary. There is always a cat-and-mouse game going on between the authorities and the banks. While the bankers may pore over stacks of regulations to comply, they are much more enthusiastic about finding loopholes. Regulations are inherently backward looking and change at a glacial pace, giving fast-moving and forward-looking bankers ample room to look for places to take risk where the authorities are not looking. Because the financial system is almost infinitely complex, it is technically impossible to regulate but a tiny part of it, leaving plenty of room for misbehavior.

Regulations may end up causing profitable activities to move to the ~~shadow~~ parallel banking system or abroad. A good example is Regulation Q in the United States from the 1960s and 1970s, which limited the interest banks could pay on deposits, the idea being that high interest rates were inflationary (this erroneous notion has recently resurfaced in Turkey). Regulation Q simply caused deposits to move to the parallel banking system—the money market funds—where market interest rates could be paid. Regulation Q was abolished a long time ago, but the money market mutual funds continue to flourish and have become a significant contributor to systemic risk in the United States. Financial activities can also shift abroad, as when the Eurodollar market first came into being in the 1950s, when the Soviet Union's oil revenue—all in US dollars—was deposited outside the United States for fear of being frozen by US regulators. This resulted in a vast offshore pool of dollars outside the control of US authorities, primarily in Europe, hence the term "Eurodollar," helping London become a world-leading financial center again.

When we regulate the financial system we often drive risk-taking behavior away from the spotlight and deep into the shadows, where it is much harder to detect. The tequila crisis in Mexico in 1993 happened because the Mexican banks were borrowing US dollars in New York to lend to Mexican borrowers in pesos. Because the Mexican banks took the currency risk, the Mexican authorities were justifiably concerned and forbade this. The Mexican banks found it easy to get around the rules by creating derivative transactions with the New York banks—Tesobonos. Because the Mexican central bank, Banco de México, did not see these transactions, it did not realize what was happening and could not step in to prevent the crisis until it was too late. It is much better if risk-taking is visible rather than hidden.

Finally, and even more insidiously, precisely because the financial authority is trying to reduce financial risk, banks have an extra incentive to take on more risk—an example of the Minsky effect. That perverse outcome happens because of the way we measure risk. If all looks nice and stable, the road is smooth—the great moderation before the 2008 crisis—and perceived risk is low. If everything is safe, what's wrong with a little bit more risk? The problem is we don't usually notice all the extra risks until much later. It was decisions taken in the low-risk, great-moderation environment at the start of the 2000s that created the conditions for the crisis in 2008. Nobody had any idea until the crisis was already under way.

The three factors—the encouragement of avoidance, the move to the shadows, and the Minsky effect—came together in 2008, helped by financial innovation: the creation of new and more complex financial instruments. The late Paul Volcker, the éminence grise of US financial policy making, alumnus of the London School of Economics, and the slayer of the 1970s inflation when he was the chair of the Federal Reserve, said in 2009, "I wish that somebody would give me some shred of neutral evidence about the relationship between financial innovation recently and the growth of the economy. . . . It was hard to think of a worthwhile financial innovation since the ATM."[4]

In 2008 it was all the various structured credit products like structured investment vehicles, conduits, and collateral debt obligations (CDOs). They allowed the buildup of very high levels of hidden risk, not least liquidity risk, that proved so damaging. The most interesting case of how financial innovation can cause trouble is the IKB bank, a small, partly state-owned, German bank. Before the 2008 crisis it was quite active in the market for a particularly dangerous financial product called a conduit. A conduit is a special purpose vehicle that invests in long-term bonds but finances itself by borrowing short term. That is highly profitable most of the time because short-term interest rates are lower than long-term interest rates, and the difference between the two is profit. Profitable so long as the yield curve is upward sloping—long-term interest rates are usually higher than short-term interest rates—and when someone is willing to lend short term. If either goes away, the strategy is no longer profitable. Naturally, the short-term lenders knew this and would normally demand high compensation for financing a conduit. The conduits found a neat way around that: a sponsor with a good credit rating that, for a fee, guaranteed the short-term lending and promised to fund the conduit if nobody else did. In good times, fantastic. The fee income rolls in, and it looks like money for nothing. But there is hidden risk. When the crisis started in 2007, the conduits could not roll over their short-term loans and hence called on the sponsor, IKB, for help. Unfortunately, IKB did not have the money needed. Facing bankruptcy, it was bailed out at the cost of €9 billion to the German taxpayers.

IKB made a name for itself the following year by transferring money to Lehmans a few hours after the latter defaulted. Apparently, IKB had automatic rules in place for transferring money to Lehmans on Monday mornings, and even if the entire world knew by Friday that Lehmans was about to fail, and it had actually failed right after midnight Monday morning, IKB didn't think to cancel its transfer.

We have become a society of regulations, ruled by the risk Panopticon. Jeremy Bentham would be proud. Many regulatory systems work well, especially in the airline industry, where continuous improvements and a culture of minimizing risk have led to a dramatic fall in fatalities even as air traffic grows. Our view of how well regulations work is shaped by our interactions with the best ones: airlines, traffic, food. Not surprisingly, despite all the abuse and exploitation and crises we want to regulate finance just as strictly. Unfortunately, it isn't all that easy, and the reason it isn't so hinges on two concepts, risk and uncertainty, and the pivotal role played by the riskometer.

5

The Myth of the Riskometer

Prediction is very difficult, especially if it's about the future.
—*Nils Bohr*

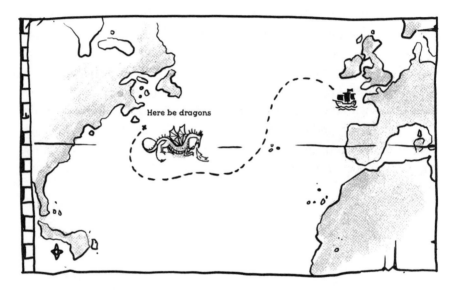

Figure 11. Credit: Lukas Bischoff/IllustrationX.

In the Middle Ages maps sometimes came with the warning *hic sunt dracones,* here be dragons (Figure 11). Where the mapmakers had little information, they warned travelers of unexpected dangers, maybe dragons. The modern riskometer should come with the same warning.

There are many ways to measure financial risk. The most accurate is to study the deep structure of the financial system, identify all the interlinkages and the hidden corners where risk is taken. That is difficult and costly, and it is much more common to use a purely statistical approach, what I called a riskometer in a blog piece I wrote for VoxEU .org titled "The Myth of the Riskometer." It is a useful little thing, the riskometer. I can plunge it deep into the bowels of Wall Street and it pops out an accurate measurement of risk.

Riskometers are used all over. Anywhere from someone investing their own money to risk managers controlling proprietary traders to a bank determining the amount of capital it holds. Financial regulators concerned with the stability of the entire financial system use one too. The riskometers promise to distill the risk of entire financial institutions into one number. It is really useful to have a single, unambiguous measurement of risk. A number with all sorts of caveats is not nearly as helpful. The decision makers, the people who run banks, and the regulatory agencies are just like President Harry S. Truman, who is widely credited as having demanded, "Give me a one-handed economist. All my economists say 'on the one hand . . . ,' then 'but on the other.'"

The prominence of riskometers is increasing by the day, and for a good reason. They are cheap, quick, and objective—scientific, really. The alternatives are subjective, slow, and expensive. In the scientific world of risk, where we have almost limitless data, sophisticated statistical methods, and all the processing power one could want, how can the riskometer not be the best way to measure risk? The problem is that riskometers can capture only a caricatured view of risk. Any particular implementation will focus on and often exaggerate some aspects of risk and ignore others. That means riskometers are not nearly as accurate as most of us think, most notably the senior decision makers. Those who are actually on the ground, designing the riskometers and reporting risk to their superiors, know better.

There is nothing new about riskometers, and we have been searching for devices for measuring risk since the beginning of time. The earliest example I know of is the riskometer the Chinese astronomer Zhang Heng invented in AD 132 during the Han Dynasty. It is a metal urn containing a bronze ball and eight dragon heads for each direction on the compass. When an earthquake hit, the ball would roll onto the dragon head corresponding to the earthquake's direction. The government was advised both of an earthquake and where it happened, allowing the emperor to send relief to the affected region.

The modern notion of risk and its applications to decision-making dates back to Blaise Pascal's work, the sixteenth-century French mathematician who both improved our understanding of risk and formally linked it to how to manage future economic endeavors. Monsieur Pascal might well be the first management consultant. The question then is whether the caricature is sufficiently accurate. Will it lead us astray by not measuring (or even hiding) the risk we care about and make us waste our efforts on risk that is not all that important? To paraphrase the statistician George Box: "All measurements of risk are wrong. Some are useful."

If I want to figure out the temperature outside, all I have to do is look at the thermometer outside my kitchen window. Right now it tells me that the temperature is 14.4° Celsius (57.9°F). If that is not precise enough, I can spend more money and be told that the temperature is 14.392°C. If I don't trust my thermometer, I can pop out to the store and buy another one. Or go to BBC's weather service, which tells me that the temperature in my postcode is 14.4°C. Thermometers are reliable and consistent, and different ones give the same answer. On top of this, everyone sees temperature the same way. Regardless of whether I am concerned about how warm my house is or am controlling some industrial process, or if I am at the North Pole or in the Sahara desert, the concept of temperature is the same. 14.4°C always has the same meaning, no matter what I, or anybody else, am up to.

What about risk? Can I use a riskometer in the same way as one might use a thermometer? No. We need three separate layers of analysis for risk, whereas only one is needed for temperature:

1. The recognition of what sort of risk is most important
2. A theory of how to quantify that risk
3. Statistical technologies for producing the actual risk measurements.

The latter two make up the concept of a riskometer, the choice of which intimately depends on what the riskometer is needed for, the first layer.

To start with, what do I want? Suppose Paul, Ann, and Mary each invest in Google stock. Their reasons for investing are different. Paul trades on his own account, his reasons are speculative, and he aims to get out in one week with a hefty profit. Ann is a fund manager, investing on behalf of her bank, and her primary concern is beating her benchmark and avoiding significant losses relative to her benchmark that would get her fired. Mary is investing for the long term and worries about getting her pension seventy years into the future when she is ninety-five years old and relying on the financial industry for her material well-being.

Even though each of the three made precisely the same investment and had access to the very same risk measurement technologies, their views on risk are very different. Paul cares about day-to-day fluctuations over the next week, Ann is worried about a substantial one-day loss sometime in the next six months, and Mary needs the Google stock price to continue to grow over the next seventy years and does not care about what happens to the stock in the meantime (and certainly not over the next week). Their investment horizons are different, their objectives are different, and therefore what risk means to them is different. Each needs a different riskometer. Unlike temperature, where Celsius is the appropriate unit of measurement regardless of what it is used for, for risk we need different concepts depending on the end use.

So the next step for Paul, Ann, and Mary is to pick a riskometer. The riskometer is a combination of two things: some concept of what risk is and a statistical apparatus to produce a risk measurement. Start with the concept. With temperature, we have three units of measure Celsius, Fahrenheit, and Kelvin. However, they all measure the same thing, temperature, and we know exactly how to go from one to the other. 100° Celsius is 212° Fahrenheit and 373.15° Kelvin. It is not the same with risk, where we have multiple concepts.

When it comes to an individual stock's risk, I may be interested in volatility, Value-at-Risk, or Expected Shortfall, just to mention the three most popular. These are not just three measurements of the same thing like Celsius, Fahrenheit, or Kelvin. It is like having three different opinions of temperature with no apparent way to compare numbers produced under one standard with another. The user has to pick the concept of risk most appropriate to her, and if she uses a generic one—a one-size-fits-all riskometer—the result will not be as good as if she picked what is the best riskometer for her purpose.

I was recently asked to address fund managers from Latin America on the idea of the riskometer and practical issues in risk management. I was appalled when one of the delegates asked me a question on the use of Value-at-Risk for pension funds. It is not often that I am speechless, but that morning I was. As it turned out, the regulators in her country had imposed a Value-at-Risk constraint on pension funds, in effect forcing them to think about day-to-day risk rather than long-term solvency. Why would they have done so? When I asked them, I was told that the reason was probably that Value-at-Risk was seen as the best practice in risk management—it is fundamental in international banking regulations, the Basel Accords—and, without thinking it through correctly, the authorities decided to apply it to pension funds.

The muddled pensions regulators are not alone. Most people, even professionals who should know better, see financial risk measurements as a single concept with no difference between day-to-day risk, the risk of extreme losses, and long-term risk. This is nonsense. One cannot go from one concept of financial risk to another without making what often are entirely unrealistic assumptions.

After deciding on a concept of risk, the next step is statistical measurement. When it comes to temperature, measurement is easy. Take some mercury, put it in a tube, and since mercury expands with heat, the mercury's height in the tube tells us the temperature. It is the same with prices. I can go to my Bloomberg terminal to check what the price of a stock is. That is it. I know the price. Both prices and temperature are real-time measurements. It is different with risk, as there is no single observable phenomenon called risk. The reason is that what is measured cannot be compared to any actual reality. In statistical language, risk is latent, meaning that it cannot be directly observed. At best, one gets an imperfect measurement by observing how risk influences the world. If a stock price fluctuates a lot, it might be highly risky, but then again it might not.

Once, when I was explaining the problem of measuring risk to my LSE students, I did the following experiment. I told them to ignore what they knew about the temperature in London at that moment and instead asked them to look out of the window and guess what the temperature was, based on how people were dressed. It was a typical October day, with a temperature of 13° Celsius. I got numbers ranging from 8° to 24°. Those on the lower end of the scale tended to come from tropical countries, where people start putting on coats when the temperature is still in the 20s. Most of the rest came from cold countries, where people are lightly dressed even when the temperature falls below 10°. The experiment shows how biased we can be when it comes to measuring latent variables like risk and how our background and experience shape the measurements.

Because risk is latent, the only way to measure it is to see what has happened in the past. If I am interested in the risk of a stock, I have to observe how the stock fluctuated in the past and infer a risk measurement. Not all that straightforward. To begin with, how far to look back? For some assets, we have a long history. The longest I know of is the exchange rate between the Dutch guilder and the British pound, starting in the early 1600s and extending to today if I allow the guilder to join the euro in 1998. Some individual stocks have been traded for over a century.

I have observations on the most important stock market index in the world, the Standard and Poor's 500 index, going back to the 1770s. Yes, the S&P 500 dates only back to 1957, but economic historians have reconstructed its older values, some of which you can find on Bloomberg. However, the US stock market was very different in the 1770s than it is today, so I may want to start measuring risk more recently. But when? Different starting points will give different risk measurements, and I have no clear way of identifying which is more correct. There is no single correct answer to the question of how much data to use. We could ask the experts, but they will probably say, "It depends," and the more expert they are, the more likely they are to say so.

If that was not enough, I also have to pick a statistical model. Here I have a large number of choices, each with its strengths and weaknesses. Some are relatively accurate but data-intensive, while others can provide less accurate measurements with little data. Some need powerful computers and highly trained experts. Others can be implemented in Excel with minimum training. Some focus on extreme outcomes, while others are more concerned with day-to-day movements. So how do we pick a model? If you ask the experts, they will just suggest their favorite methodology. Not very helpful.

When it comes to risk, the objectives, the concept of risk, and the statistical methodology should be considered simultaneously. This means that different end users, all with the same investment and technical skills, ought to measure risk differently. In the example above, what is risk to Paul is irrelevant to Mary and vice versa. There are a lot of riskometers out there. Because it is not very hard for someone who knows programming and statistics to create yet another one, it is not surprising that academia and consultancies are full of people churning out riskometers, all producing different measurements of risk for the same assets. It can be an easy way of getting a PhD in statistics, physics, computer science, or economics. The same PhDs tend to get jobs in the financial industry, producing riskometers for their government agencies and banks.

The European Central Bank's Risk Dashboard

Far better an approximate answer to the right question, which is often vague, than an exact answer to the wrong question, which can always be made precise.
—*John W. Tukey (1962)*

There are few better places for seeing riskometers in action than the European Central Bank's risk dashboard. The dashboard is full of interesting numbers (Figure 12). On the day after the Brexit vote in June 2016, it told us that systemic risk was 0.321853, on a scale of 0 to 1. That was indeed much higher than the 0.185922 the week before, not to mention the 0.058941 at the start of 2016, when we seemed to be especially safe. The historically safest date was 27 September 2013, at 0.02106. Fortunately, the Brexit systemic risk is not as bad as it was in December 2008, when it hit 0.838846, worse than the number after Lehman failed in September 2008, when it was "only" 0.554620. These figures look exact. The six significant digits tell us so: 0.321853 is much more accurate than a mere 0.3 and suggests the European Central Bank has pretty precise measurement technology. But is that precision realistic? As Warren Buffett once said, "We don't like things you have to carry out to three decimal places. If someone weighed somewhere between 300–350 pounds, I wouldn't need precision—I would know they were fat."

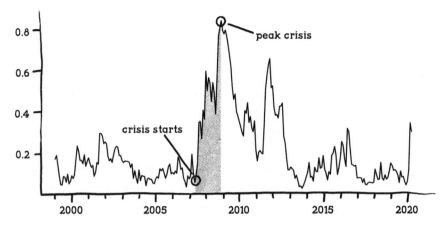

Figure 12. ECB composite indicator of systemic stress (CISS) systemic risk indicator. Credit: Lukas Bischoff/IllustrationX.

The 0.321853 is no more an accurate measurement than 0.3, and the extra precision serves only to mislead. Despite the dashboard's apparent precision, there is a strange omission from it in that it does not tell us anywhere what the numbers mean. Presumably the numbers are ordinal, so 0.321853 is worse than 0.02106 and better than 0.838846, but by how much? Is it a lot worse or almost the same? In other words, it omits any analysis of statistical significance.

When I took my first course in statistics at university, the professor hammered into us the importance of significance testing. Create confidence intervals. If the standard deviation of the numbers on the systemic risk dashboard is 0.1, the change in systemic risk from 0.185922 to 0.321853 on the day of the Brexit vote is not statistically significant. If the standard deviation is 0.3, the Brexit systemic risk is not statistically different from the December 2008 number of 0.838846. If it is 0.5, the historically highest and lowest numbers are not statistically different from each other. If we require our undergraduate students to produce confidence bounds, is it too much to ask the European Central Bank to do the same? How should we, or anyone, make use of the dashboard otherwise? I could forgive all of that if the dashboard gave a warning, indicating that risk was building up and a crisis might be on the horizon. It does no such thing (see Figure 12).

On 22 June 2007 it told us systemic risk was very low at 0.042938. That is the month when the crisis was already under way, when the quant funds faced difficulty, and when Northern Rock was starting to run into difficulties selling its securitized mortgages. Indeed, measured systemic risk was quite low in the five years before 2007. The indicator sent the signal that everything was fine, and it was okay to take on risk at precisely the same time all the bad decisions that led to the crisis were being made.

Meanwhile, the highest number was recorded in December 2008, after the worst was over: the peak of the crisis was late September and early October. Imagine you observe a dam bursting. When is the risk highest? Before it breaks or after? Before, of course, because the dam can't burst twice. It is the same with the highest risk measurement in December 2008, when it tells us the risk is at its all-time high at the time the crisis was already subsiding. The measurement is misleading.

The European Central Bank could save itself a lot of trouble by taking out a subscription to the *Financial Times* or perhaps the ECB's home newspaper, *Handelsblatt*. Because both the press and the dashboard react to market prices, the newspapers' front pages will tell us a crisis is under way at the same time the systemic risk dashboard does. It would be much cheaper, and the European Central Bank could reassign all its systematic risk analytics team to something productive.

The First Riskometer

The riskometer was born in October 1994, when the investment bank JP Morgan released Value-at-Risk to the world, along with a statistical technology to measure it. Two things, a concept and method, make up a riskometer, and JP Morgan was the first to make one. The reason JP Morgan created Value-at-Risk in the first place was that its chairman at the time, Dennis Weatherstone, asked the bank's quants (finance lingo for statisticians working with financial data—experts in quantitative methods) to come up with a single number representing how much money the bank might lose over the next twenty-four hours. The number was to be ready in time for JP Morgan's treasury meeting in New York at 4:15 pm every day and hence has the informal name "the 4:15 report."

Value-at-Risk promises to improve on the traditional risk measure, volatility, which answers the question, How much fluctuation in stock returns can we expect? The quants created Value-at-Risk based on the query, What is the minimum loss on a day when we suffer large losses? To illustrate how this works in practice, suppose the price of Apple stock is $200, and I own fifty shares, so my portfolio has a value of $10,000. A 99 percent daily Value-at-Risk might be $200, meaning that one day out of a hundred I expect to lose $200 or more, and on the other ninety-nine days I will either make money or suffer losses smaller than $200. There is nothing magical about the 99 percent, but it is the most common probability and the one mandated by financial regulations.

The idea behind Value-at-Risk dates back to the 1920s, but JP Morgan made two notable contributions. It connected Value-at-Risk to a statistical apparatus in order to estimate it and made it freely available. It took something that used to be proprietary and in-house, really known only to a handful of people inside banks, and gave it to the world. From that point on an army of researchers not only enthusiastically embraced the Value-at-Risk riskometer but also created many new ones. Why would a bank do such a thing? They are not exactly in the business of altruistic creation of knowledge. The reason is regulations, according to Jacques Longerstaey, one of the creators of Value-at-Risk: "All the banks would go to the regulators and ask to be allowed to use internal models to lower their capital requirements," he said.[1] So, JP Morgan gave us Value-at-Risk so it could lower its capital and hence increase its profits.

Value-at-Risk became wildly successful and was almost immediately adopted by the financial regulators when it was incorporated into Basel I in 1996, two years after its debut. It is one of those concepts that attract a lot of criticisms, if not outright hate. Pablo Triana wrote a book called *The Number That Killed Us* about all the evils of Value-at-Risk. Value-at-Risk has few serious defenders (even though some are staunch defenders), but the received wisdom is that it is very hard to do without it because the alternatives are worse. As is so often the case, the usefulness of Value-at-Risk depends on where it is to be used; in some cases it is useful, in others useless and sometimes outright dangerous. Longerstaey came to regret his creation, telling Dennis Weatherstone that "[he] created a monster by asking for that one number."[2]

The Dragon Bites—Fat Tails

There are two main challenges for any designer of riskometers: fat tails and fluctuating risk. When Hurricane Harvey flooded Houston, Texas, at the end of summer 2017 the meteorologists told us that it was a once-in-five-hundred-year flood. One might think this was an extreme and infrequent outcome, except that it was the third once-in-five-hundred-year flood to hit Houston in a row. The meteorologists underestimated the flood risk in Houston so badly because they used rainfall observations over a century to project what might happen in half a millennium. In the absence of data, all they have is an educated guess.

The most difficult problem in measuring risk is how to deal with very large and infrequent negative outcomes. Because these significant losses don't happen very often, it is quite difficult to exploit historical observations to predict what sort of losses we might expect in the future: the fat-tail risk problem. In the words of the former chairman of the Federal Reserve Alan Greenspan: "As you well know, the biggest problems we now have with the whole evolution of risk is the fat-tail problem, which is really creating very large conceptual difficulties. Because as we all know, the assumption of normality enables us to drop off the huge amount of complexity in our equations. . . . Because once you start putting in non-normality assumptions, which is unfortunately what characterizes the real world, then these issues become extremely difficult."[3]

At this juncture it becomes useful to define the term *tail risk*. The most common way we describe statistical outcomes is by the bell-shaped curve, often called the normal or the Gaussian distribution after Johann Carl Friedrich Gauss, who came up with it in the late eighteenth century. The bell curve's tails sit on the far left and right side of the curve, away from the middle part. They represent the likelihood of outcomes that are either very large and positive—the right tail—or very negative—the left tail (Figure 13). We say the tails are fat if the probability of a very large outcome is higher than we would expect if the data followed the bell-shaped normal distribution. This means that if I plot the normal distribution curve and a fat distribution curve together, the fat will lie above the normal on the left and right sides, as shown in the figure, but be lower in the middle. The fat tails are the unknown areas with dragons.

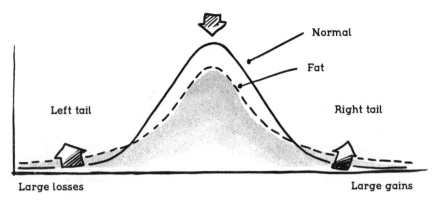

Figure 13. Fat tails and large losses. Credit: Lukas Bischoff/IllustrationX.

I have daily observations on the S&P 500 index dating back to 1928. What is the most obvious way to translate these daily observations into some measurement of risk? If you ask someone who has just taken a university course in statistics, they might say "easy." Calculate the standard deviation, assume the data follows the bell-shaped normal distribution, and voilà, we can calculate the likelihood of any possible outcome.

The standard deviation of stock market returns has another name: volatility. Using my statistical package of choice, R, I find that the daily volatility of the S&P 500 is 1.1 percent. Knowing the volatility is really cool. I can calculate once-in-five-hundred-year losses, just like the meteorologists did for Houston, Texas. Suppose I invest $1,000 in the S&P 500. Based on this analysis, I would expect the typical worst day every year to give me losses of $26, while the worst day in my 88 year sample should be a loss of $39, and over a millennium $45. Not so shabby! Except, of course, it is not like that. If I take my eighty-eight-year history of daily returns on the S&P 500, I find that the average annual worst loss is $47, not $26. These differences become bigger with time. The worst day over the past eighty-eight years, 19 October 1987, would give me losses of $229, not the $39 from the normal. Using volatility and the normal to measure risk would have lulled me into complacency—the dragons would have eaten me. This is summarized in Figure 14, which shows both the type of losses I would expect if I used the normal distribution versus what actually happened.

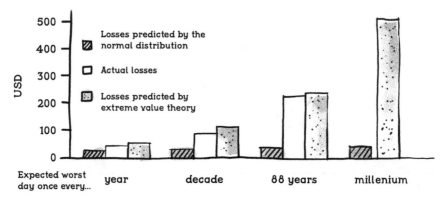

Figure 14. The largest losses. Credit: Lukas Bischoff/IllustrationX.

Volatility can be an accurate measure of risk if and only if returns are normally distributed. Since they are not, volatility is an insufficient and misleading measure of risk.[4] Often it does not really matter all that much, as the simplicity of volatility is all we need in most cases, situations in which we care about day-to-day movements and not the dragons, as with Paul in my example above. However, if we care about the dragons, be aware: they bite only in times of stress. The next time you hear someone use volatilities or standard deviations as measures of risk, especially extreme risk, remember the dragons.

So if volatility and the normal distribution are not sufficient, what can we do? There are strategies, but none is easy. Dealing properly with fat tails requires well-trained researchers, a lot of data, fast computers, and considerable time. Meanwhile, it is more expensive to hedge against tail risk, and it is harder to explain. So, it is about time and resources and communication and expectations. It is difficult enough to talk about volatility in an accurate way to nonspecialists, yet, as this text perhaps indicates, most discussion of fat tails tends to go over the heads of decision makers. That said, all is not lost: there are two other avenues one can take. The first is based on understanding the deep nature of where risk lies, how the people who work in the financial system interact, and how they create risk.

If that is too complicated, we can go down the purely statistical route. Here, we can do no better than follow the Dutch lesson because they are the world leaders in predicting an especially deadly type of risk: flood risk. For good reason, 26 percent of the land area of the Netherlands and 21 percent of its population are below sea level, and every once in a while the sea rises so high that it floods all the areas below the sea level. The last time this happened was in 1953, when 1,863 people drowned. As a consequence, the Dutch government decided to build a tall seawall called the Delta Works. I went to see the Delta Works in the summer of 2021. It is an impressive structure, and if you find yourself in the Netherlands, I recommend paying it and the memorial museum to the 1953 disaster a visit.

The problem was that while it is possible to build a sufficiently high wall to protect against all flooding, it is really expensive. Therefore, the government of the time decided that it would be acceptable for the Netherlands to flood once every ten thousand years. The Dutch statisticians and engineers were tasked with determining the Delta Works' height to meet that once-every-ten-thousand-year requirement. No surprise the Dutch have become world leaders in tail risk. The mathematical technique they came up with is formally known as extreme value theory (EVT), also called the power law after the underlying mathematical equation, or even Pareto analysis after the Italian economist Vilfredo Pareto, who formulated it in the nineteenth century.

Over the years I have spent a lot of time at Erasmus University in the Netherlands working with my good friend Casper de Vries, the first person to apply EVT to finance.[5] Suppose I use the methods we developed to estimate the losses on the S&P 500 index. As the S&P 500 risk figure above shows, we get much closer to what has been observed in history, and the once-in-a-millennium prediction is undoubtedly much more realistic than the normal distribution predicts.

Even with all that EVT expertise, all the Dutch experts can capture is an imperfect measure of risk. When they decided on the Delta Works' height, they used historical observations on sea height, and, being Dutch, they had records stretching back almost a millennium. Unfortunately, the world had changed since then—even the 1953 numbers are no longer accurate, given climate change. It is the same problem that faced the meteorologist predicting Houston's rainfall. The statistical analysis can be correct only if the world does not change very much.

Fluctuating Risk and the World of ARCH

ARCH and its ilk are fair-weather riskometers.

If we study a long history of financial returns, it becomes clear that volatility is sometimes very low and, at other times, much higher. In my eighty-seven-year sample of daily S&P 500 returns, annual volatility is the lowest in 1964, at 4.8 percent, and the 1960s is the decade with the lowest volatility. The 2006 volatility was also relatively low at 9.5 percent, only to quadruple in 2008. We have to go back to the Great Depression to observe similar magnitudes. History shows that we alternate between periods of low and high volatility. The specialists call it *volatility clustering* (see an example in Figure 15).

Until 1982 the way one obtained volatility was by calculating the standard deviation of financial returns. Such analysis ignores volatility clusters, so what was needed was a method that captures these changes in volatility, and that was provided by Robert Engle while visiting the London School of Economics. In 1982 he published a paper with the inauspicious title "Autoregressive Conditional Heteroskedasticity with Estimates of the Variance of the United Kingdom Inflation." The first three words

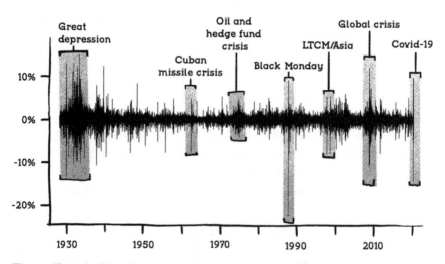

Figure 15. Volatility clusters. Credit: Lukas Bischoff/IllustrationX.

of the title are abbreviated ARCH. The ARCH model was a revolutionary step in the estimation of risk, and in 2003 Engle got a well-deserved Nobel Prize for developing it. His key insight was to assign weights to historical observations. Suppose we have three days of data and give today a 50 percent weight, yesterday 30 percent, and the day before that 20 percent in the volatility calculation. By doing so, we see that the ARCH model kills two birds with one stone. It both captures the volatility clusters, and its mathematical formulation allows for returns to be fat-tailed. At least that is the promise.

How well does the ARCH family of models work? Reasonably well. It certainly fits historical data better than if one simply uses the standard deviation of returns as volatility. For many applications that is all that is needed, a reasonably good idea of what type of volatility to expect tomorrow. For fat tails or systemic risk, we have to look elsewhere. Because ARCH and its ilk are fair-weather riskometers.

Misusing History

A riskometer should not aim to explain the past well. Instead, its purpose is to look for currently unknown future mistakes.

The final element in creating a riskometer is data. Data that describes the infinitely complex financial system. In a perfect world we would have detailed observations on how market participants see the world: all their information, models, and analysis; which asset classes are popular and receiving money and which are deserted and sold; which bankers are in ascendance, and who is on the way out; the regulatory environment and how it is expected to evolve. Data of this type would give us a reasonable understanding of what is happening today and allow us to make solid guesses about likely future scenarios. Well, we don't have these data.

Mostly we have the outcomes, the prices, and quantities that distill all the information out there into risk measurements. Inevitably, a lot gets lost in the process. The question is what. It depends on what the riskometer is meant to capture. All riskometers use historical data to predict what sort of risk we can expect in the future. How informative are these historical outcomes? They capture how the market reacts to news but also how it expects news to evolve. They are a good snapshot of what is happening at any given time. What such data misses are deep vulnerabilities. Take the European Central Bank's systemic risk dashboard yet again. It told us that systemic risk was, on average, 0.06677640 in 2004, the safest year in its history. What is missed is revealing. We now know, with the benefit of hindsight, that a crisis was around the corner. The critical hidden vulnerabilities were all the structured credit products composed of subprime mortgages and other high-risk assets, all the excessive risk nobody knew about, the hidden liquidity risk that bites only in times of stress. The relevant information was out there somewhere, but information is not the same as knowledge. If nobody connects the dots, information is irrelevant. Every financial institution saw only its own exposures, not everyone else's, and nobody thought to add up the numbers. The information was out there somewhere, but trying to make sense of all the data coming out of the financial system in real time is like drinking from a fire hose. We have to pick and choose. And in 2007 almost nobody picked subprime and structured credit. It is easy, with the benefit of hindsight, to ask, "How could you miss that? It was all in front of you." But in real time, not all that easy. Ultimately, most riskometers use just trading prices and volumes, disregarding all the other relevant bits of information. It is not because someone is deliberately trying to obfuscate. It is just all we can do technically.

The primary challenge in creating riskometers is that risk comes from the future, but we only know the past. That creates particular problems, not least what is known in statistics as data snooping. The problem arises because before using a riskometer to make important decisions, we would like to know how good it is. We would ideally put it in practice, wait a few years, and then pass judgment. We are too impatient for that, and what is usually done instead is to figure out how well a riskometer measures history using a procedure called backtesting.

Suppose I take my long sample of S&P 500 prices and use all the observations from the beginning of the sample until the end of the year 1999 to forecast risk with a riskometer on the first day of the new millennium. That gives me one forecast observation, which I can compare to the actual market outcome that day. I then move up one day and use all the information up to and including the first day of the year 2000 to forecast risk on the second day. By repeating this every day until today I will get a few thousand observations and then use that information to evaluate the quality of my riskometer. That is backtesting, something routinely done in practice.

However, while it sounds like a fantastic way to evaluate the quality of a riskometer, there is a problem. I know what happened between the year 2000 and now—risk was very low in the mid-2000s, we had a big crisis in 2008, and all the other things that happened. The temptation is then to try to explain as much as possible of what happened in the past—especially finding a way to predict the crisis of 2008.

When I was in graduate school, I took a course in Soviet economics, and the professor told us a Russian joke: the best Soviet historians are experts in forecasting history because government policies were justified with reference to history. Thus history had to be "correct" if the historians were to survive. If I try enough riskometers, I will explain history well, and I will predict the crisis in 2008 years in advance. A lot of research has done precisely that. All of that work is useless because of what statisticians call spurious correlation, in which variables seem related to each other even though in reality they have no such causal relationship. There are many examples of spurious correlations; the correlation between divorce rates in the American state of Maine and the consumption of margarine is 99.3 percent.[6] When I told this to someone, he responded by saying, "It is a good thing I stopped eating margarine," thereby falling for two fallacies: spurious correlations and assuming that this general observation applies to the individual.

What explains the 99.3 percent correlation between divorce rates in Maine and margarine consumption is that if I calculate the correlation between every possible economic time series available—and there are hundreds of thousands of them—I will find some that are highly correlated purely by random chance. Some of these might even appear to be more sensible than the spurious margarine and divorce correlation, leading the unwary, or unethical, analyst to the wrong conclusion. As H. L. Mencken put it: "For every complex problem there is an answer that is clear, simple, and wrong." When it comes to riskometers, if I try one out and one only I will get the correct confidence intervals for my risk measurements. If, however, I arrive at the same riskometer as a result of trying out a large number of explanatory variables and model specifications, these confidence intervals will no longer be accurate. Any riskometer that performs poorly in forecasting history will be changed, leaving us with those that explain history well, like the Soviet historians. The problem is that such riskometers will tend to do poorly in forecasting the future. Not much more accurate than 99.3 percent is about the future relationship between margarine and divorce in Maine.

Why Risk Is Hard to Measure

All models are wrong, but some are useful.
—*George Box*

A few years ago, when I was reading the Basel III proposals for the global postcrisis financial regulations, I asked myself: How well does what is being proposed work? How accurate are the riskometers that important regulations are founded on? To my surprise, I found almost no public research on this, and as far as I can tell, nowhere in the thousands of pages of Basel III is the accuracy of the mandated risk measurements discussed. There is plenty of work on the various technical aspects of riskometers, along the lines of "Does Method A work better than Method B in some particular situation?" Indeed useful, but it does not answer the more fundamental question of how accurate the riskometers we depend on to keep us safe from finance are.

First, I did a blog piece on this question and then joined forces with Chen Zhou, a coauthor of mine now working in the Netherlands.[7] Our paper is called "Why Risk Is So Hard to Measure," and what it does is to investigate how the most common riskometers work in practice. We started by taking daily prices of all publicly traded stocks in the United States from the early 1960s, measuring both the risk and the accuracy of those risk estimates by the 99 percent confidence bound, that is, the range of values where the risk measures will lie 99 percent of the time. We then did a Monte Carlo experiment, simulating random outcomes from our computer world based on our assumptions of how the world works, measuring the risk in those outcomes. The benefit of such an approach is that because we created the world, we knew exactly what the risk was and therefore how accurate the riskometer's estimations were.

What we found is that the number of observations used is crucial to estimating risk accurately. Not unexpected, but what was surprising is how many observations one needs. To get a reasonably accurate measurement of risk, we require many thousands of daily observations. Considering that there are about 2,500 days when the financial markets are open every decade, we need many decades of data. When we use four years of data, the Value-at-Risk estimates are between $74 and $151, where the true value is $100. Now four years of data are a lot; we usually see much less used in practice. Three hundred trading days, or fifteen months, is much more common, and here the Value-at-Risk measurements range from $61 to $246.

What this means in practice is that two banks holding the same assets could come to very different conclusions about risk. One might get $61 and the other $246. The bank with $61 would think all is fine and sharply increase its risk. The other bank faces $246 and would be forced to scale down its risk. Very different outcomes when the underlying risk is precisely the same because, after all, the two banks hold the same assets. The only difference is that they use different riskometers. The bank with the high numbers might want to switch to the low-number riskometer and even do so in consultation with the regulators. The result would be a race to the bottom, all banks chasing the same riskometer. Still, there is no guarantee that the riskometer with the lowest number today will do the same tomorrow; it might even provide the highest. Gaming the riskometer in this may not be all that useful in the long run. The reason is model risk.

When the Covid-19 crisis started in February 2020, it didn't take long for research explaining the virus's propagation to emerge. Many models were created, and while Covid-19 is a virus, the modelers weren't limited to epidemiologists, as computer scientists, physicists, doctors, statisticians, economists, and financiers all got in on the action. Their models were initially quite contradictory, and it seemed like the policy makers often picked the models that best explained what they wanted to do in the first place. Over time, as more and more information emerged, the models started to converge.

The technical name for the degree of inaccuracy in the Covid-19 models is model risk, the risk of making wrong decisions when relying on models.

Model risk is inversely related to the complexity of the problem at hand. In the Covid-19 crisis the models were desperately needed at the outset, as nobody knew how to counteract the virus. A lot of the early modelers came under unfair criticism for the low quality of their initial predictions. Yes, they turned out to be wrong in the end, but it is often better to have poor predictions than none. And by the time the models become reasonably accurate they are no longer needed. It is always like that. Model risk is lowest when the thing being modeled closely resembles something already well understood, like with airplanes. It is easy to simulate the movement of aircraft in the computer because all the applicable laws of physics are well known. Only the details differ. With a new disease like Covid-19 model risk is inevitably very high.

The same applies to the financial models that underpin the riskometers. We are quite good at measuring day-to-day risk in highly liquid stocks, when nothing much is going on in the markets, having a lot of data to train the models and quick feedback if the models fail. Model risk is then low. It is much harder to measure tail risk, and methods for doing so have a lot of model risk. I looked at model risk in risk models for the stocks of all American financial companies from 1970 to 2012 in a recent paper titled "Model Risk of Risk Models." We measured model risk by taking the six most commonly used statistical methods for estimating risk, defining model risk by how much they disagree. What we found was quite striking. Model risk is lowest when the financial markets are quiet, as in the years before the crisis in 2007, the mid-1990s, and the late 1970s. Model risk is highest in times of crises, as in 2008. In other words, riskometers have the annoying tendency of being reliable when all is good and failing miserably when needed the most. Just like European Central Bank's systemic risk riskometer, almost every riskometer in use in 2006 told us risk was at a historical low. The riskometers all agreed, and model risk was low. Unfortunately, they all agreed on the wrong thing.

Riskometers are used to make crucial decisions: regulating banks, controlling pension fund investments, managing insurance company reserves, and the day-to-day investment decisions of every financial institution. They are fundamental to the robo-advisors now increasingly common in investment management. The financial system as we know it today could not function without riskometers. Those who understand the riskometer, its strengths and weaknesses, know when it is a useful tool: perhaps in the short-run comparison of portfolios where the underlying financial market conditions are stable.

Unfortunately, too many people treat the numbers produced by a risk-ometer as being akin to sacred truth and don't question them nearly enough. Riskometers are too often used inappropriately to make deci-sions on tail risk in long-run investments, precisely the types of risk most likely to negatively impact banks, pension funds, insurance companies, individual savers, investors, and indeed the entire financial system. These are the types of risk that riskometers are least useful for—when we get bitten by the dragon.

6

Ideas Matter:
Risk and Uncertainty

Stability is destabilizing.
—*Hyman Minsky*

Figure 16. Credit: Lukas Bischoff/IllustrationX.

Uncertainty is not risk, an important distinction made by three early twentieth-century economists: the American Frank Knight, the Briton John Maynard Keynes, and the Austrian Friedrich August von Hayek. It is one of the most important methodological breakthroughs in the field of economics. The three economists expressed their disquiet with the established economic dogma at the time—nineteenth-century classical economics—which maintained that the economy obeyed Newtonian-like laws of nature. Such laws could be described with precise mathematical equations spanning the entire range of possible outcomes, discoverable by a simple measurement. An example is the classical theory of prices, which says that prices are determined solely by the level of output, technology, and wages.

A crucial but implicit assumption of such nineteenth-century thought is ergodicity, a mathematical concept of stability. Ergodicity, a key assumption in the natural sciences, implies that by doing repeated experiments or observing the same phenomena over time we learn nature's laws. All we need are enough observations. The three thinkers rejected the assumption of ergodicity for the economy as too simplistic and plainly wrong. In doing so, they were a part of the wholesale revision of nineteenth-century values and assumptions about society brought about by the World War I.

It started with Professor Frank Knight of the University of Chicago arguing that the concept of risk was fundamentally different from uncertainty. Risk is something one can quantify, describe with mathematical and statistical models, and hence translate into numbers. If the economic world is ergodic, risk is the correct way to describe it. So long as something is risky, one can make confident statements: there is a 1 percent probability that England will win the next football World Cup, there is a 25 percent chance Greece will need another bailout in the next three years, there is a 48 percent chance we will make money by investing in Amazon over the next six months. The only way we can make such accurate declarations is if the statistical and mathematical models comprehensively describe the world, and every observer of the economy sees risk in the same way. There is no room for subjective judgment. If one cannot quantify the probabilities, we can say only that Greece may need a bailout. The Greek bailouts lie in the realm of uncertainty, not risk.

Uncertainty captures outcomes that cannot be adequately described mathematically. When it comes to making decisions, uncertainty implies that it is not sufficient to simply observe the world around us and process those observations with statistical techniques. Something is missing. We need to recognize that each person is different and sees and understands the economy differently, via their own information and objectives and abilities. If we do not, we will simply end up making decisions based on how we think the world is or ought to be, not how it is. Uncertainty, not risk, drives economic activity. Investments and profits and losses happen because we do not anticipate perfectly how events occur. Since every person has different expectations about the future, their expectations drive the uncertainty that drives the economy.

The same year Knight published his work on risk and uncertainty, John Maynard Keynes took a more nuanced view, which he then further refined in his *General Theory of Interest, Employment and Money* (1936): "By 'uncertain' knowledge . . . I do not mean merely to distinguish what is known for certain from what is only probable. The game of roulette is not subject, in this sense, to uncertainty. . . . The sense in which I am using the term is that in which the prospect of a European war is uncertain, or the price of copper and the rate of interest twenty years hence, or the obsolescence of a new invention. . . . About these matters there is no scientific basis on which to form any calculable probability whatever. We simply do not know!"[1]

His starting point was that humans are not naturally rational beings able to anticipate and forecast everything perfectly, as the nineteenth-century classical economists would have it. Instead, people routinely follow animal spirits, instincts that guide human behavior. Keynes came to be rather dismissive of statistical analysis, rejecting the notion that decisions can be made on the basis of the frequency of past events—ergodicity. Instead, he focused on the "degrees of beliefs" that humans can have, given their knowledge at a given time, about the occurrence of future events.

My favorite expression of that sentiment comes from an economist customarily thought of as being very far from Keynes: Ludwig von Mises, one of the leaders of the Austrian school. Mises criticized econometrics—the statistical analysis of the economy—in 1962: "As a method of economic analysis econometrics is a childish play with figures that do not contribute anything to the elucidation of the problems of economic reality."[2] It is delightfully ironic that many of Keynes's followers went on to do exactly what Mises and Keynes argued against, creating statistical and mathematical models of the economy, treating uncertainty as risk in the same way the nineteenth-century classical economists did.

The Nobel Prize winner George A. Akerlof, in a paper called "What They Were Thinking Then: The Consequences for Macroeconomics during the Past 60 Years," makes the point that Keynes's disciples deliberately ignored his warnings about risk and financial crises so they could derive simple mathematical models of how the macroeconomy works—models which soon were proven to be not only wrong but also dangerous.

In 1945 Friedrich von Hayek, while a professor at the London School of Economics, published an article titled "Use of Knowledge in Society" in which he expressed views similar to those of Akerlof, agreeing with both Knight and Keynes that quantifying risk was impossible. Hayek, however, came to the point from a different direction. Instead of people being motivated by Keynes's animal spirits, he argued that it was technically impossible to describe the world with precise mathematical statements: "*If* we possess all the relevant information, *if* we can start out from a given system of preferences, and *if* we command complete knowledge of available means, the problem which remains is purely one of logic. . . . This, however, is emphatically *not* the economic problem which society faces."[3]

Hayek was writing during World War II, when the economic policy debate was between believers in central planning and Soviet-model scientific socialism and those preferring a market-based economy. Most thinkers of that era advocated central planning, seeing the capitalist system as crisis prone and inefficient, where the Great Depression was caused by the failure of capitalism, while the Soviet Union escaped the Depression because it was centrally planned. Almost every country in the world at the time was actively considering central planning.

Hayek disagreed. To him, knowledge is dispersed among the various individuals who make up society, information that is impossible to aggregate into perfect knowledge. The farmer knows much more about his fields than anyone else, he knows how best to plant his crops, and he has a direct economic incentive to be as knowledgeable about his land as possible. No central authority can acquire such information; all they can hope for is some high-level summary information. This is why collective farming does not work. The farmer makes better decisions than the ministry of agriculture, and central planning of the economy cannot be successful. In Hayek's view, as long as markets are free of government interference, market prices solve the problem of uncertainty, distilling essential information into one number: the price.

Even though Keynes and Hayek are often seen as having very different economic philosophies—a distinction much amplified by their disciples—their views on uncertainty are quite similar. Keynes focused on how uncertainty affects decision-making, while Hayek was more interested in understanding how one can minimize and overcome uncertainty. These views are highly complementary. Not surprisingly. They were both working in England at the same time, remained friends, and corresponded extensively.

Where Keynes and Hayek diverge is in their policy conclusions. Keynes argued that because of the markets' animal spirits, they tend to get into an undesirable state, justifying corrective government intervention. If we don't know how to quantify the risk of future investment decisions, they "can only be taken as a result of animal spirits." If the animal spirits are too pessimistic, the government needs to increase confidence and reduce uncertainty, thereby increasing investment. Hayek came to the opposite conclusion, maintaining that while individuals and organizations might know little about the future, the government knows even less. A company knows the business it is in and hence has a better idea of future uncertainties than the government. Because the government knows less about the economy, its decisions are worse on average if it intervenes.

It therefore seems likely that if Keynes were writing today, he would be in support of the objectives of the macroprudential regulators, the crafting of rules to ensure a robust and safe financial system. After all, his magnum opus, *The General Theory*, came out in 1936, right after the Great Depression, which is often seen as having been caused by the free market's failure. Yet I suspect Keynes would not like how the regulations are conceived today, at least to the extent they are based on risk measurements; he would see them in the same way he saw nineteenth-century classical economics. I do not think Hayek would like either the objectives or the implementation of today's financial regulations. He might argue that because the regulators do not and cannot know all the risks in the financial system, all they accomplish is increasing costs as well as inefficiency and higher risk of crises. The central banks are making the same mistakes as the central planners of yesteryear.

Hayek and Keynes, perhaps the two most influential economists of the twentieth century, are among the most misunderstood thinkers in economics. They have legions of groupies who delight in misrepresenting their views. A friend of mine, Hannes Gissurarson, recalls in his new book a dinner he had with Hayek in 1980 during which Hayek said to him, "We should not become Hayekians, as the Keynesians were much worse than Keynes and the Marxists much worse than Marx."

The views of Knight, Keynes, and Hayek on risk and uncertainty were mostly ignored after World War II. The disciples of Keynes, the most influential of the three, disregarded this aspect of his work, preferring instead to draw on the classical nineteenth-century views on risk in building the Keynesian models of the era. When Keynes himself stressed the importance of uncertainty, the disciples paid little attention. Of course, they did not see it that way—most economists of the era saw themselves as the intellectual heirs to Keynes.

There are many reasons for this rejection of uncertainty in favor of risk. Much better data collection after the war, new statistical techniques, and the availability of computers to do calculations all led to a sense of can-do. It was inevitable that we neglected uncertainty in our constant attempts at controlling our environment. Risk and mathematical descriptions of the world are essential for that, and uncertainty just gets in the way. It tells people what they do not want to hear: it is not as easy to measure and control. Invariably, the risk view wins out.

The person who formalized that best was Wassily Leontief, an economist educated at the University of Leningrad who became a Harvard professor and eventually a recipient of the Nobel Prize. He saw the objective of economics as the collection of facts and figures followed by mathematical models describing the relationships. This culminated in an approach he called the input–output model, which reduces the entire economy into a set of equations. The output of one sector becomes either an input into other sectors or final consumption. Leontief's model became very influential in the mid-twentieth century and was one of the foundations of central planning as practiced by the Soviet Union and other communist countries to this day.

The input–output model had a significant impact on the development of a method called linear programming at the statistical control group of the US Army in World War II. It was successfully put into practice in organizing the Berlin Airlift. The army flew the maximum amount of cargo into Berlin, given constraints like the number of available runways in Berlin and the prevailing weather. A small set of equations can describe the problem, and what matters is risk, not uncertainty.

One member of the army's linear programming team was Robert Mc-Namara, who became the secretary of defense in the 1960s and was famous for using Leontief's philosophy in conducting the Vietnam War.[4] His management philosophy was based on measuring everything that could be measured, most famously body bags, and then using those measurements to control outcomes. What could not be measured did not matter. The problem with this approach was ably demonstrated by the sociologist Daniel Yankelovitch, who called it the McNamara fallacy: "The first step is to measure whatever can be easily measured. This is OK as far as it goes. The second step is to disregard that which cannot be easily measured or give it an arbitrary quantitative value. This is artificial and misleading. The third step is to presume that what cannot be measured easily really is not important. This is blindness. The fourth step is to say that what cannot be easily measured does not exist. This is suicide."[5] In all fairness, McNamara was trying to put structure on a very complex problem, using quantitative methods as tools in all the Johnson White House's political battles. He was not the first to use statistics that way and not the last. It has been quite common in the Covid-19 crisis.

One of McNamara's successors, Donald Rumsfeld, expressed a much better understanding of risk and uncertainty in 2002. While widely ridiculed for it at the time, it has come to be seen as a brilliant statement of decision-making in a period of uncertainty: "Reports that say that something has not happened are always interesting to me because as we know, there are known knowns; there are things we know we know. We also know there are known unknowns; that is to say, we know some things we do not know. But there are also unknown unknowns—the ones we do not know we do not know. And if one looks throughout the history of our country and other free countries, it is the latter category that tends to be the difficult ones."[6]

The problem with Leontief's input–output model is the same as that of nineteenth-century classical economics, McNamara's warfighting philosophy, modern financial regulations, and risk measurements. They all create a simple, caricature view of a world that is infinitely complex. The models assume all relevant factors can be summed up into simple mathematical equations and do not leave any room for uncertainty or complexity or technological progress. Perhaps most important, they depend on accurate measurements.

When I studied quantitative methods in graduate school, my professor, James Henderson, told us the story of when he used to work at the IMF on Latin America. The fund had encouraged the Latin American countries to create input–output models of their economies. This worked quite well until Henderson noticed that, according to the input–output model, the Latin American economies were not only very similar to each other but also rather resembled the US economy. This was surprising because the Latin American countries were much poorer than the United States and their industries quite different. When Henderson looked into this, he was told by the Latin countries that their statistical collection was not as detailed as that of the United States, and when a number was missing they would just use the US number.

The quality of measurements is only as good as the person making them. A common problem, as noted by Josiah Stamp, one of the leading statisticians in the United Kingdom in the early twentieth century: "The government are very keen on amassing statistics. They collect them, add them, raise them to the nth power, take the cube root and prepare wonderful diagrams. But you must never forget that every one of these figures comes in the first instance from the village watchman, who just puts down what he damn pleases."[7]

Subjective Probabilities

One person who continued the work of Keynes and Hayek on risk and uncertainty was George Lennox Sharman Shackle. Shackle started writing his PhD at the London School of Economics in the 1930s, with Hayek as his advisor. However, after Keynes published his *General Theory*, Shackle dropped Hayek and did his thesis on Keynes's ideas. Hayek did not hold it against him, and they remained friends. Shackle is one of the great underrated economists. I don't recall seeing him mentioned anywhere when I was in graduate school, and it was not until my LSE colleague Charles Goodhart brought him to my attention that I started reading his work. Shackle argued that it was not possible to calculate the probability distribution of all outcomes and thereby make rational economic decisions. Economic data is not ergodic.[8]

Unlike Knight and Keynes, however, and their sharp distinction between risk and uncertainty, Shackle argued that something in between existed, a degree of knowledge about an outcome's probabilities. He called this subjective probability, the confidence in the future occurrence of a particular event. Subjective probability incorporates the probability of someone's judgment being incorrect, implying that an economic variable, perhaps prices, can diverge from what should be expected. This foresaw what has become known as psychological and behavioral economics. Many observers have echoed Shackle's views on probability, one of whom, Warren Buffett, voiced his own notion of reasoned probability: "The riskiness of an investment is not measured by beta (a Wall Street term encompassing volatility and often used in measuring risk) but rather by the probability—the reasoned probability—of that investment causing its owner a loss of purchasing power over his contemplated holding period. Assets can fluctuate greatly in price and not be risky as long as they are reasonably certain to deliver increased purchasing power over their holding period. And as we will see, a nonfluctuating asset can be laden with risk."[9]

Stability Is Destabilizing

An important element is missing in the work of the four thinkers discussed above, and that is how uncertainty arises and affects the likelihood of outcomes. Hyman Minsky provided that link. Focusing on financial crises, he argued that perceptions of risk affect peoples' risk-taking behavior and hence the likelihood of financial crises far into the future. Minsky developed his theories in the context of the mid-twentieth-century economic theories of his time, such as Leontief's input–output models. Minsky rejected these as being too simplistic because they ignored how investment decisions are made and how firms are financed. His theory of investment and crises was based on distinguishing between three types of financing. The first, which he called hedge financing, is the safest. Firms borrow little, and when they do they repay the loans directly out of cash flow. The second type is speculative financing, riskier since firms rely on cash flow to repay interest but roll the principle over. The most dangerous, Ponzi financing, is where the cash flow is not sufficient to repay either principal or interest, so firms are betting that the underlying asset will appreciate enough to repay their liabilities. The current trend in Britain for buy-to-let real estate is a prime example of Ponzi financing: people buy properties to rent them out, financing mortgage payments out of rent and increases in the price of the property.

Hedge financing is the most stable, but the other two are much more tempting to investors. Moreover, when the economy is growing there seems to be little reason to give up profits and play it safe. Indeed, it is difficult to do so. Suppose an economy starts safe, using only hedge financing. This installs confidence and motivates people to take more risk and use speculative financing. In the beginning, it all looks good; economic growth increases, making Ponzi financing increasingly attractive. But over time we run out of feasible investments, and ultimately it all ends abruptly and a crisis ensues. Financial crises happen because we think the good times will last forever, and there is no reason not to make use of Ponzi financing. Investors want to take on more risk, often helped by a lax regulatory environment and government encouragement. Ultimately, this culminates in an unsustainable speculative bubble and a crisis.[10]

The conditions for a crisis are, therefore, ripest when we think risk is low. This means that one of the best predictors of a financial crisis being around the corner is when the pundits start talking about the current prosperity as lasting forever, such as the permanent era of stability in the 1920s and the great moderation in the two decades before 2007. Often justified by arguing that the laws of economics do not apply because "our country has just such fantastic economic policy" or "we have become so clever that we have learned how to prevent crises, investing optimally and behaving rationally, ensuring permanent stability and high growth." Not so fast. When we start seeing cultural reasons for prosperity, it is time to run.

Not surprisingly, Minsky did not get much recognition in his lifetime. He was not doing mainstream economics and was rejected by the Keynesian school he came from, both because of his emphasis on uncertainty and because of his criticism of deterministic economic models. Yet he was never wholly forgotten, and after the global crisis in 2008 he became quite the celebrity. People in the know often call crises a Minsky moment because his theory explains them so well. "If there is excessive optimism in the boom period, it will lead to an accumulation of conflicts [in the economy], which may end up with a so-called Minsky moment," said Zhou Xiaochuan, then governor of the People's Bank of China, in

October 2017. Meanwhile Minsky's critics and those who shunned him are long forgotten.

Minsky's instability hypothesis implies that an observation of low risk should create the conditions for a future crisis. This proposition was expressed in 2014 by the then chairwoman of the Federal Reserve Janet Yellen: "Volatility in markets is at low levels. . . . [T]o the extent that low levels of volatility may induce risk taking behavior . . . is a concern to me and to the Committee."[11]

The relationship between low volatility and crises has remained conjectural, not verified empirically. That got me curious, and I joined forces with a couple of coauthors, Marcela Valenzuela and Ilknur Zer, to see if such a relationship existed, writing a paper on the subject titled "Learning from History: Volatility and Financial Crises." There are two reasons this had not been done earlier. The first is that we need a very long history of volatilities and crises, and the necessary data was not readily available. To that end we collected data on monthly stock market observations, spanning 60 countries and 211 years.

Still not sufficient. If we test a statistical model of the relationship between volatility and crises, we find it does not exist. That, however, does not mean there is no relationship; it is merely more complex. What matters is volatility being different from what people have come to expect. To test that hypothesis, we first need to estimate expected volatility and then use deviations from that in a statistical model. Low volatility is, then, when volatility is below expectations and, conversely, high volatility is where volatility exceeds expectations. And low volatility turns out to be statistically significant.

We find a clear chain of causality. Unexpectedly low volatility sends the all-clear signal. We therefore have no qualms about taking on more risk. To do that, we borrow money to make risky investments. In the short run, all is fine, but over time, some or even many of the loans turn out to be dodgier than expected. Perhaps they were used to invest in real estate, creating a house price bubble that eventually bursts. Not surprisingly, loan defaults mount, banks get into difficulty, and a crisis ensues (Figure 17). Unexpectedly low volatility predicts both rapid credit growth (increasing leverage in the banking system) and the incidence of crises up to ten years into the future. Perhaps surprisingly this causal relationship

Figure 17. Volatility and crises. Credit: Lukas Bischoff/IllustrationX.

holds only for unexpectedly low volatility. High volatility has no predictive power for crises. It is only associated with them. In other words, high volatility happens at the same time as crises and cannot be used as a crisis predictor, only as a crisis indicator.

Goodhart's Law

The last step in the evolution of how we see risk and uncertainty is the analysis of what happens when governments try to regulate economic activity by targeting measurements of the economy. This link was made by my LSE colleague and, I am privileged to say, coauthor Charles Goodhart. Very few are as adept at distilling complicated government policies into the bare essentials, identifying what works, and clearly demonstrating why other policies are destined for failure.

He is best known for Goodhart's law: "Any observed statistical regularity will tend to collapse once pressure is placed upon it for control purposes."[12] His law has a natural implication for regulations. Once the government tries to regulate some activities, they immediately become unreliable as indicators of economic trends. The context of this statement relates to the use of monetary policy to achieve the optimal trade-off between inflation and unemployment. This all started when Bill Phillips, a professor of economics at the LSE, wrote a paper implying that there might be a long-term, stable, and negative relationship between unemployment and inflation. The lower the unemployment, the higher the inflation. Various economists then suggested that central banks and the fiscal authorities—because fiscal policy was thought to be the more powerful at that time—could use their policy instruments to choose the optimal trade-off between inflation and unemployment.

Putting his training as an engineer to work, Phillips developed the Monetary National Income Analogue Computer (MONIAC) in 1949, using hydraulics to model the British economy's workings. The MONIAC was a large contraption, about 2 meters high, 1.2 meters wide, and 1 meter deep, composed of several transparent plastic tanks linked by pipes. Each tank captured some aspect of the UK economy, and the flow of money was represented by colored water flowing through the pipes. Economic principles determined the flow of water between the tanks. The MONIAC operator could set various economic parameters, such as tax rates and investment rates, by turning the valves controlling the flow between the tanks. Fundamental to the MONIAC was the negative association between inflation and unemployment, a relationship that the central banks could exploit. If unemployment was too high, all the central banks had to do was print money.

Although the mechanical MONIAC was too unwieldy for practical use, the underlying mathematical equations were soon translated into the then recently available digital computers. Unsurprisingly, the idea behind the Phillips curve was quite attractive to policy makers. The central bank can control the level of economic activity simply by tweaking inflation. The resulting activist monetary policy became quite popular in many countries.

I experienced Phillips's notion of monetary policy firsthand in my first job as an economist. A summer intern at the Central Bank of Iceland in 1987, I was asked to work on a model of optimal currency devaluations. It was based on taking the five most important sectors of the economy and finding out by first approximation how they would be affected if the Icelandic krona was devalued. A 1980s version of Phillips's MONIAC and based on macroeconomic models that were already twenty-five years out of date and proven to be wrong. I did manage to upset my superiors, not by telling them the model was wrong—which I did—but by programming it with a menu-driven spreadsheet so that they could simply plug in a number and immediately see pretty charts and tables for how the economy would react. They got upset because the very simplicity of the spreadsheet exposed the naïveté of the central bank's economic model. You see, the previous version of the model was programmed fifteen years earlier in an obscure programming language called Fortran that nobody understood, allowing the senior staff in the central bank to believe the analysis was rigorous.

The problem with Phillips's model and the other macro models of the era is that it is not possible to exploit the negative correlation between unemployment and inflation for policy purposes. The Nobel laureate Robert Lucas expressed that most clearly in his "Econometric Policy Evaluation: A Critique," in what has come to be known as the Lucas critique: "Given that the structure of an econometric model consists of optimal decision rules of economic agents, and that optimal decision rules vary systematically with changes in the structure of series relevant to the decision maker, it follows that any change in policy will systematically alter the structure of econometric models."[13]

The observed relationship between monetary growth, inflation, and real economic activity holds only as long as the central bank is not trying to use monetary policy to achieve and reduce unemployment. Once it tries to do so, the relationships immediately break down. The reason is that the causality runs in one direction only. Inflation is high because the economy is growing rapidly, but not the other way around. If the central bank tries to exploit the association, it might succeed once because people mistake the new money for actual prosperity. But they are not going to be repeatedly fooled by the fact that the central bank is printing money. Instead, the freshly printed money just ends up increasing inflation because people understand that the central bank is pulling the wool over their eyes, and they will simply demand higher wages to pay more for the same goods but will not work any harder, so the economy does not grow. The relationship between unemployment and inflation breaks down precisely when the central bank tries to exploit it.

While Goodhart originally phrased his law in the context of monetary policy, he has since extended his interpretation to financial regulations. He argued in *Risk, Uncertainty and Financial Stability* that, following Shackle's approach, measurements of risk may be useful for the control of day-to-day outcomes in financial markets while being mostly useless for anyone concerned with the risk of large, infrequent adverse outcomes—

systemic risk or tail risk—because such analysis needs to be forward look-ing. By definition, no risk measurement based on historical data is ever able to adequately capture the probability of future outcomes and will especially miss out on large and infrequent events; events that include an element of surprise—the unexpected and unexpectable.

Suppose a regulator observes that banks with high-risk readings have historically been more prone to fail than those with low risk. In response, she persuades her agency to impose a rule whereby any bank with a high-risk reading will be subject to extra scrutiny and required to hold ad-ditional levels of capital. Will doing so make the financial system more stable? Not necessarily. First, the relationship between the high-risk read-ings and bank failures could be misleading. More important, the bank is likely to target the measurements and try to make its readings look as low as possible while not changing its risk-taking activities. And they will not find this all that difficult to do. Banks find it easy to manipulate risk measurements in a way that is fully compliant with the letter of financial regulations, and there may be nothing the authorities can do about it even if they find out. Therefore, if the financial authorities use some risk measurements to control the financial system, they may just end up dis-covering that the measurements cease to be reliable: a direct application of Goodhart's law.

The idea that the economy obeys laws akin to the laws of physics is seductive. All we have to worry about is risk, and we can ignore uncer-tainty. We then can control an unruly economy, allocate resources in the best possible way, manage risk, and prevent calamities. If only it were so. The economy is different from the physical world. It is based on the behavior of human beings, many of whom are intent on doing exactly what they want to do—rules or no rules. Recognizing that fact is the genius of the six thinkers discussed above. They all understood it is only in the physical world that we can describe the relationship between out-comes and probabilities precisely—where all that matters is risk and un-certainty is irrelevant. In physics, math captures all; not so in the society of humans that form the economy.

7

Endogenous Risk

A data-driven risk management process cannot capture endogenous risk, only exogenous risk.

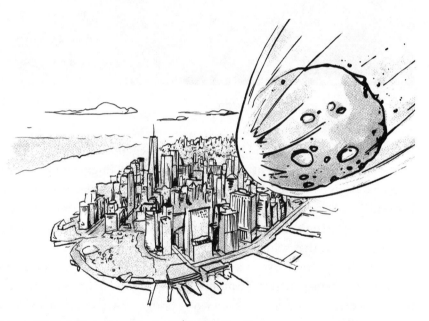

Figure 18. Credit: Lukas Bischoff/IllustrationX.

The pedestrian Millennium Bridge, opened by Queen Elizabeth II on 10 June 2000, was the first new bridge to span the River Thames in London for a century. Thousands of people crowded onto the bridge on the day of its opening, supposedly not a problem, as the bridge was designed to cope easily with such large numbers. However,

Figure 19. Albert Bridge in London.

within moments of the bridge's opening it began to wobble violently, to the great embarrassment of its designers, Arup Engineering and the architect Norman Foster. In the process it earned the nickname the Wobbly Bridge. The swaying came as a surprise, as no such outcome had been predicted by Arup's extensive computer modeling and human testing. It is well known that soldiers marching across bridges can cause them to collapse—the reason they are asked to break step when crossing bridges. Marching soldiers generate harmonized frequencies that can create feedback between the internal frequency of a bridge and soldiers' steps, leading to a collapse. If you look closely, you can often see signs on bridges telling soldiers to break step when marching (Figure 19).

The problem caused by soldiers marching across bridges is well known, and Arup did consider that in their modeling. They even had a precise number: it would take 167 marching soldiers for the Millennium Bridge to wobble. But those crowding on the bridge on opening day were not soldiers, but people from all walks of life who, for the most part, did not know each other. The chance of them spontaneously marching was considered next to impossible. But the designers missed something important. Every bridge is designed to move with the elements, and the Millennium Bridge was supposed to sway gently in response to the Thames breeze. Soon after it opened it was hit by a gust of wind and moved sideways, as expected. The pedestrians' natural reaction was to adjust their stance to regain balance—lean against the movement. Herein lies the problem. They pushed the bridge back, making it sway even more. As an ever-increasing number of pedestrians tried not to fall, the bridge swayed more and more. What happened was that when at least 167 pedestrians crowded onto the bridge in windy conditions, a feedback loop emerged (Figure 20). It was always present, lurking in the background, but needed particular conditions to emerge.

It is the same in the financial system. The distinguishing feature of all serious financial crises is that they gather momentum from the endogenous responses of the market participants themselves, like a tropical storm over a warm sea gains energy as it develops. As financial conditions worsen, the market's willingness to bear risk disappears because the market participants stop behaving independently and start acting as one. They should not do so, as there is little profit and a lot of risk in just following the crowd, but they can be forced to by circumstances.

So, how did Arup miss the potential for the Millennium Bridge wobbling? For the same reason, most financial regulations fail to prevent systemic risk. Arup modeled the impact of individual members of the crowd

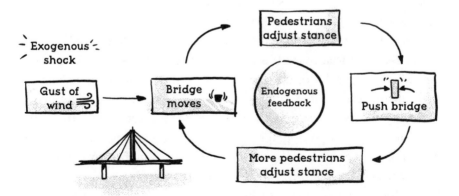

Figure 20. Millennium Bridge feedback loop. Credit: Lukas Bischoff/ IllustrationX.

in isolation. But to properly understand the risk, it is necessary to study every aspect jointly: the weather, the bridge's mechanics, pedestrians' behavior, and the danger arising from individuals acting as one. All of these factors have to be studied simultaneously or, as we economists say it, in equilibrium. The Arup engineers were aware of the danger arising from soldiers marching across the Millennium Bridge. They just never imagined a couple of hundred civilians who didn't know each other would end up doing precisely that. Apparently, these feedback effects were known in some civil engineers' circles, but the natural instinct of companies to keep information proprietary meant it was not made public. It took Arup eighteen months to figure out what had happened, and it eventually came up with two separate solutions. They could either put a dampener on the bridge's movements or create noise—some mechanism that creates random movements to cancel out the synchronized swaying. Arup opted for the former, and it is working well. Still, the random noise solution would have been more interesting, at least from a financial system point of view.

There is a moral lesson in all of this. When something goes wrong, we always want to find someone to blame, someone to punish. On the Millennium Bridge, the natural self-preservation instinct of the people on the bridge caused the wobble—the precautionary principle. Nobody did anything wrong. They were just trying not to fall. Paradoxically, doing the right thing can bring about the worst possible outcome, and we often see that in crises. Market participants' self-preservation instinct causes liquidity to dry up in times of strain, taking us over the precipice into a full-blown crisis. Who was to blame for the Millennium Bridge's wobble? The engineers and the architects. Certainly not the pedestrians. Who is to blame for a financial crisis? It is not as clear-cut, but the financial authorities who set the rules of the game do share the blame. How to find the fundamental causes of instability? Studying beauty contests might help.

Beauty contests were popular in British newspapers in the 1930s. They published pages of photographs of women, encouraging readers to vote for whomever they thought was the prettiest. But there was a twist: a lottery ticket was given to those who voted with the majority. This inspired John Maynard Keynes when he was writing in his *General Theory* about how market prices are formed: "It is not a case of choosing those [faces] which, to the best of one's judgment, are really the prettiest, nor even those which average opinion genuinely thinks the prettiest. We have reached the third degree where we devote our intelligences to anticipating what average opinion expects the average opinion to be. And there are some, I believe, who practice the fourth, fifth and higher degrees."[1] The readers did not choose their favorite based on whom they thought the prettiest. Rather, they voted strategically to maximize the chance of voting with the majority and so get a lottery ticket. In the same way, speculators don't choose stocks on the basis of the fundamentals of the company, they try to out-think other speculators.

In 2002 Hyun Song Shin, then a professor at the London School of Economics (and now the economic advisor and head of research at the Bank for International Settlements, the central banks' central bank), and I proposed a new direction for the literature on risk and uncertainty. We focused on the origin of risk and how the behavior of people leads to risky outcomes. In our view risk can be either endogenous or exogenous.

A dictionary definition of the term "endogenous" refers to outcomes having an internal cause or origin. How an infectious disease spreads through a population is endogenous to the nature of that same population. If we always keep a safe distance between ourselves and our fellow countrymen, we will not get infected, but if we choose to live cheek by jowl with other people, our chance of infection is high. Your chance of getting a cold is endogenous to your behavior and those around you: one reason why taking the New York subway can be hazardous to one's health; and why social distancing was so important in the Covid-19 crisis. The opposite of endogenous is exogenous, whereby outcomes have an external cause or origin. When an asteroid hit the Gulf of Mexico sixty-five million years ago, wiping out the dinosaurs, that was an exogenous shock. There was certainly nothing the dinosaurs did to cause their demise. The risk of an asteroid hitting Wall Street is exogenous.

Suppose I wake up this morning and see on the BBC website that there is a 50 percent chance of rain. If I then decide to carry an umbrella when leaving my house, my doing so has no bearing on the probability of rain. The risk is exogenous. Suppose, instead, I wake up this morning and see on the BBC website that there is some negative economic news about the United Kingdom, and in response I decide to buy a put option on the pound sterling—I profit if the pound weakens. My actions make it more likely the pound will fall. Not by a lot, mind you, a tiny, tiny amount. But tiny is not zero—there is an endogenous effect.

I would not be doing anything wrong. On the contrary, I am behaving prudently, hedging risk, like the pedestrians on the Millennium Bridge, who were trying not to fall into the water. Just like a single pedestrian on the Millennium Bridge did not make it wobble, me alone buying this put option will not make the pound sterling crash. Another ingredient is needed, some mechanism coordinating the actions of many people so when we act in as one, our combined impact is strong. The chance of that happening is endogenous risk. All that is needed to turn some shock—the financial market version of the gust of wind hitting the Millennium Bridge—into a crisis is for a sufficient number of people to think like me (all wanting to prudently protect themselves) for the currency to crash. It is the self-preservation instinct of human beings that so often is the catalyst for crises.

No crisis is purely endogenous or exogenous: they always are a combination of an initial exogenous shock followed by an endogenous response. The same initial exogenous shock can one day whimper out into nothing, and the next blow up into a global crisis. When Covid-19 infected the first person in Wuhan, all the subsequent events could have been averted if that person had behaved differently. But nobody knew at the time. The reason the exogenous shocks blow up into a crisis is that they prey on hidden vulnerabilities no one knows about until it is all too late.

The Dark Side of Well-Meaning Rules

The twin roles of market prices drive endogenous risk. The first is familiar, an idea fundamental to Friedrich Hayek's theories, that market prices embed all relevant information in the economy into one variable: the price. In a simple investment example often used in introductory undergraduate finance courses, the price of a stock is determined by the present discounted value of future dividends, where the discount factor embeds the uncertainty about the future.

Less familiar is the notion that prices are also an imperative to action, forcing us to behave in a particular way, perhaps even against our self-interest. This happens because most market participants are subject to a myriad of regulations, codes of conduct, and restrictions imposed by their trading partners and other stakeholders. These include accounting rules, legal obligations, disclosures, bank capital, risk constraints, and mark-to-market guidelines.

Suppose a bank holds some asset that falls in price by an unusually large amount (Figure 21). The measured risk of that asset will then increase, and risk weights will go up, so the bank's risk-based capital ratio might fall dangerously close to the minimum set in regulations. To protect itself, the bank may have no recourse but to sell that asset. In other words, a change in prices causes riskometers to show higher risk, which in turn triggers forced selling, an example of how prices can be an imperative to action. That is exactly what happened in the Gamestop market turmoil in January 2021 when speculators fought each other, some shorting, others going long. Small speculators trading on the Robinhood platform were eventually unable to trade because Robinhood itself was forced to limit trading because it clears its trades via the Depository Trust and Clearing Corporation (DTCC), and the heightened price volatility prompted DTCC to demand $3 billion in collateral from Robinhood.

A bank may not react to market outcomes in the way we expect it to because the constraints it is under dictate a certain type of behavior. If the bank is large its trading activities will have a significant price impact. One could say that the presence of constraints undermines the integrity of the

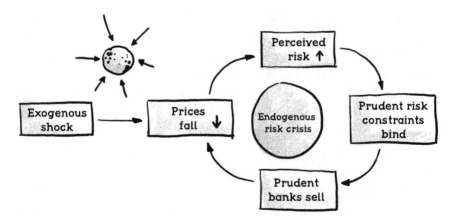

Figure 21. Prudent banks and endogenous feedback. Credit: Lukas Bischoff/IllustrationX.

prices, taking them away from their fundamental values. In extreme cases, prices can become so distorted that they lead to undesirable extreme outcomes, like bubbles and crashes. That said, these constraints don't bite all of the time, not even most of the time. It is only in times of stress that they significantly affect market prices. That observation goes a long way toward explaining why we decide to use riskometers and why they perform so poorly. The riskometers describe the world quite well when everything is quiet but do not capture behavior changes in times of stress: why they are fair-weather instruments.

What does this mean for regulations? That we should do away with all the rules and constraints? Far from it. The rules are by and large very beneficial: helping to keep the financial system orderly, protecting investors, and preventing abuse. However, they do have a dark side. Well-meaning rules can act as a catalyst for making market participants act in unison, just like the Millennium Bridge's design made all the pedestrians march like soldiers. A good example is buying stocks on margin.

The first time stock markets became accessible to the general public was in 1920s America, as buying stocks was the preserve of the wealthy and connected before that. After World War I anyone in America could buy stocks. Not only that, but they also didn't have to invest much money. One could bring $100, borrow $900, and buy $1,000 worth of stock—be leveraged nine times. This buying on the margin became very popular. Money poured into the stock market, and since the United States was the only country where stock markets were fully open to the general public, money flowed to Wall Street from all over the world. The result was the mother of all stock market bubbles, one that came to a sticky end in September 1929, triggering the Great Depression.

The dark side of the well-meaning margin rules shows its face when the bubble is bursting. Suppose I buy ten shares of IBM at $100 each, $1,000 in all. I put up 10 percent, or $100, of my own money and borrow $900. The entity financing this transaction will want some protection against the stock falling in price, insurance called a margin. Suppose the margin is equal to the initial $100. If IBM's price falls by 5 percent to $95, the investment is now worth only $950. I still owe $900, while my net value ($1,000–$950) has fallen to $50. However, the entity financing the transaction insists on 10 percent of the original amount, $100, so I

have to make up the $50 shortfall. This is called a margin call, an immedi-
ate demand for $50. I have two choices: sell enough of the stock to pay
back the borrowed funds or find $50 elsewhere. Many investors will have
no choice—they can't find the $50 in time and have to sell. How likely
is a day like that? I looked at the history of daily IBM stock prices and
got 22,696 observations. Out of those, there are 117 days when the price
of IBM fell by 5 percent or more, so the likelihood of a 5 percent price
drop is 0.52 percent, or about once every 9½ months. If the price falls by
10 percent or more, we are wiped out; such days have happened 13 times,
or almost one day out of every seven years.

Investors may have no choice but to sell the stock to meet the margin.
Yet if a large number of investors are in the same situation, a significant
volume of sells hits the markets simultaneously. Prices fall even more,
creating yet more margin calls, more investors have no choice but to sell,
and prices fall more. An endogenous risk vicious feedback loop emerges
from the dark (Figure 22).

Here, the margins work like the wobbly Millennium Bridge. Pedestrians were trying not to fall, leaning against the swaying of the bridge,
perversely causing it to sway even more. In the case of margins, it is the
automatic protection for the lenders that is at the root of the damage.
One of the enduring images of the crash of 1929, even if now debunked,
is desperate investors jumping out of the sky-high windows of their Wall
Street offices. The putative reason was margins. Investors got margin
calls, their capital was wiped out, and they were set to be declared bankrupt by the end of business that day.

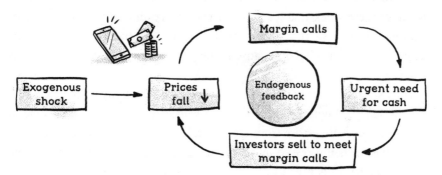

Figure 22. Margin call feedback loop. Credit: Lukas Bischoff/IllustrationX.

Some rules, like margins, constrain market participants only in particular situations. Others work all the time, having a rather surprising impact on prices by making investors continually react in unexpected ways to market developments. The way prices and quantities are supposed to relate to each other is clearly illustrated in an example economics professors are fond of. When the price of oranges increases, we buy fewer (and farmers want to sell more), and when the price falls, we buy more (and the farmers want to sell fewer)—the law of supply and demand. There is no exception. We will buy some goods almost without considering cost—goods economists call highly inelastic, like tobacco and heroin. We buy them almost regardless of the price, but we don't buy more when the price goes up.

Are there any goods that we buy more of when the price goes up? Yes, a strange asset called a Giffen good, named after the nineteenth-century Scottish economist Robert Giffen. It is a hypothetical good, useful to illustrate weird behavior in markets, something that exists in theory but not in practice. Every other good exhibits the intuitive property that we buy less when the price goes up. If you are thinking of counterexamples like high fashion, yes, demand can go up when prices increase. But that is because the good's exclusivity is also valued—if I want to be the only person on my street with a posh handbag, I am willing to pay more for it.

However, the constraints I have been discussing can make investors buy more when prices increase and sell when prices fall: the law of supply and demand apparently gets reversed. Sometimes these constraints can even be self-imposed, for instance, when investors use automatic trading rules. My favorite example of how constraints can cause unfortunate outcomes is the biggest stock market crash in history, commonly known as Black Monday. On 19 October 1987 stock markets around the world fell by 23 percent. The underlying cause is the best example of endogenous risk I have ever seen.

It all started in 1976, when two professors at the University of California, Berkeley, Hayne Leland and Mark Rubinstein, came up with a clever idea to protect investors from stock market crashes: portfolio insurance. If an investor is interested in buying insurance against a large price drop, all she has to do is buy a put option, which gives her the right (but not the obligation) to sell a stock at a preagreed (strike) price at some point in the future. Suppose the price of Apple is $200 today. If we buy a five-year put option on Apple with a strike price of $180, we get the right to sell an Apple stock for $180 whenever we want for the next five years.

What if no option is available? Or the option is too expensive? Leland's and Rubinstein's portfolio insurance solved that with the magic of financial engineering: what is formally known as dynamic replication, whereby one can create a financial instrument that looks and behaves like an option. So, if it looks like a duck, swims like a duck, and quacks like a duck, it must be a duck, right? Not quite. There is a key difference. In portfolio insurance, one has to buy or sell the asset being insured every day to replicate the option correctly. If the price increases, we have to buy, and if the price falls, we have to sell. In other words, a buy dear–sell cheap strategy—we apparently violate the laws of supply and demand.

All that was needed for portfolio insurance to cause a crisis was for a sufficient number of people to use it as a trading strategy. And that is what happened in September 1987. The US government postmortem of the 1987 crash estimated that around $100 billion was placed in formal portfolio insurance programs, representing around 3 percent of the precrash market capitalization. From Wednesday, 14 October to Friday, 16 October 1987, the market declined by around 10 percent. The sales dictated by those who used portfolio insurance strategies amounted to $12 billion, but actual sales were only $4 billion. This meant a substantial amount of pent-up selling pressure accumulated over the weekend, causing the S&P 500 index to fall by 23 percent on Monday, 19 October.

The stock market crash of 1987 is a classic example of the destabilizing feedback effect on market dynamics of concerted selling pressure from mechanical trading rules, like the sell-on-loss considered here. Again, just as in the Millennium Bridge example, the underlying destabilizing behavior is entirely invisible so long as trading activity remains below some critical but unknown threshold. It is only when this threshold is exceeded that the endogenous risk becomes apparent, causing a market crash.

A common view of crises maintains that they arrive from the outside, like the above asteroid that is about to hit Wall Street. That is not true. The main driver of crises is endogenous risk, underpinned by the system's hidden mechanisms, just like sell-on-loss trading rules. Unfortunately, there is too much of a tendency to focus on the triggers of crises, not the mechanism. The problem is that there is a tiny number of mechanisms but an almost infinite number of triggers. They are visible but not all that important. Some are even human.

Andreas Georgiou used to be Greece's chief statistician but then committed the crime of accurately reporting the size of the Greek budget deficit in 2009 without allowing the board of the statistics agency to first vote on the size of it. One might think a politically appointed board should not decide on statistical measurements. But it got worse for Andreas. He was pursued in the courts for this crime and convicted in June 2018 by the Greek Supreme Civil and Criminal Court and sentenced to two years on probation. Why did the Greek authorities get upset? Because he reported the true number of 15.4 percent and not the finance ministry's estimate of 13.6 percent, thereby triggering the Greek crisis. Andreas may have been the trigger, but he was certainly not to blame, and the crisis would have happened anyway, even if he had fudged the numbers. The crisis mechanism was already in place. The Greek crisis was not the first time the trigger was confused with the underlying cause: see the 1914 crisis following the assassination of Archduke Ferdinand and, in 1763, the end of the Seven Years' War. In both cases a crisis was inevitable: it was not a question of if, but when.

We should not focus on the trigger but on the underlying vulnerability, the mechanisms that cause crises. When getting too concerned about the triggers, we risk what my skiing instructor once called paralysis by analysis. If one thinks about skiing down a one-kilometer, 45° slope, one might conclude it is best to take a lift down. Paralysis by analysis. It is the same with triggers because there are so many of them; if you start searching for and protecting yourself against all potential trigger events, that will end up being all you do. Focusing on the triggers can lead policy makers seriously astray, But that is often what they end up doing. The press reports on the triggers, the public demands that someone be blamed, and the likes of Andreas Georgiou get prosecuted. Meanwhile, those responsible, like the Greek politicians, get off scot-free. Our attention should be focused on the mechanisms, and the financial authorities and hedge fund managers should know that. Sadly, they are often no better than the Greek prosecutors.

Bubbles 101: Perceived and Actual Risk

Crises take (almost) everybody by surprise. It could not be any other way because if many people anticipate a crisis, they will get out of the market—either preventing the crisis or causing it to happen immediately. However, even if we are surprised, crises don't happen randomly. They are the culmination of the accumulation of risky behavior over years and decades. Few people have said it better than the former head of the Bank for International Settlements, Andrew Crockett: "The received wisdom is that risk increases in recessions and falls in booms. In contrast, it may be more helpful to think of risk as increasing during upswings, as financial imbalances build up, and materializing in recessions."[2]

In a paper I wrote with Hyun Song Shin and my LSE colleague Jean-Pierre Zigrand, we applied endogenous risk to the measurability of risk, classifying risk into two categories, perceived risk, what the riskometer measures, and actual risk, the underlying hidden risk that is undetected until it suddenly materializes in a crisis. Riskometers, by definition, can measure only perceived risk because they are based on using fluctuations in market prices to infer the riskiness of the underlying assets. If the fluctuations are low, the risk measurements will follow. If the market is confident, prices are rising, fluctuations are low, and perceived risk is low. The use of riskometers based on perceived risk is one reason bubbles happen. Market prices get increasingly disconnected from the underlying reality, and the risk of a significant correction (actual risk) steadily increases. Suppose some investors buy an asset. Consequently, the price of it increases slightly, which in turn encourages more people to buy, making prices rise a little more. The result is a series of small price increases, which, when translated to price fluctuations, imply volatility is falling.

If we then use a common device to measure risk-adjusted returns, the Sharpe Ratio, proposed by the Nobel laureate William F. Sharpe, the asset looks better and better.[3] Prices increase steadily, perceived risk falls—a fantastic investment, steady profits at low risk. "Money for nothing," as the 1980s Dire Straits song would have it. A bubble born of the positive feedback between rising prices and falling perceived risk. Prices continue to rise faster and faster until some trigger event causes them to crash. Because everybody wants to sell before the prices drop, they all rush to

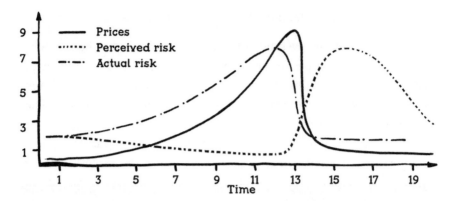

Figure 23. Money for nothing. Actual and perceived risk. Credit: Lukas Bischoff/IllustrationX.

the exits, and the prices crash immediately. When things are good, we are optimistic and buy, which endogenously increases prices—the bubble feeds on itself. This eventually goes into reverse, and negative news preys on falling prices, with the markets spiraling downward much faster than they went up. Yet again, prices go up the escalator and down the lift (or elevator if in America). Only after the prices have crashed does perceived risk increase. By then it is too late.

So, what happens to actual risk through all of that? It increases along with the bubble. After all, it captures the fundamental risk, the risk of a market crash, hence falling when the bubble deflates (Figure 23). I often wish someone could have convinced the financial regulators that the risk after 2008 was much lower than the risk before, and they should have been encouraging risk-taking and not derisking the system.

~~Long-~~Short-Term Management and the Perfect Storm

In the summer of 1998 the financial markets were turbulent, not least due to the hedge fund Long-Term Capital Management (LTCM).[4] LTCM was the most celebrated hedge fund of its time. It was founded in 1994 with illustrious partners like Myron Scholes and Robert C. Merton (of Black-Scholes fame), who shared the 1997 Nobel Prize. LTCM started with over $1 billion in capital and was very successful despite its exceptionally high fees. A typical hedge fund charges "2 and 20," 2 percent of an investor's assets as fees plus 20 percent of profits earned. LTCM charged 2 and 25, and its investors were required to commit their funds for at least three years. In the first two years investors enjoyed 43 percent and 41 percent returns, respectively, after fees, and $10 million invested in 1994 was worth $40 million four years later. In September 1997 LTCM's net capital was $6.7 billion, and the value of its investments was $126.4 billion, the difference being borrowed money. It returned $2.7 billion to investors in December 1997 to focus on investing its partners' own money.

LTCM's success created the impression that it would make extraordinary profits from applying technical expertise unavailable to anyone else—just magic. Scholes summed up the strategy thus: "LTCM would make money by being a vacuum sucking up nickels that no one else could see." LTCM drove tough bargains on financing and got very low rates and special deals because its prime brokers did not want to be left out of the LTCM business. They were prepared to cut corners both on the rates charged and on the amount of collateral demanded. The mainstay of LTCM's trading strategies was convergence or relative value trades, which seek to exploit differences in the price of similar assets. The underlying principle is that two fundamentally identical assets should have identical prices, as otherwise there is a profit-making opportunity: arbitrage. LTCM's risk management system indicated in 1998 it would take a ten-standard-deviation event (otherwise known as a 10-sigma event) for it to lose all of its capital in a single year. This means the risk system expected LTCM to go bust once every 3.3×10^{20} years.[5] By comparison, the age of the universe is only 1.3×10^{10} years. No wonder the partners returned funds to the investors to focus on their own money. They just did not expect to fail—their riskometer told them so. Meanwhile, LTCM's trading environment was increasingly choppy, as its very success spawned copycats. More and more players with similar trading strategies piled into the market, and profit-making opportunities started disappearing. In response, LTCM ventured into new areas, most notably the volatility on the S&P 500, measured by the Chicago Board Options Exchange's Volatility Index (VIX). The long-run average VIX until the middle of 1998 was 16.8, and the VIX exceeded that level throughout 1998. Volatility is mean reverting, and with volatility way above average, money was to be made by betting the VIX would fall.

On the day I am writing this, the VIX is 35. Suppose you see the same value when you read this and get the brilliant idea to log onto your online broker and buy a short VIX fund—betting it will fall to the long-run average. Think twice. While it is almost certain the VIX will fall, the cost of maintaining the short VIX fund might exceed 35 percent a year, so unless the VIX falls relatively soon you are in for losses.

That can happen quite quickly. Just ask the unfortunate investors in Nomura's *Next Notes S&P500 VIX Short-Term Futures Inverse Daily Excess Return Index ETN*, which lost 96 percent the very same day Nomura launched the fund on 5 February 2018. What happened is that the VIX had fallen from 28 at the start of 2016 to 13.54 by the end of January 2018, and, if one follows the basic principles of momentum investing, the VIX was destined to fall more. Nomura launched its short VIX fund on Monday morning Japanese time with the previous week's VIX value and quickly sold ¥32 billion worth to investors. Unfortunately, heightened uncertainty hit the US market the same day, so when the US stock market opened the VIX quickly rose to 37.32—boom, Nomura's luckless investors lost ¥32 billion in the blink of an eye.

Back to LTCM. It was eyeing the steady increase in VIX throughout 1998 and decided to get in on the action. However, because the profit margin on betting that the VIX would fall was too small for LTCM it opted to borrow to increase leverage. LTCM became so prominent in the volatility market that it earned the nickname "The central bank of volatility."

Except, as LTCM piled into the market, the VIX continued to rise. LTCM suffered losses of −6.42 percent in May 1998 and −10.14 percent in June. Then Russia defaulted in August, triggering a market panic, and the VIX continued to rise, reaching 45 in August. By early September LTCM's equity had tumbled to $600 million. As the debts were constant and the positions worth less, leverage rose sharply, reaching 125. LTCM was in serious difficulty, getting margin calls it did not have the cash to cover and hence was forced to liquidate its positions. That made the VIX rise even more. A vicious feedback loop was set in motion: higher VIX causing margin calls, leading to liquidation, making the VIX rise further, repeat.

Realizing the disastrous consequences of letting LTCM fail, the New York branch of the Federal Reserve organized a $3.6 billion bailout from its major creditors to avoid a wider market collapse. The participating banks got a 90 percent share in LTCM in return. After the bailout, the panic abated, and the positions formerly held by LTCM were eventually liquidated at a small profit to the bailers. In light of the 2008 crisis a decade later, it is quite amusing that the LTCM bailout was controversial; the government did not put up any of its funds—only LTCM's counterparties did—but even that was seen as beyond the pale.

One LTCM partner said, "What happened to LTCM was a perfect storm—a 100-year flood."[6] But does that stand up to scrutiny? Endogenous risk analysis suggests otherwise. The unprecedented price movements in the summer of 1998 were not the results of terrible luck, just as the Millennium Bridge did not wobble because of bad luck. Instead, it was only a matter of time before a small exogenous shock would hit LTCM, causing its failure. Once the bubble started bursting, the internal dynamics of the feedback loop took hold with a vengeance. Under the right conditions, the crisis was a near certainty because of the endogenous feedback loops between margin calls and distress.

LTCM bet on the mean reversion of an asset that fluctuates around its long-run mean. Profits were made, but only by those who bailed LTCM out. Why did LTCM not profit? The explanation is provided by an observation often misattributed to Keynes, who supposedly said when asked by an investor in 1931 about market conditions: "The market can stay irrational longer than you can stay solvent." The very high VIX levels were caused by the uncertainty created by the very existence of LTCM. A necessary condition for the VIX to return to its long-run mean was for LTCM to fail. A perfect storm did not hit the fund. Its failure was a near certainty.

Endogenous Risk and the Financial System

Endogenous risk doesn't usually leave much of a footprint on the financial markets. While it lurks in the dark corners of the system, most of the time all we see is exogenous risk. When markets appear to be efficient, with prices that follow random walks, as in Burton Malkiel's book *A Random Walk Down Wall Street*. But the good times don't last. Endogenous risk will show its face when some trigger pushes us to act in concert with each other, like the pedestrians on the Millennium Bridge. Price movements will be amplified—bubbles and crashes.

The spirals of coordinated selling that are unleashed by endogenous risk are normally held back by the inherent stabilizing forces in the markets: the arbitrageurs, the hedge funds, the sovereign wealth funds, the Warren Buffetts, the Soroses. They step up to the plate in crises to buy cheap assets, putting a floor under prices. An excellent expression of this is from Baron Rothschild in the eighteenth century, who is reported to have said, "Buy when there's blood in the streets, even if the blood is your own." The self-interest of the speculators benefits society, as in Adam Smith's classic statement, "It is not from the benevolence of the butcher, the brewer, or the baker that we expect our dinner, but from their regard to their own interest."

What lets endogenous risk off its leash is decisions and policies that serve to harmonize market participants' behavior. Rules that prevent them from erecting a floor under the markets by buying all the assets that are so undervalued because of the crisis. The riskometer puts the contrast between endogenous and exogenous risk in the sharpest relief. Almost all methods of measuring risk are based on the assumption that risk is exogenous because that is the easiest way to deal with risk. All one has to do is to collect some daily historical financial data—market prices, credit default swap spreads, interest rates, trading volumes—and feed them into a riskometer. Nothing wrong with that if all we care about is exogenous risk: short-term fluctuations.

If, however, we care about tail risk, banks failing, and crises, we have no choice but to find some way to measure endogenous risk. That is not easy. Large losses and crises happen because of risk everybody missed, so identifying endogenous risk before it is too late is like searching for a needle in a haystack, except that we don't even know what the needle looks like. We know only that the needle is there when we stick our hand into the haystack and it gets pricked. After a crisis, everybody knows what went wrong, and we prevent a repeat: closing the barn door after the horse has bolted. Meanwhile, the forces of the next crisis start gathering strength somewhere where nobody is looking.

The 2008 crisis is an excellent example of how we missed all the warning signs. While I suspect many people thought financial products based on the American housing market were dodgy and opted not to buy them, a few profited from it. The book (and movie) *The Big Short* by Michael Lewis tells the story of a few plucky players who did exactly that. Meanwhile, no government authority had an inkling of the danger lurking right under their noses. The lesson from 2008 is that the buildup of endogenous risk happens almost wholly out of sight. Eventually, the vulnerabilities hit the hidden trigger—risk got a little bit too high on a certain day when the markets had little tolerance for it—and it all blew up.

The challenge for investors and the financial authorities is that while endogenous risk is ever-present, it cannot easily be measured. As endogenous and exogenous risk move in opposite directions, the riskometers get it wrong in all states of nature, reporting too little risk before a crisis and too high after it, just like the European Central Bank's systemic risk dashboard.

Outcomes in the financial system are determined by the interaction of the institutions and individuals that make up the financial system. That's why my colleagues and I proposed the term "endogenous risk" to capture the resulting risk. However, even though endogenous risk gives a useful description of the world, it is difficult to work with in practice. It cannot readily be quantified or incorporated into riskometers or put onto risk dashboards. The general practice is to assume risk is exogenous, that it arrives from outside the financial system, impacting the system but not being affected by it. Like an asteroid hitting Wall Street (see Figure 18).

As a practical matter, it may be perfectly okay to assume most risk is exogenous. It just depends on our objectives. Anyone concerned with day-to-day risks or risks of frequent small losses would not be very far off by focusing on exogenous risk. It is only those who care about tail risk—the infrequent large outcomes that cause significant losses, the failure of banks, and financial crises—who should focus on endogenous risk. What is worrying is how easily the riskometers based on exogenous risk can be manipulated.

8

If You Can't Take the Risk, Change Riskometers

Beauty is skin deep.

Figure 24. Credit: Copyright © Ricardo Galvão.

We often run into street artists who, for a small fee, will draw a caricature of us. One that exaggerates facial features for comical effect, perhaps emphasizing the nose and diminishing the chin. One example is the caricature of me made by Ricardo Galvão, who did many of the drawings in this book (Figure 24). Risk measurements are just like those street caricatures. The riskometer is the creation of its designer, who makes all sorts of decisions, balancing ease of implementation with accuracy, emphasizing what he cares about, and dismissing the rest. Riskometer design is highly subjective, and two designers faced with the same problem will create riskometers that measure risk quite differently.

The reason for all of the subjectivity is that risk is not directly measured, like prices or temperature. It can be inferred only by how prices move, and to do that we need a model. And since by its very nature every model is subjective, the risk measurements are a product of the underlying assumptions. And that means the accuracy of risk measurements is much lower than is generally presumed. Certainly much less reliable than the thermostat that keeps the risk manager's office at a steady 22°C. More important, all that subjectivity makes riskometers easy to abuse. Perhaps with blatant dishonesty, as when someone deliberately tweaks the models, so they tell us risk is $1 million when it is really $5 million. Plenty of that going on, but I think intellectual laziness is more common. Using riskometers to pretend risk is measured and managed so we can demonstrate we are diligent and compliant. We follow all the regulations while doing something else. And because it is so hard to verify that the riskometers are accurate there is little the regulators, the compliance officers, and all the other guardians of good practices can do.

A friend of mine, Rupert Goodwin, used to make a living selling risk systems. One day he went to a bank that had just been audited by the local financial authority. The regulator came in and asked the risk manager if he used a riskometer. When the risk manager said yes, the regulator ticked off a box and left. The most obvious way a riskometer goes wrong is when it is simply a tick-the-box exercise:

1. Is a risk model used? ✓
2. Is the Value-at-Risk number below $1 million? ✓

I suspect laziness is the usual explanation for such tick-the-box risk management, but deliberate misunderstanding of what riskometers can and cannot do is much more interesting. The powers that be have opted for deliberate ambiguity. Senior bankers and regulators generally have a limited understanding of statistics, and even when they do it's likely out of date and won't cover the detailed mechanics of the modern riskometer. They have to make decisions and are much more comfortable not knowing—the deliberate ambiguity. Like sausages. If you are going to eat them, you are better off not knowing how they are made. Some two decades ago I made exactly that mistake when I read a book called *Fast Food Nation* by Eric Schlosser, which went into the gory details of how fast food is made. Not many books have changed the way I live my life, but this one did, and I have studiously avoided fast food ever since. I would have been happier if I hadn't read *Fast Food Nation*—ignorance can be bliss. I suspect most senior bankers and regulators take the same view, happier not knowing how the riskometers that govern their world work. The easiest way to do that is to choose a measurement of risk that somehow maps all the portfolios' complexities and even entire financial institutions' risks into one number—Value-at-Risk. So long as the Value-at-Risk number is within an acceptable range, all is fine.

The creator of the all-important Value-at-Risk riskometer, the JP Morgan bank, came to get badly hit by its creation three decades after bringing it into the world. That is when a member of the bank's London staff, nicknamed the London Whale, caused a $5.8 billion loss because he was apparently trying to profit from the bank's Value-at-Risk. It started with Bruno Iksil, a senior trader in a division called the chief investment office (CIO), whose function was to hedge the bank's credit risk. That year the Value-at-Risk for the CIO division exceeded $95 million, problematic since the total target Value-at-Risk for the entire bank was only $125 million.[1]

There are two ways to deal with this problem. Either reduce the risk of the portfolio or change the riskometer. JP Morgan seems to have chosen the latter. How do we know this? The person in charge of the Value-at-Risk model at the CIO, Patrick Hagan, sent an email to his colleagues with the subject "Optimizing regulatory capital," using his private Yahoo account. The email was subsequently made public by the Senate committee investigating the loss.[2] And that exposes the crucial difference between thermometers and riskometers. A favorite saying of President Truman was, "If you can't take the heat, get out of the kitchen." When it comes to risk: If you can't take the risk, change riskometers.

As it turned out, JP Morgan's new riskometer missed out on some of the critical risks facing the CIO, risks that soon would lead to the $5.8 billion loss. In the words of JP Morgan's quarterly securities filing: "This portfolio has proven to be riskier, more volatile, and less effective as an economic hedge than the firm previously believed." Of course, if one deliberately picks a riskometer that signals the lowest risk, the portfolio will be riskier than we think it is.

Manipulating Riskometers 101

A few years ago I addressed a small group of very senior financial regulators, telling them that when I lecture to my LSE students on risk forecasting, I like to give them the following anecdote: "Suppose my job is to forecast the risk of some portfolio, measured by Value-at-Risk. One day my boss calls me into her office: 'Jón, the Value-at-Risk is too high, and you have to make it lower. However, our traders are doing a fantastic job, and I want to keep the nice returns. Now go and play with your computers and make it happen. And by the way, ~~don't get caught~~ make sure you comply with all regulations.'"

And then I show the students how to make it happen. The senior decision makers were aghast: both that I would have the audacity to show the students how to do such a thing and that it was easy to do. The answer to why is that these are simple tricks a lot of people know. If the students become risk managers, they should learn those schemes so as to know what to keep an eye out for.

The easiest way to manipulate the risk measurements is to pick a riskometer that delivers a lower number. On my website, extremerisk.org, I forecast risk for several assets every day with the most commonly used techniques. Let's focus on the S&P 500 index, where we find today that our Value-at-Risk is $22 million, supposing a $1 billion portfolio, getting the Value-at-Risk from a common technique called historical simulation. Historical simulation is just one of many techniques one can use to calculate Value-at-Risk, and one of the most commonly used. Suppose I use the six most common calculation methods (Figure 25).

By switching from historical simulation to another method, exponentially weighted moving average (EWMA) (incidentally, created by JP Morgan in the same report in which it proposed Value-at-Risk), the Value-at-Risk falls from $21.8 million to $8.5 million—accomplished without doing anything else. There are two problems with this trick. To begin with, there is no guarantee EWMA will continue to result in the lowest

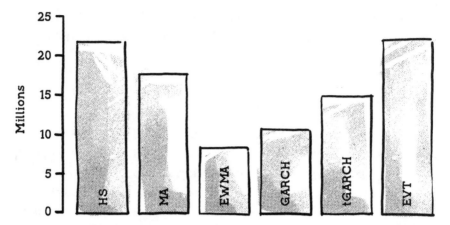

Figure 25. Value-at-Risk on a $1 billion portfolio of S&P 500 on 2 January 2018. Credit: Lukas Bischoff/IllustrationX.

Value-at-Risk. Indeed, on some days it will be the highest. Even worse, it does not meet our criteria for not being detected. The bank's compliance people and the regulators will take notice and likely take a dim view of such switching of riskometers, especially if done often.

A better way to manipulate riskometers is to cherry-pick the assets one puts into the portfolio. Choose stocks that robustly provide the juicy returns we want but do not contribute very much to the measured risk. Technically, we add another constraint into the portfolio optimization problem: maximize returns subject to two constraints, low reported risk and high true risk. This is possible because the riskometer is a caricature, and what we are doing is searching for assets that exploit the weaknesses in our riskometer: the tiny chin and big nose. It is easy enough to do by anyone with moderately good quantitative skills and is practically un-detectable by both the compliance department and the regulators. When I tried to do this for a sample portfolio, it took me only a few minutes to reduce the Value-at-Risk by over 70 percent—without changing the expected returns much.

The final way to manipulate is to use options. I show a particularly egregious example in my book *Financial Risk Forecasting*. This approach is based on judiciously buying and selling options around the actual and desired Value-at-Risk numbers to minimize measured risk and not affect much else.[3] Doing exactly that is a blatant abuse of the bank's risk management system and presumably would be picked up by the risk controllers. However, if one goes about it more subtly, it will likely never be detected.

There are many similar ways one can manipulate riskometers. Some are easy to detect, others are known only to the person taking the risk. If you are skeptical and think I am just an academic making up extreme examples that would never see the light of day in the real world, think again. The reason the UBS bank failed in 2008 was precisely because of what I'm describing here.

Many banks failed in the 2008 crisis, but the most interesting for the topic at hand is the Swiss bank UBS. We are quite fortunate that the Swiss Federal Banking Commission had UBS produce a postmortem titled *Shareholder Report on UBS's Write-Downs*. It is a fascinating document, clearly and clinically highlighting all that went wrong: a superb example of a desire to manipulate the risk management process and, ultimately, self-delusion. The main culprit was $19 billion in losses on collateralized debt obligations (CDOs) composed of US subprime mortgages in 2007.[4]

Given that it used Value-at-Risk to measure the risk, UBS apparently did not realize the CDOs were risky. Value-at-Risk is the worst risk-measurement methodology for CDOs because by construction it cannot pick up the risk in an asset with a steady income and the occasional substantial losses.[5] The bank could have done much better. It had comprehensive details on each mortgage it bought, and nothing prevented it from analyzing these data, which would have told it that something was fishy. Indeed, some of UBS's competitors did avoid large losses on subprime mortgages by carefully analyzing the data they had on them. The UBS risk managers opted for a riskometer that was tailor-designed not to capture subprime mortgage risk. This fed into the calculations of the bank's overall riskiness and was dutifully reported to senior management, the Swiss authorities, and UBS's auditor, Ernst & Young. None was concerned. UBS lost sight of the fact that it was deceiving itself when it thought it was fooling the regulators.

Another exploit of riskometers is to take advantage of the risk management techniques that are meant to protect us. Use the regulations to hide risk. Under the Basel regulations, banks are supposed to measure their trading risk and report the risk numbers to the authorities. The technique for doing so is one beloved by consultants and designers of dashboards: traffic lights. The traffic-light rule says that a bank is allowed to have three days a year where its losses exceed the Value-at-Risk measurement. The banks are given some leeway, and so long as they exceed the Value-at-Risk only four times a year they stay in the green zone. If they exceed it between five and nine times they are in the amber (yellow) zone and if they exceed more than nine times, the red zone.

A bank in the green zone must hold capital at least equal to three times the Value-at-Risk; if in the amber zone, three to four times Value-at-Risk; if it hits the red zone, four times the Value-at-Risk plus the likelihood of being subjected to intrusive scrutiny. Obviously, the higher the Value-at-Risk, the more the bank has to invest in low-yielding capital and less in high-return, high-risk assets. It's no surprise that the bank wants to minimize its measured risk, hence the amount of costly capital it has to hold. Recall the example of the London Whale.

Imagine the following: Suppose a bank knows its true Value-at-Risk, but the regulator knows only what the bank tells it. Further, suppose the bank fully intends to comply with the letter of the regulations, the traffic lights, but still wants to take on more risk. What will happen? Chen Zhou, a coauthor, and I looked into this question in a paper titled "Why Risk Is So Hard to Measure." As it turns out, it is quite easy to underreport risk while remaining fully compliant with the traffic lights rule. Particularly interesting to us was how banks react to being controlled by the traffic rule. They will change the composition of assets, shifting from assets that fluctuate a lot in price (but not excessively) to assets whose prices are usually relatively stable, but on occasion are subject to substantial losses. In the language of finance, the banks come to prefer assets with lower volatility and higher tail risk. Such assets have the advantage of making the bank look good, but at the expense of making it more likely the bank will fail. Like UBS's CDOs.

Finding such assets is easy. As we had CRSP, the entire database of daily stock returns in the United States, on hand, we simply searched for stocks that simultaneously matched some profitability criteria and standard risk management standards while staying in the green zone. The results confirmed the theoretical prediction. Because of how the regulations worked, the best way to bypass them was to increase the very risk we don't want the banks to take. In all fairness, the example above applies to Basel II, which now has been surpassed by Basel III, which also replaces Value-at-Risk with Expected Shortfall, which is not subject to this particular exploit.

Capital Structure Arbitrage

One of the best ways to see how riskometers get abused in practice is in what is called capital structure arbitrage, the manipulation of capital rules to make the capital ratio look as high as possible while keeping it very low in practice: all without violating the letter of the law or drawing the attention of the authorities. What makes capital structure arbitrage possible is the very complexity of bank capital. As there is considerable scope for mistakes and even outright manipulation of the capital calculation, it is no surprise banks are quite adept at such machinations. Any bank wanting to be seen as having high capital while actually holding little capital can use clever financial engineering tricks to make bank capital appear to be almost anything the bank wants. There are consulting firms entirely dedicated to helping them do precisely that.

Such capital structure arbitrage helped many banks get into difficulty in the 2008 crisis. I looked at this in detail in my last book, *Global Financial Systems: Stability and Risk,* when I saw that banks that appeared to be highly capitalized were going bust. That should not have happened because if they were making risky loans, the risk weights and hence capital should have reflected that risk. As it turned out, the capital was illusionary because of capital structure optimization.

The capital ratio comprises two parts, capital in the numerator and risk-weighted assets in the denominator. Capital structure arbitrage involves maximizing the numerator and minimizing the denominator to make the ratio as high as possible. The denominator captures the interaction of the value of assets, often loans, and their risk weights. Since most loans are illiquid and have no market price, the only way to find their value is to use a valuation model. It is even harder to calculate the risk weights because we have to use a riskometer. Since both parts of the denominator calculation are based on models, the banks have ample scope to pick models that make the denominator as small as possible. Similarly, the numerator is

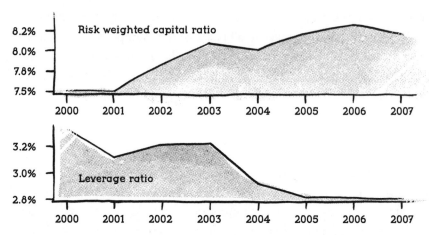

Figure 26. Capital ratios for European banks before the 2008 crisis.
Credit: Lukas Bischoff/IllustrationX.

easy to manipulate because capital is composed of both equity and capital instruments that turned out to be not very equity-like, not the least hybrid instruments.

I can illustrate this by looking at two ways of calculating a capital ratio: tier 1 capital divided by risk-weighted assets and equity divided by total assets (leverage ratio). The former allows plenty of scope for manipulation, but the latter does not. The leverage ratio is always smaller because of the risk weights (Figure 26 shows the two ratios over time). The risk-weighted capital ratio is trending upward, sending the signal that the banks were becoming more capitalized and safer as time passed. The leverage ratio trends downward, indicating that the banks are becoming less capitalized and riskier.

The Inevitable Crisis in Quantland

Wednesday is the type of day people will remember in quant-land for a very long time. Events that models only predicted would happen once in 10,000 years happened every day for three days.
—Wall Street Journal, *June 2007*

The June 2007 crisis in Quantland heralded the opening shots of the global crisis that reached its peak fourteen months later. The term

"Quantland" refers to the activities of a particular type of investment fund that replaces decisions by human beings with computer algorithms. These funds are often called quant funds, short for funds that use quantitative strategies.

The classical way to manage a fund is to do what one of the world's most successful investors, Warren Buffett, does with his Berkshire Hathaway fund: use fundamental analysis to analyze companies' relative strength. Quant funds dispense with that, instead collecting vast amounts of statistical information: prices of every conceivable asset, the state of the economy, and whatever else they can get their hands on. This data is fed into algorithms that identify how all this data affected prices in the past, and use the result to forecast prices. The algorithm is then let loose on the markets, automatically buying and selling assets of all types—stocks, bonds, derivatives, and so on—much faster than any human being can. Humans take only an indirect role by monitoring the algorithms' decisions to make sure they don't go too crazy.

The people working for quant funds differ from those working for more traditional fund managers. Not accountants or economists or finance experts, they are more likely to have studied technical subjects like computer science, physics, and statistics, often holding doctoral degrees from the world's best universities. All the quant funds think they have the best information and algorithms and computers and human capital, stealing a march on their quant competitors, not to mention the much slower traditional funds.

By the summer of 2007 the quant funds had been very successful, with the average fund outperforming its benchmarks by 2 percent. Some did much better. Goldman Sachs's flagship Global Alpha fund made 48 percent from April 2005 to March 2006, not quite as impressive as the 140 percent it made in its first year, 1996. The quant funds got their comeuppance in June 2007 when prices began to move in ways that were the opposite of those predicted by the computers. The algorithms were programmed to get out of losing investments, so when prices fell, they automatically sold. And because they sold, prices fell, and because prices fell, they sold more. They were all selling simultaneously, so prices moved in lockstep, as they usually do in crises. Figure 27 shows a typical endogenous risk feedback loop.

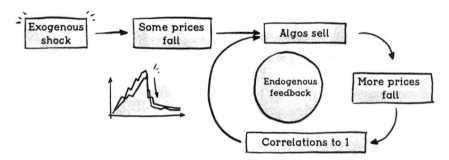

Figure 27. Quant crisis, 2017. Credit: Lukas Bischoff/IllustrationX.

All the riskometers and clever pricing models failed to anticipate such an eventuality. Losses were substantial. Global Alpha lost 7.7 percent in July 2007 and a further 22.7 percent in August. It was not alone, as most other quant funds suffered similar losses. By comparison, the US stock markets fell 3.3 percent in July and increased 1.3 percent in August. Global Alpha was eventually closed in the autumn of 2011 after even more losses. What happened was that the masters of the quant funds overestimated their cleverness. Each thought it was the smartest, using unique and state-of-the-art techniques to make money. They weren't, as underneath they were all doing the same thing. It wasn't visible when nothing was happening as in the tranquil years of the great moderation. All that was needed was a trigger. Typical endogenous risk crash, just like the wobble of the Millennium Bridge.

Crises happen when a hidden risk factor hits an unseen trigger, precisely what happened here. The hidden risk factor was how all the algorithms were programmed to react in the same way to market turmoil. Completely unknown until a sufficiently large price drop triggered their self-preservation tendencies: David Viniar, the then Goldman chief financial officer, was tasked with explaining Alpha fund's losses to the world. "We were seeing things that were 25-standard deviation moves, several days in a row." Under the normal distribution, the only way such a statement has any meaning, a 25-standard-deviation loss is expected to happen one day out of 10^{137}, which is 1 with 137 zeros after it. For comparison, NASA tells us that the universe's age is about 14 billion years, while the Earth is a lot younger at 4.5 billion years.

Either the quant funds got really, really unlucky or they weren't nearly as clever as they thought they were. Through the lens of endogenous risk, the 2007 Quantland crisis was inevitable. The combination of the great moderation with aggressive market participants aiming to exploit the tranquility. After all, what is our natural reaction when we perceive risk as being very low? Certainly not to sit on our hands and be conservative. No, we follow Minsky and take more risk. In the beginning with no impact on the markets, but eventually more and more funds pile into the action. Hugely profitable at the start. Returns are higher and higher because everybody enters the markets, while measured risk remains low because the prices are going up steadily but with little volatility.

The riskometers couldn't fathom such an eventuality in 2007. Because it wasn't in the data, it wasn't detected. It wasn't in their DNA. Fundamentally, when the quants started to use the riskometers to make investment decisions they changed the financial system, undermining the quality of the risk measurements. The 2007 quant crisis was inevitable. Risk is endogenous even if the riskometers assume otherwise.

Demand for Junk–Financial Alchemy: CDOs and the 2008 Crisis

Before Dmitri Mendeleev published the periodic table in 1869, the concept of the chemical element was not well understood. People even believed in alchemy, the turning of cheap base metals into gold. They just had to find the right recipe. Fabulous riches awaited. While Mendeleev showed alchemy is not possible in the physical world, the modern practice of alchemy in finance is still alive—turning cheap, unloved assets into something everybody desires.

Financial alchemy was at the heart of the global crisis in 2008, not least the CDO. The CDO gets its name because it uses various types of debt, such as mortgages, loans, or bonds, as collateral for a CDO. It became increasingly apparent in the early 2007s that CDOs were a cause for concern. That is when I was asked to do a new course in LSE called Global Financial Systems and started to look into CDOs. I found practically no background reading on how they work and especially what the risk in them is. The only material out there was technical discussions about creating CDOs and marketing blurbs on why they were fantastic. All about alchemy: the ease and benefit of turning high-risk junk assets into gold. Nothing about risk.

I ended up calling around former students working in the financial industry who were kind enough to connect me to experts willing to talk me through the mechanics of CDOs. What I learned was decidedly frightening. If I want to get the current price of a stock, all I have to do is to look up the price on Bloomberg. Not that simple for CDOs, as there is no market price to be found there. Instead, I need a complicated model just to get the price. And an even more complicated model is required to get the risk. Plenty of places for things to go wrong. Not only that, but the models used to get the prices and risk of the CDOs contained a fatal flaw. The way a CDO works is that a bank buys risky debt. Subprime mortgages, junk bonds, or anything, so long as it is risky. Suppose I buy one hundred subprime mortgages. Over time some of the mortgage borrowers may get into difficulty. They may get sick or lose their job or whatever, and default. However, it is quite unlikely that all one hundred default.

Now comes the alchemy. Every month I expect one hundred mortgage payments to be made. I then promise Mary the first five payments, no matter which mortgage they come from. Yiying then buys the right to get the next twenty payments. The important thing is that if ninety-five of the mortgages default, Mary gets all her payments but Yiying nothing. Morgane buys the right to the next sixty-five payments, and Paul buys the right to the payments from the last ten mortgages to be paid every month. Mary's investment is the safest and Paul's the riskiest, so Mary will pay the most for her right and Paul the least. These rights are called tranches (French for "slices").

Mary's right to the first five payments is very safe and gets a AAA rating from the credit-rating agencies. These tranches are often called super senior because it is so certain they will pay out. Yiying's tranche is less safe and gets only a AA rating, while Morgane's are even lower at BBB. The middle tranches are known as mezzanine, Italian for "intermediate floor." Paul is the last to be paid, and his tranche is called equity or, colloquially, toxic waste. Suppose we assume that if one family defaults on its mortgage, that says nothing about the likelihood of any other family defaulting. Usually an innocent assumption, as each family's default is specific to them, perhaps illness, disability, or death. Even though individual families are likely to default, the likelihood that *all* default is very, very low.

Alchemy. We have taken high-risk assets and turned them into super-safe assets. What's missing? The chance of an economic slowdown. When the economy is doing well, mortgage defaults are mostly independent of each other. But in recessions factories close and people get laid off. Because all the employees lose their jobs, they no longer patronize the local restaurants and supermarkets and hairdressers, so the economic misery spreads. A sizable number of families in that community can end up defaulting on their mortgages.

When things are good, mortgage defaults are individual, in recessions contagious. The problem is that the previous recession in the United States was in 1992, and subprime mortgages only really took off in 1993. The data used to train the riskometers didn't contain any recessions, so the riskometers didn't know about the possibility of factories closing and people being thrown out of their jobs. The common practice of sourcing subprime mortgages from a single county in the United States made the problem worse because people living in the same geographic area are likely to depend on the same employers.

But why would one want to put subprime mortgages into the CDOs in the first place? The reason is that some tranches are easier to sell than others. The safest and the least safe—super senior and toxic waste—had few buyers, while the mezzanine was the most popular, so it makes sense for the CDO's creator to make the mezzanine tranches as big as possible. However, that means that the assets cannot be too safe. For instance, if you put US government bonds into the CDO, the safest tranche's size increases. Consequently, the CDOs created a demand for junk. A friend of mine worked in the treasury office of a bank in 2008, and one day he got a phone call from a large international bank offering to lend him a rather substantial amount of money. My friend was a bit taken aback by this and asked the banker if he had seen Bloomberg that day and noted his bank's very high credit default swap (CDS). The banker said, "Yes, that's why I'm calling you. I need something risky to structure." My friend took the loan and told me the large international bank took a 96 percent loss when the global crisis hit a few months later.

Not many buyers wanted the equity tranches, so some smart bankers found a way to tranche them up in a product called CDO-squared. Clever, except the model risk is amplified because now we have the model risk of the initial CDSs and the model risk of the CDO squared. Madness. We even got some CDO-cubed!

Because the super senior and equity tranches were hard to sell, the banks often held them on their books. Naturally, because the super senior were AAA rated, no problem. While the equity tranches were risky, the models didn't find them excessively risky, so the capital charges were limited. That is what caused all the bank problems in the second part of 2007. As the CDOs got downgraded, all of a sudden the banks were holding much riskier assets and they had a much lower value than initially assumed. The banks found themselves in serious difficulty and close to violating their capital constraints. The technical reason why UBS failed.

If one of the criteria for high profits is maximizing the use of junk assets, it shouldn't be surprising that it did not end well. Richard Bitner describes this eventuality in his book *Confessions of a Subprime Lender: An Insider's Tale of Greed, Fraud, and Ignorance.* Nobody cared about quality. All they wanted was the highest possible number of the riskiest mortgages imaginable.

Cat and Mouse Games

When I used to do executive education courses on risk forecasting, most students worked in supervisory agencies, risk management, or compliance and wanted to get up to date on the latest techniques. But one day I got a trader. We got talking, and when I asked her why she was taking the course, she said that her risk manager was using Value-at-Risk, and she wanted to know how he arrived at the risk numbers so she could do what she wanted without interference from the pesky risk controllers. While we are used to thinking about the regulators arguing with banks about how much risk they can take, a much more adversarial debate occurs between traders and risk managers. The former want to invest in what they like when they like, while the latter are tasked with ensuring the traders take risk in line with what the company wants. Not too little and not too much. There is a perpetual tension between the risk managers' and traders' objectives, what economists call a principal-agent problem.

Because both the traders and risk managers know all about the strengths and weaknesses of riskometers, a cat and mouse game ensues. The traders try to exploit these weaknesses, whereas the risk managers try to close the loopholes. One trick used by the risk managers is Chinese walls, a term dating back to the Great Depression when the US government wanted to minimize the conflict of interest between a bank producing supposedly objective research on a company while also handling its initial public offerings. Banks were allowed to keep both functions in the same bank but were required to put the Great Wall of China between them. The risk manager's ideal case is when the riskometer is entirely hidden from the traders—the Great Wall of China stands between them. The nightmare for any risk manager is exercising control over a trader who is an expert in riskometers. Even worse is when the traders used to work in risk management or compliance before being promoted to trading and know all the tricks. Jérôme Kerviel, the Société Générale trader who cost his employer $6.9 billion, started his career in compliance before being promoted to trading.

If Mary is a proprietary trader, all the risk manager should tell her is that her risk is too high or too low or just right. He should not tell her that her Value-at-Risk is $2 million and should be only $1.5 million or even that he is using Value-at-Risk, and he should certainly not tell her that he got the $2 million from a GARCH model. The more the trader knows about the risk measurements, the easier it becomes for her to manipulate the risk management process. This is precisely what the student in my executive education course was trying to accomplish.

The practical problem is that while Chinese walls sound great in theory, they don't work well in practice. After all, the risk model cannot be hidden because it must produce results. Meanwhile, as profits are threatened the Chinese walls lead to accusations of unfairness, discretion, and incompetence. The resulting political game will be won by risk managers only immediately after a crisis, when memories of past losses are fresh and fears widespread. In normal times the profit-making trader will have much more political power than the risk manager. Senior management turns a blind eye to transactions when significant profits are made. Just like Credit Suisse, which muzzled its risk management department and for its trouble lost at least $4.7 billion on Archegos Capital and cost its clients up to $3 billion from the collapse of Greensill Capital. All in early 2021.

The Four Principles of Correct Riskometer Use

Risk comes from the future, but we know only the past.

Soon after I wrote "Risk and Crises," a blog piece on the problems of riskometers, I got an interesting comment from a risk manager: "As a risk manager I fully recognise the shortcomings of any model based on or calibrated to the past. But I also need something practical, objective, and understandable to measure risk, set and enforce limits, and encourage discussions about positions when it matters. It is very easy to criticise from the sidelines—please offer an alternative the next time."[6] He is right. It is easy to fall into the trap of excessive nihilism, criticizing without providing alternatives. The riskometer is useful, we have to manage risk, and if we don't use the riskometer to do so, we might as well stick a wet thumb in the air. So, in response I joined forces with a friend, Robert Macrae, and wrote a couple of blog pieces titled "Appropriate Use of Risk Models." Our fundamental point is that risk is defined only in terms of outcomes we wish to avoid, and that how best to estimate risk critically depends on what we want. In chapter 5 above on the myth of riskometer, I gave the example of Paul, Ann, and Mary, who each invest in Google stock but for very different reasons. Even though each holds the same portfolio and has access to the same technology, they measure risk differently. Simply because Mary cares about risk seventy years in the future, Ann in the next six months, and Paul the following week.

Robert and I came up with five principles of the appropriate use of riskometers. The first is that risk comes from the future, but we know only the past. All a riskometer can do is project the past into the future, and many conditions have to hold for the projection to be accurate. The actual history has to represent the future, with no nasty surprises in store—ergodicity. Meanwhile, the person creating the riskometer has to be respectful of history and avoid data snooping. If we don't think history is a reliable guide to the future, don't use riskometers; do something else.

The second principle is that the point of a riskometer is not to predict bad outcomes. All it is supposed to do is tell us something bad *may* happen. So, even if everything goes wrong or nothing goes wrong, we do not have sufficient grounds to criticize or praise the riskometer. A principle that is violated frequently, for example, in postmortems on big losses. The benefit of hindsight is that after a bad outcome everyone is an expert, and criticizing is easy.

The third principle is that how one should calculate risks depends on what one fears. Avoid at all costs one-size-fits-all approaches when it comes to risk, like Value-at-Risk. We are all different and have different needs, so other users need different riskometers. Unfortunately, everything pushes toward the one-size-fits-all riskometer. When the same riskometer is used by everybody, individual failure is covered by collective failure.

The fourth principle is, don't probability shift. It is easy to estimate a model for short-term risk (like 95 percent daily Value-at-Risk) and use that to get an estimate of a once-in-a-millennium event, as I explained earlier. While easy enough to do, for the numbers to have any meaning we need at least two strong assumptions—ergodicity and the correct parametric form—both of which are violated in practice.

The final principle is that financial risk is endogenous, created by the interaction of the human beings who make up the financial system. Endogenous risk limits what any riskometer can do in that risk forecasting involves predicting the behavior of people. As a general rule, a riskometer performs best when focused on short-time horizons and nonextreme outcomes, in cases where a lot of people are trading an asset. The riskometer fails when asked about illiquid, long-term, and extreme risk because that involves predicting human behavior, too much to ask of a computer algorithm.

Riskometers ought to come with warnings, like medication does: If used correctly, the drug will help you, but there is a risk of side effects and even death, so be careful. Just like the chance that medication might kill you is not a good reason not to take medicine, the riskometers' side effects don't mean we shouldn't use them. Not measuring risk just means sticking the proverbial wet thumb in the air. While not perfect, risk-ometers indicate risk and, if used correctly, can be quite useful. And if abused, it can similarly cause a lot of damage. Just like medication. Good risk managers tell me they use many riskometers simultaneously. By getting multiple measurements of the same risky position and knowing how each of the riskometers performs, they can combine subjective judgment with the objective output of the riskometers in their decisions.

The potential for manipulation is real, as the examples of JP Morgan's Whale and UBS show, not to mention all the rogue traders. Manipulation is hard to detect until everything goes awry, no matter how well intentioned a bank is. Even if the senior management fully intends to obey the spirit and the letter of the rules, internal incentives such as bonuses and promotions will lead traders to take advantage of the risk management system: to abuse the riskometer. What is especially worrying is how regulations can encourage banks to take the worst type of risk—tail risk—and so perversely make it more likely the bank will fail. The reason is simple: the tendency to use riskometers not as a risk-control device but to maximize profits: the London Whale problem.

Does anyone care? Despite all the colossal failures in 2008, riskometers are still in widespread use, and banks and regulators are increasingly using them. The simple truth is that the modern financial system would not function without riskometers. If we ask someone to manage our money, we need to monitor and control the risk they take. In practice, that means using riskometers. Just remember not to ask for too much. To those whose job it is to care about the entire financial system's stability, the riskometers' failings are especially pertinent.

9

The Goldilocks Challenge

What do you see? Light. Darkness. The balance is so much bigger.
—Star Wars: The Last Jedi *(2017)*

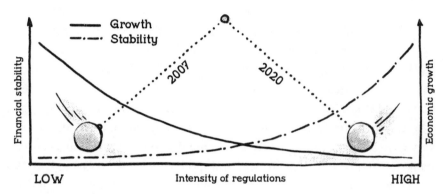

Figure 28. Credit: Lukas Bischoff/IllustrationX.

When I lecture on bank bailouts in my LSE masters course I ask my students to imagine they are the finance minister of their country. Suppose, as the finance minister, you receive the CEO of your country's biggest bank one morning, telling you that her bank will go bankrupt by five o'clock that day unless you give her a $50 billion bailout. And if her bank fails, it will take your economy down with it, causing a systemic crisis. You have two clear choices. Call her bluff and refuse, risking a financial meltdown, or give some of the wealthiest people in your country $50 billion. Not an easy decision. At that moment, it would not matter what your political leanings are, right or left wing. A libertarian who believes the government should not regulate or bail out private entities;

or a socialist hating the right-wing financial elite who would like nothing more than to tax and regulate them out of existence. The only question to consider: Is the banker telling you the truth? If you think she is, you have no choice but to give in.

The reason is that no government can ignore a systemic crisis. The consequences are so severe that we would do almost anything to prevent one. Perhaps the worst outcome is that the empirical evidence suggests that governments lose power after a major crisis. You would be out of a job, and that would not do. When faced with the $50 billion ~~request~~ demand, the more information you have about your financial system and the bank in question, the better. That will not only help you figure out whether you are being played, but also aids you in finding a better, cheaper solution. If you had had access to good information earlier, you might even have been able to prevent the bank from failing in the first place.

The nineteenth-century US federal government did not impose much in terms of regulations on banks, leaving that to the states. The United States did not even have a central bank. When a crisis came along, the private sector would sort it out. Not surprisingly, the United States was very crisis prone, and there were increasing demands to establish a central bank and start regulating finance. Still, politics was not in favor. It took the severe financial crisis of 1907 to finally overcome the political opposition, and that was because of how the private sector dealt with the crisis. In 1907 the most important banker in the country was John Pierpont Morgan, the founder of the eponymous bank, which was later split by the Glass-Steagall Act in 1935 into JP Morgan and Morgan Stanley. He acted as the de facto central bank, providing liquidity himself and leaning on other bankers to do the same, in the process enriching himself and his buddies while punishing his enemies. The way he behaved in the 1907 crisis was seen as being beyond the pale, and the political leaders realized that a central bank could not be avoided. It could not be called a central bank for political reasons, but the Federal Reserve System, or the Fed, was set up in 1913.

Even then, the Fed did not get many powers, nor did it want them. During the Great Depression the Fed did everything it could to do nothing. The definitive 1963 study by Milton Friedman and Anna Schwartz showed that the Fed's failure to increase liquidity in the Depression was the main reason it became so severe. Their conclusions determined why we had so much liquidity created during and after the 2008 crisis: the central bankers were dead set on avoiding their Great Depression predecessors' mistakes. I once talked to a central bank governor who told me that what motivated him in the 2008 crisis was the portrait of his Depression-era predecessor in the main conference room. He would look at it and say to himself, "What would you have done? I will do the opposite." Not until President Roosevelt took office did the US government give the Fed both the mandate and the obligation to respond to crises.

Being forced to intervene in times of crisis without adequate planning is the worst-case scenario, as the Argentinians learned to their cost in 1994. A few years earlier their government had proclaimed it would never bail out any bank, only to reverse course embarrassingly following the tequila crisis in Mexico in 1994. It is far better to be prepared for the eventual crisis—it will happen.

It is not enough to ensure the central bank understands the system and is ready to step in if a sufficiently bad event happens. Even that decision has secondary consequences requiring further regulations, and so forth. Once they have taken one step, they need to go the whole way. It is like getting married. I cannot just pick the things I like about my partner and leave the rest—she is a package deal. It is the same with financial regulations. Still, we should not expect too much. The authorities can never be fully prepared, and they will make mistakes. Big, costly, stupid ones. It is easy to criticize with the benefit of hindsight, but regulating finance is a tough job. It is difficult, perhaps outright impossible, for any financial authority to stop the excessive risk-taking that leads to a crisis, as bubbles make everybody feel warm and cuddly. Since the public sees only the benefits, the politicians follow. So do the bankers, even if they should know the danger the bubble poses.

The technocrats should be in the know. However, if they warn the public, they risk being denounced, losing their income, or even being prosecuted, as Greece's former chief statistician, Andreas Georgiou, learned. In my native Iceland, when the pending crisis became clear for all to see in the spring of 2008, government ministers still denounced those warning it was all going to end in tears, with some even calling on the banks to increase risk. Ultimately, it is tough to follow the advice of William

McChesney Martin Jr., the former Fed chairman, who said the Fed's most important job was "to take away the punch bowl just as the party gets going." The financial authorities face a difficult Goldilocks challenge: not regulate too little, as the United States did in the nineteenth century; and not too much, like Cuba or North Korea today. It has to be right.

The 1866 Lesson

No country had any financial regulations to speak of at the start of the nineteenth century. When they thought of banks at all, the governments cared only about forcing them to buy government bonds. The only financial crime was theft, sometimes punishable by death, which applied only to poor people stealing to eat, not bankers robbing their business partners, clients, the government, or the general public. There were no rules on disclosure, and it was perfectly legal and morally acceptable to lie in public statements. This way of life changed after the 1866 crisis, when Overend & Gurney (O&G) went bankrupt. O&G was one of London's most respected financial institutions and the largest bank in the world focused on commercial lending. The day after it collapsed, on 30 September 1866, it was called the "greatest instrument of credit in the Kingdom."[1]

The development of a commercial credit market was a major reason the United Kingdom became the world's first industrialized country. Budding British capitalists found it easier to raise money—the venture capitalism of the day—than their counterparts anywhere else in the world. One of the riskiest and most profitable types of venture was shipping, and the development of new ships and shipping lines was the high-tech industry of the mid-nineteenth century. For most of its existence O&G didn't participate in such high-risk lending, but the partners eventually came to desire an increase in their already immense wealth and decided to finance shipping technology. But they bet on the wrong technology and soon faced bankruptcy. To save themselves after O&G was effectively bankrupt the partners decided to incorporate, selling shares to the public and telling potential shareholders the bank was completely safe, with no bad loans. At the time, this was legal, and there was no obligation for any firm to publish accounts, reveal its actual financial situation, or tell the truth.

When O&G failed, Walter Bagehot, then editor of *The Economist,* wrote that the partners ran their business "in a manner so reckless and foolish that one would think a child who had lent money in the City of London would have lent it better." The partners believed they would be bailed out by the Bank of England, which sent three bankers to look at O&G's books. It did not take them long to realize O&G was broke. The Bank of England faced a delicate decision: if O&G failed, there would be panic; if it were saved, the other firms in the finance game would also expect to be rescued. The Bank of England chose to let O&G fail. It is not clear why it made that choice. Moral hazard was clearly a significant concern, but other factors weighed on it as well. The Bank of England was a private institution competing with the likes of O&G, and its future profits were likely to be enhanced by the failure of an important competitor. Because the Bank of England did not do any bailouts nor provide support of any kind, even refusing to grant loans against government securities, panic spread through the banking system. The market for otherwise safe assets like government bonds—gilts—dried up.

The financial institutions of the nineteenth century were partnerships, with the notable exception of the Bank of England. This meant that O&G's partners should have been liable for all losses, except they managed to incorporate in the nick of time. The third senior partner had the surname Barclay, and a few years later he started a bank with the eponymous name, where the last Overend became the largest shareholder. The partners of O&G eventually faced private prosecution because the government did not feel they had done anything wrong and refused to prosecute them. The only crime they could be charged with was theft. In the private prosecution, the partners hired the government's most senior lawyer to defend them, so the same lawyer both represented the accused and was the boss of the judges ruling on the case. The partners were acquitted.

At the time, there were no established procedures for dealing with the failure of a big bank. But as the O&G 1866 crisis turned out to be one of the worst crises of the century, the government had no choice but to do something. It made the Bank of England commission Walter Bagehot to investigate how it should respond to future crises. He published a white

paper in 1873, establishing three principles enshrining the Bank of England's role as a lender of last resort:

1. The central bank should lend freely
2. At a penal rate of interest
3. On good banking securities.

Bagehot's advice proved to be good, and the Bank of England successfully dealt with the banking panics of 1878 and 1890 by following his rules,
while the panics of 1847, 1857, and 1866 led to acute financial crises. Bagehot's analysis of the 1866 crisis and his recommendations for how the
government should resolve crises are the first modern analysis of financial stability and policy remedies. It has been hugely influential and has
shaped policy throughout the world ever since. The refusal of the Federal
Reserve to follow Bagehot's rules was a significant contributor to the
Great Depression from 1929 to 1933. We see the influence of Bagehot's
principles to this day, and he was frequently invoked in the 2008 crisis.

Bubbles and Our Amazing Capacity for Self-Deception

One of the trickiest Goldilocks challenges is bubbles. Are they
simply the consequence of speculation gone sour and should hence be
pricked? Or is all the rapid price growth real, to be appreciated and nour-
ished, not stamped out? Japan and China give nicely opposite answers to
this question.

The land the Imperial Palace in Tokyo sits on is not very large—when
last in Tokyo, I walked all the way around it in less than an hour. In
1989 that land was more valuable than the entire landmass of the state
of California. Japanese home buyers needed multigenerational loans to
buy homes. That was at the very tail end of an extraordinary economic
boom that started right after World War II and ended in 1992 with one
of the biggest financial crises ever seen. In the three decades before 1992,
the average annual economic growth in Japan was 5.1 percent. It has been
0.7 percent since. The stock market has fared even worse. The annual
return was 9.9 percent but only about 0.5 percent since.[2] The Japanese
bubble is typical of financial bubbles. In the beginning Japan's rapid economic growth was based on sound foundations, high-quality human

capital, and the rebuilding of a war-devastated economy. But because the growth was so rapid it looked like the Japanese businessmen and policy makers could do no wrong, a perception that masked the underlying vulnerabilities. When Japan ran out of productive industrial investments, real estate became the logical target, which explains the astronomical value of the land under the Imperial Palace in 1989.

Real estate bubbles are often the last thing to happen before a crisis. When Robert Aliber, a professor at the University of Chicago, one of the best-known experts on financial crises, and the coauthor of the book *Manias, Panics, and Crashes: A History of Financial Crises,* visited Iceland in the spring of 2008, he caused a scandal when interviewed on television. What Robert did was to count the number of building cranes in Reykjavík, and use that number to predict a crisis. Everybody said he was wrong. The Icelandic crisis, the worst in the global crisis that year, started four months later.

The Japanese themselves didn't see a bubble, finding all sorts of reasons why things were different in Japan. One of the best crisis predictors is people invoking their culture. Japan had a unique economic model, rejecting outdated European and American short-term capitalism and creating a unique, sustainable Japanese economic system. The Japanese businessman had morphed into what the Japanese liked to call the economic man, uniquely able, working in a superior system. Then reality came knocking. The laws of economics are universal.

Bubbles are insidious. We start by taking a little risk. Things turn out okay. We take more and more risk at a faster and faster rate until it all collapses. Bubbles happen all the time. Internet stocks in the late 1990s, subprime mortgages and structured credit products before the 2008 crisis, the Roaring Twenties, the Nifty Fifty stocks in the early 1970s, real estate in Spain in the 2000s. We can go far back in history. The Dutch tulip mania in the 1600s is the first documented bubble but surely there were many before. Is the financial market Covid-19 boom simply a bubble destined to burst? Is *China: The Bubble that Never Pops* in Thomas Orlik's book or as George Magnus has it in his *Why Xi's China Is in Jeopardy?*

Who is right? Looking back after a bubble bursts, it is easy to act wise and say, "We had this huge bubble. Why were the speculators so stupid, and why did the authorities not do anything? All we had to do was to restrict credit. Really simple stuff." Yet bubbles still happen. The problem is that their very existence can be verified only after they burst—we need the benefit of hindsight. We can never be certain before the bubble bursts. The cost of getting it wrong, calling something a bubble incorrectly—what statisticians call a type I error, the incorrect rejection of a true hypothesis—can be very costly.

Suppose the Chinese authorities had decided in 1995 that "oops, China is overexpanding, we are in a bubble and have to slow down." Then China would not have enjoyed the 470 percent economic growth over the next couple of decades. One can just as easily become dazzled by all that growth. China will stop growing one day, and then its market will be seen as having been in a bubble. But crying wolf is a game one is destined to lose. It could happen tomorrow or in twenty years.

Even supposedly well-identified bubbles, like the internet dot-com bubble of the 1990s, might not necessarily be such a bad thing. Bubbles can cause prices to explode, but they also release a lot of funds for risky investments, some of which end up being the seed money for the leading companies of the future. The online giants of today, like Amazon and Google, originated from the dot-com bubble. Intel and many of the semiconductor companies came out of the Nifty Fifty bubble in the early 1970s, while many companies like Coca-Cola had their IPOs during the Roaring Twenties bubble. We don't even know if we should call these episodes bubbles. The Nobel Prize–winner Fama French, the godfather of the theory of efficient markets and the person just about least likely to believe in bubbles, argued recently, "For bubbles, I want a systematic way of identifying them. It's a simple proposition. You have to be able to predict that there is some end to it. All the tests people have done trying to do that don't work. Statistically, people have not come up with ways of identifying bubbles."

It is difficult for the financial authorities to meet the Goldilocks challenge posed by bubbles. The political economy is always in favor of allowing the bubble to grow. And the authority aiming to prick them faces a dual risk. If they prick the bubble, they will always be accused of destroying growth. If they allow it to happen and things then blow up, they will be accused of incompetence or worse.

How Iceland Failed the Goldilocks Challenge

One of the first questions facing a designer of regulations is whether to use rule-based or principle-based regulations. The former focuses on preventing undesirable behavior, much like a speed limit that prohibits us from going too fast. The latter says it is better to focus on the outcomes, that we should drive in a way that does not lead to a crash, taking into consideration things like the weather, the state of the road we are on, traffic, and the quality of the car we are driving. Neither approach is satisfactory, and we need some combination of both. If we go too far in either direction we are likely to end up in trouble. The Icelandic crisis in 2008 exemplifies this conundrum.

After the Icelandic banking system collapsed in October 2008, the head of the banking regulators was asked in a television interview what the financial supervisor's job was. He replied, "To ensure the banks don't break the law." To a lawyer, that is the right answer, but to me, an economist, the journalist asked the wrong question. It should be "What is the purpose of regulations?" a question with a straightforward answer. The objective of regulations is not to make sure banks don't break the law. Instead, it is to ensure they provide essential functions to the economy, efficiently and at a reasonable cost while not behaving in a way that harms society. The Icelandic banks violated all the regulations' objectives while not breaking any law—and got away with it.

The emphasis on not breaking the law might not be too problematic if the law is sufficiently general, allowing the regulators to enforce the law's spirit. The problem in Iceland is that its legal system has an unusually strong focus on literal interpretations of the law and is very reluctant to take into account the purpose of the law. In most countries the regulator would determine the law's spirit and issue instructions to achieve that. Hard to do in Iceland. This led to some curious outcomes. A few years before the crisis, the banking supervisor told a bank, call it bank A, that it needed to increase its equity—issue and sell new shares—but the bank did not want to do so because it would dilute existing shareholders. The most direct way around this was for the bank to issue new shares and purchase them itself. But that is a fake transaction and is not allowed.

The Icelandic banks found a neat way around this. Bank A sold the newly issued equity to bank B, and bank B sold its newly issued equity to A. While this might mean the banks are now exposed to each other, they then made a contract for difference, compensating each other for losses and reimbursing each other for profits. If the price of A fell, A would make up B's losses, and, conversely, if A's stock price went up, B would give the profits to A. To the Icelandic regulator and its strict tick-the-box legal point of view, no problem. Of course, it was all fake and, while legal, did not afford any protection. Even worse, it gave the appearance of protection, encouraging market participants to engage with these banks *as if* they were safe. After the crisis, I mentioned this to a few acquaintances in supervisory agencies in other countries. They were aghast, all saying that this sort of transaction would not have been allowed in their country. Even if not explicitly forbidden, it would be seen as a violation of the regulations' spirit.

But if the regulators were too relaxed before the crisis, there is a danger of going too far in the other direction after it has happened. The Icelandic regulator again shows this better than most. Ever since the 2008 crisis its main preoccupation has been to impose rules that would have prevented the crisis, closing the barn door after the horse escapes. Iceland has some of the world's highest bank capital charges and extensive restrictions on what the financial system can get up to. Consequently, financial services in Iceland are the most expensive in Europe, and it is really hard to make the sort of risky investments so necessary to underpin future growth. Instead, Iceland bet its fortune on tourism, an industry that does not need a lot of capital, only to see it come crashing down with the Covid-19 crisis in 2020.

The Icelandic regulators are hardly unique in failing the Goldilocks challenge, even if they fell for it particularly hard. It has happened in all jurisdictions and exemplifies a particular form of procyclicality. During upswings, regulations become increasingly lax, amplifying the boom; after a crisis, they become excessively strict, magnifying the downturn. By 2020 the cry for fewer regulations was getting increasingly loud, and, with Covid-19 everywhere, financial stability played second fiddle to economic prosperity. Many countries already have relaxed capital standards, and most signs point to even more relaxation. Unfortunately, the last crisis episode always has an undue influence on how we think about future crises. The policy makers are always at risk of falling for the successful general's syndrome, just like the French army in the 1930s.

The Maginot Line: Preparing for the Past

When the French military after World War I was preparing for another German invasion, they thought the best way was to construct a great defensive barrier along the French–German border. They called it the Maginot Line. There was only one problem: while the French prepared for another World War I with trenches and heavy artillery, the Germans came up with Blitzkrieg. They invaded via the Ardennes Forest—which the French assumed was impenetrable because they had not stayed on top of new technology—bypassing the Maginot Line entirely and eventually capturing it from behind. The French fell for the successful general's syndrome—preparing for the last war while the enemy prepares for the next.

It is difficult for financial authorities to avoid the successful general's syndrome. The last crisis dominates the headlines and is studied intensely. Inevitably, prevention of the past dominates the regulations of the future. The problem is that while there will be a crisis, it is almost certain that the next crisis will happen in a different place, somewhere no one is looking, like Covid-19.

That is precisely what happened in the years and decades before 2008, when old-fashioned financial crises were thought to be a thing of the past and what really mattered to the central banks was inflation. It is understandable why central bankers would think that way. High inflation was endemic in the 1970s and early 1980s, and there seemed to be no way of conquering it. Everyone was obsessed with inflation. As far as I know, the only time a US president has talked about the third derivative—the rate of change of the rate of change of the rate of change—in a public speech was Richard Nixon in 1972: "The rate of increase of inflation is going down." Stagflation—a combination of stagnation and inflation—was the word of the 1970s. With all the effort focused on inflation, the central bankers eventually defeated it, and by 2007 they were patting themselves on the back for having solved their main problem. They had reduced monetary policy to an engineering problem: small tweaks in interest rates would allow them to hit their target inflation rates. As it turned out, they hadn't mastered inflation all that well either: they did not hit their 2 percent inflation target for over a decade afterwards.

Most central banks thought it essential that their mission not be polluted by other dirty objectives such as financial stability. I remember being in central bank conferences in the mid-2000s in which senior central bank officials debated whether financial stability belonged within their remit and most argued no. After all, the main problem of their forefathers, financial stability, had been solved. Crises happened only in developing countries, not in the United States or Western Europe. Echoing the French army's backward-looking preparations in the 1930s for the next war, most central banks scaled down their financial stability divisions in the 1990s and early 2000s. The Bank of England was among the most aggressive, laying off or pushing out those not doing macroeconomics, the reason why it was so badly prepared in 2007. In doing so, the central bankers forgot the lessons of the previous crisis. Macroeconomics had evolved in the second half of the twentieth century as if the financial sector didn't exist. When I was in graduate school, my macroeconomics courses completely ignored the financial system. The father of macroeconomics, John Maynard Keynes, must have rolled over in his grave because his magnum opus, *The General Theory of Interest, Employment and Money*, strongly emphasized the financial system's importance in the macroeconomy. When 2008 came along, the central bankers and macroeconomists rushed to the library to dust off the history books and the economic texts of half a century earlier. They were no better than the French generals in the 1930s in falling for the successful general's syndrome.

It is so easy to fall for the successful general's syndrome because most information we have about financial stability relates to what happened in the past. A bureaucratic entity charged with creating transparent rules will find it much easier to make rules preventing recurrence than anticipating what might happen. Central banks are rigid, bureaucratic, and formal, well suited for precise processes that don't often change, not so much for out-of-the-box thinking. One might then try to solve this state of mind by using principle-based regulations. A bank is supposed to behave in a way that meets the broad objectives of financial regulations, not take on too much risk, finance the all-important small- and medium-sized enterprises, and at the same time not go bust. It is one of those things that sound good in theory but are not so easy in practice. It is hard to figure out what the objectives would be and practically impossible to verify whether a particular bank is complying.

Principle-based regulations require innovation, and if the authorities try to be too innovative in their regulatory designs, they run the risk of fostering spectacular regulatory failures. This does not mean that creativity in financial regulation, like principle-based regulations and light touch and sandboxes or whatever the buzzword du jour is, is a bad idea. The alternative can be just as bad and even worse, as the tick-the-box-obsessed Icelandic regulator shows. So we need some balance between the tick-the-box approach and abstract, principle-based regulations if we are to meet the Goldilocks challenge.

After the 2008 crisis, the word—in the UK and in places that take its lead—is *conduct*. We even have a Financial Conduct Authority in the United Kingdom, the idea being that financial institutions should behave properly and avoid doing anything untoward. That means focusing on individual behavior, with a special emphasis on compliance. After the financial 2008 crisis, the LIBOR, foreign exchange, and terrorist financing scandals, financial institutions have beefed up their compliance functions. The number of risk and compliance staff in HSBC in 2014 was 10 percent of its entire workforce. Every bank intensively monitors its staff. Computers and senior managers read messages and emails, telephone calls are recorded, and the banks are spending enormous efforts to ensure that employees behave properly. Many senior managers must read daily emails and messages from their underlings, selected by an artificial intelligence engine. In his 2016 book *Why Aren't They Shouting?* Kevin Rodgers mentions the anecdote of a Russian quant working for him in his Deutsche Bank office, saying, "It's great. I was too young to be spied on under communism, but now I have the chance to experience it under capitalism. I guess you could say that's progress." Even so, banks can't prevent some employees from going rogue, and abuse is inevitable. When the next scandal comes along, are we willing to ratchet up monitoring of bank employees even further? Will the cost of doing so in both financial and civil liberties terms be acceptable? Even then, will that prevent future scandals? Francesch Castello, the banker beheaded in Barcelona in the 1300s, might suggest it does not. The Goldilocks challenge will not be solved by finding the right balance between principles and rules. Because it is not enough to focus on the behavior and the incentives of the regulated. We should also look at the motives of the financial regulators. Are they captured or excessively risk averse like the Chinese air traffic controllers?

Over the years, as a happy consequence of its rapid economic growth, the airspace above China has become extremely crowded. One reason is that the military controls a substantial part of it, but the other (of bigger interest to me here) is Chinese air traffic controllers' incentives. Their job is stressful, having to maintain constant high concentration, juggling a large number of aircraft, and managing the limited airspace efficiently.

The problem is that accidents are inevitable, and the only way to prevent them is not to have any air traffic—just like the only way not to have financial crises is not to have a financial system. Well, that is not feasible, but the instinct of any air traffic controller who wants to minimize the likelihood of accidents is to maximize the spacing between aircraft so they will not collide. If taken to the extreme, air traffic will become very slow. To solve that particular Goldilocks challenge, American and European air traffic controllers are incentivized to manage traffic efficiently, tasked with simultaneously maximizing the volume of air traffic while maintaining acceptable higher levels of safety. Air traffic controllers who make mistakes and report them promptly benefit from leniency programs. The aviation authorities have created a highly effective risk culture. It is different in China. Their air traffic controllers are severely punished when they make mistakes but get no benefit when air traffic flows smoothly. Thus they like to keep the space between aircraft between ten and sixteen kilometers, not the five in America.

Bank regulation continually pushes toward the Chinese air traffic model. When the banking system is functioning well and with no scandals, the supervisors don't get much credit. Even worse, we harp on the cost of regulations. Then, when something goes wrong we blame the regulator. The head of the regulatory agency will be roasted in the press and summoned to give testimony before the senate on live television. The type of question she is going to get is, "You had all the information and all the powers, why did you let the bankers exploit the public?"

The danger is that the supervisors' incentives end up being focused on the prevention of failure at all costs: the supervisor becomes too risk averse. In other words, the supervisor's incentive problem is the inverse of that of the banker, and it is essential to have some mechanisms in place to prevent excessive supervisory risk aversion. One way to do so is through a cost-benefit analysis of regulations, easy to conceive of, hard to do in practice. The opposite also frequently happens, what is known as regulatory capture, whereby a supervisory agency no longer services society but instead works in the interests of the regulated. The best recent example is the American Federal Aviation Administration (FAA) and the troubles of the Boeing 737 Max aircraft. The FAA seems to have out-sourced most monitoring of the 737 Max to . . . Boeing. When foreign regulators started to prohibit the 737 Max from flying, the FAA resisted. A classic case of regulatory capture. Regulatory capture is all too common. In Britain a recent case is the horsemeat scandal, in which food processors got away with selling horsemeat as beef. The Food Standards Agency not only failed to discover the substitution despite frequent inspections, but also did not want to punish the guilty nor change practices afterward.

The banks are superb lobbyists, aiming to create banking regulations favoring themselves while discouraging entry into the banking system. And for good measure protect banks' profits and ensure the odd bailout. If the supervisors don't play ball, the banks just go directly to the politicians in charge of the supervisors. If that wasn't enough, governments have many other reasons for regulating besides keeping the financial system running efficiently. Most, if not all, like to have "national champions"—the reason we have the systemically important financial institutions (SIFIs)—and that political desire gives the banks considerable power over the regulators. The government may have altruistic ulterior motives, such as requiring banks to provide unprofitable banking services to disadvantaged sectors of society. Charles Calomiris and Stephen Haber argue in their book *Fragile by Design: The Political Origins of Banking Crises and Scarce Credit* that the political objective of providing housing for low-income families in the United States led to an unholy alliance between left-wing advocates of the poor and the bankers, preventing effective regulations and thus creating fertile ground for the 2008 crisis. They further argue that some countries suffer an excessive number of crises because bankers and politicians join forces to create a financial system favoring well-connected special interests at the expense of society.

Why Bail Out Banks and Not Carmakers?

When the finance minister in the archetypal example gets the request for $50 billion (see above), the banks are demanding a bailout. The main problem for the government is that giving in results in moral hazard. Even the remotest possibility of a bailout creates a moral hazard. Moral hazard happens when we benefit from taking risk while someone else bears the cost of that risk. Insurance is a typical example. When one is insured, the insurance company pays out if something terrible happens. Moral hazard is where being insured induces us to misbehave. Perhaps a guy's laptop is old and gets conveniently lost when he is on holiday, the type of moral hazard insurance companies face continuously. But they know this, and their fees reflect the risk. That is the key: the risk is priced in.

So why even contemplate bailing out the banks in the first place? When the global crisis hit in 2008, I remember listening to BBC's main current affairs program, *Today,* on the topic of carmakers in difficulty. The spokesperson for the carmakers' association made a strong case that carmakers were strategically important for Britain and had to be bailed out if they failed. We see many such demands in the 2020 Covid-19 crisis. We have all these businesses that are innocent victims of the virus demanding bailouts and quite often getting them. One of the worst legacies of the Covid-19 crisis will be the lingering expectation of state support for private industry when things go wrong.

I don't think we should bail out carmakers or any other private firm, except perhaps banks. The reason is that there is a crucial difference between a bank and a carmaker. The failure of even the largest carmaker is quite unlikely to be a vital public concern. The shareholders, creditors, and possibly the employees suffer, but competing carmakers benefit. There is no significant damage to the economy, and the failure may be good for the economy if it leads to more innovation. The role of the government should be limited to managing the bankruptcy process. That doesn't stop it from interfering, and the government routinely bails out corporations, like the United States' bailing out of General Motors in 2009 at the cost of $11 billion. While there might be good political reasons for bailing out carmakers, there is little economic sense in doing so. Failure is an essential part of the capitalist economy. Inefficient companies fail, and other, better ones take their place—Joseph Schumpeter's creative destruction.

While the economy can quite easily cope with even the largest corporations' failure, it is not the same with banks. Modern society cannot function without continuous banking services. We depend on debit cards to pay for lunch every day, and companies need to pay employees and suppliers on Fridays. It all goes via banks, so any hiccups in the services provided by banks are quite disruptive to society at large. While it is relatively straightforward to transfer control of failing corporations to the creditors, it is not the same with banks because their business is moving money. In a bankruptcy, ownership of money and obligations need to be clear. It can take a long time to establish claims; Lehman Brothers is still in litigation a decade and a half after its failure.

It gets worse. Bank failures are contagious. The only reason a bank stays in business is because its clients believe in its solvency and permanency. If the clients lose that faith, they will all rush to withdraw their money or terminate their business relations—a bank run. The social cost of a bank failure vastly outweighs the money lost in a bankruptcy because any disruption in the provision of banking services directly hits everybody. The result is what we economists call externality. The private cost or benefit is dominated by the cost or benefit to society at large.

Bank bailouts also create moral hazard. If the government steps in when banks fail, the banks are likely to take on more risk than they otherwise would. Unfortunately, the moral hazard from bank bailouts is different from that in insurance because it is usually not possible to charge those receiving bailouts for the privilege. After all, the bank is already failing, and we have to give it money: there is no point in kicking it when it is down. So why not charge them an insurance premium that protects the government in case it has to give a bailout? Easy in theory, hard in practice. The reason is that the insurance premium should reflect the bank's riskiness, but if it was so risky why didn't we prevent it in the first place? Besides that, it isn't that easy to measure the risk in the first place. If we then charge a fixed insurance fee, we are merely punishing the prudent.

The hardest decision to get right in the Goldilocks challenge is bailouts. Bailing out banks means rewarding the very entities that got into trouble in the first place, but not bailing them out can cause a much more costly crisis. All is not lost, and there are ways to do bailouts right. A bailout is a transfer from one part of the population to another—someone pays and another benefits. How to determine the winners and losers is a political question, why the government, not a bureaucrat, has to decide to do a bailout. Once a bailout is decided on, who should do it? The central bank or the ministry of finance? The central bank might be ideal because it can print money on demand and so cannot run out of money. However, there is no such thing as a free lunch. The consequence of monetizing bailouts is inflation, and the cost is borne by people on fixed incomes, like retirees. That might seem somewhat academic now that the central banks can apparently print all the money they want without consequences. But the central question remains: Even if the central banks could run the printing presses at full speed 24/7 without worry, who should benefit? Do we build a hospital or school, lower taxes, or do a bailout with the freshly printed money?

To get a handle on the question of bailouts, I came up with a classification scheme for bailouts in my book *Global Financial Systems*. To start with, some bailouts should be done by the ministry of finance and others by the central bank. The central bank should do the bailout in liquidity crises, where everybody is clamoring to convert liquid assets into cash—as in 1907, 1914, and 1866. In a liquidity crisis, the market for even the safest of assets disappears, as when investors went on strike in the autumn of 2007. A solvent bank with tangible assets might fail simply because it cannot sell them at a reasonable price to meet immediate demands for cash.

Suppose the crisis was not only about liquidity but also solvency, as in 2008. The banks made bad decisions, some of their loans are worthless, and they are facing bankruptcy. The banks' difficulty is caused by their misbehavior, so they are not merely the victim of the crisis. A liquidity injection is not sufficient. The government needs to directly support the banks to shield the economy from the worst. That is best done by the ministry of finance, not the central bank, because it involves using taxpayers' money to bail out a private entity, needing political support to be legitimate.

So what is the best way for the ministry of finance to bail out a bank if another bank can't take it over? It has five choices:

1. Guarantee the bank's debt
2. Take over (buy) the bank's bad debt
3. Lend money to the bank
4. Buy the bank's preference shares
5. Force the bank to recapitalize by issuing new shares sold to the government at a nominal cost or just nationalize the bank if it is in a particularly bad way.

For taxpayers, option 5 is the best, followed by 4, all the way to the worst, 1, since the taxpayer gets the upside if things go well. The banks, of course, see it differently. They prefer the taxpayer to absorb all the losses and will lobby for debt guarantees and, barring that, the government assuming bad debt. The last thing they want is equity dilution or preference shares. So which outcome prevails? It depends on a bank's power. If it can force option 1 it will do so, whether via lobbying, scaremongering, or bribery. Perhaps the same family that owns the bank runs the government? It's been known to happen.

In the 2008 crisis the European banks were generally successful in forcing the government's worst options, 1 and 2. Why? Scaremongering and the authorities' inexperience. The banks knew what was happening, and the government was not prepared, so the banks maneuvered the authorities into their preferred option. Ireland made the worst choice, guaranteeing bank debt and earning a sovereign default for its trouble. Europe since then has tried to find better outcomes for the taxpayer. The Spanish government brilliantly managed to implement option 5 in the summer of 2017 when it resolved Banco Popular and sold it to Santander for one euro. It is not easy to be so ruthlessly efficient, as is shown by the European country with the highest number of bank failures in recent years, Italy. Their politics gets in the way, as in the resolution of the world's oldest bank, Banca Monte dei Paschi, in 2017. It had been failing slowly, and anybody following Italian banks knew it was only a matter of time until it failed. Unfortunately for the Italian taxpayers, the government vacillated while the costs mounted, eventually deciding to bail it out at a cost of €5.4 billion.

The Monte dei Paschi case and many other bank failures in Italy and elsewhere illustrate how easy it is to take advantage of the taxpayer. The reason is shown in *The Wealth Effect: How the Great Expectations of the Middle Class Have Changed the Politics of Banking Crises* by my LSE political science colleague Jeff Chwieroth and his Australian coauthor, Andrew Walter. They argue that bailouts have become a middle-class good. Rescuing banks benefits the middle classes, which then lobby in favor of bailouts, which is why the Italians continue to spend money they can ill afford to bail out their banks.

It is easy for the financial authorities to adopt a principled position when nothing is happening, proclaiming they will protect the taxpayer and minimize moral hazard. It is much harder to stick to it when push comes to shove, as the Argentinians learned in 1993 and the Italians today. The political pressure is enormous. Perhaps the investors are pension funds or grandmothers as in Italy, and by having them take a hit the economic and political consequences will be severe. The temptation is always to give in: the taxpayers can surely afford it.

Goldilocks enters the Bear family's house, tasting the porridge of Papa bear, Mama bear, and Baby bear. She finds Papa bear's porridge too hot, Mama bear's too cold, and baby bear's porridge just the right temperature. The Goldilocks challenge is to find the appropriate balance between too hot and too cold. The most important and the most challenging part of the regulators' job is the Goldilocks challenge. Regulate too much, and the economy doesn't grow; regulate too little, and we get damaging crises. We need the right regulation intensity.

It is not easy. Of all the human activities we try to regulate, the financial system is by far the hardest to control. The incentives of the regulators and bankers do not align well with society's interests. The mission's complexity means it can be difficult to avoid regulators who fall into one of two extremes, either excessive risk aversion or getting captured by the regulated. The regulators are under constant pressure from lobbyists, pundits, and politicians, all demanding action, disregarding the need for an integrated approach to regulations. Meanwhile, those who are regulated react unpredictably, in some cases driving risk-taking into the shadows or perhaps not taking the right type of risk.

10

The Risk Theater

Over the past decade, G20 financial reforms have fixed the fault lines that caused the global financial crisis.
—*Mark Carney (2017)*

Figure 29. Credit: Copyright © Ricardo Galvão.

In the movie *Minority Report,* a special police unit called Pre-Crime predicts murders before they occur and thus arrests killers before they kill. Premeditated murders do not happen, leaving only crimes of passion, unplanned and hence not preventable. By 2008 almost everybody—policy makers, politicians, bankers, journalists, pundits, and academics—thought the problem of financial crises, at least in developed countries, had been solved. We now know better, and the financial authorities have a firm mandate from the highest levels of the political leadership: "Do something about finance. We will give you the resources and powers and political support to make it happen." In response, we got

a new breed of PreCrime—macropru—financial regulators put in charge
of macroprudential policy, tasked with preventing premeditated misconduct before it all goes wrong.

A vast agenda of regulation has been created. Leading the way is the
G20, the forum for the governments and central banks of the twenty
largest economies. The G20 delegates the job of dealing with finance
to the likes of the Financial Stability Board and the Basel committee.
Almost every country has set up its own financial stability board and put
its central bank in charge of macropru. It is still early days, but a clear
picture is emerging of the next generation financial policy. We have new
authorities and older ones with a bigger role. They have more data, more
resources, and more power. The financial sector retains a formidable lobbying power but has only partially succeeded in resisting the push for
regulations. So, how well does it work? Some parts are quite successful,
others a waste of resources, and others are outright damaging. What we
have gotten is a lot of risk theater. I take the term "risk theater" from the
notion of the security theater, coined by Bruce Schneier, referring to the
practice of implementing measures supposed to improve security while in
practice doing little to achieve it. A highly visible demonstration of security: checkpoints, guards, cameras, the banning of products. Restricting
people's behavior, privacy, and liberty. But when scarce resources priori-
tize visible security, actual security is deemphasized.

Turning Banks into Volvos Will Not Help

The safest carmaker in the world is Volvo. It was the inventor of
the seat belt, which it made freely available to the world in the 1950s. The
Volvo XC90 was crowned the safest car in the United Kingdom: no driver
or passenger deaths occurred since its launch in 2002. Volvo's objective is
zero fatalities. Ironically, a woman named Elaine Herzberg was killed by a
self-driving Volvo XC90 in 2018, but it wasn't the Volvo's fault. Uber, the
company testing the self-driving XC90, had disabled the car's automatic
self-breaking. The XC90 knew it was supposed to break, but Uber's software didn't allow it to.

Suppose the financial authorities manage to make every financial institution prudently run—as safe as Volvos. Nobody makes crazy investments. Everybody follows the rules and measures risk correctly—all are

prudent. Surely, then, no bank will fail, and financial crises will not happen, just as there would be very few car crashes if everybody followed the speed limit, nobody texted while driving, nobody drove drunk, everybody obeyed all the traffic laws, and we all had Volvos.

Can regulations prevent financial crises? The evidence from the years after World War II, the Bretton Woods era of 1944 to 1972, superficially suggests yes. The financial system was then very heavily regulated, and although banks failed, only two banking crises are recorded anywhere in the world over those twenty-eight years. But the financial system was almost entirely national, with little cross-border banking and very expensive financial services. Perhaps suitable for its era, but not the twenty-first century. The world changed. After the collapse of Bretton Woods in 1972 and the emergence of the Washington Consensus, banking became global. Regulations followed. But the new regulations were different from the Bretton Woods ones. The focus was no longer on tight controls; instead, we aimed to control risk. Making sure the banks were prudently run—Volvos.

It was all fine for a while, but then in 2008 banks started to fail for completely unexpected reasons. That should not have happened since Volvos are safe. The problem was that the prevailing regulatory thinking focused on each bank's behavior in isolation. What the authorities missed was the importance of the system. A financial system composed entirely of prudent banks is inherently unstable. We now know there were plenty of hitherto unknown risks, especially liquidity risk, so fundamental to the 2008 crisis. The system is not merely the sum of the individual banks. But financial regulations still mostly focus on each financial institution in isolation, using the riskometer as their main tool.

An interesting case study of what this means in practice happened on Thursday morning, 15 January 2015. That day Switzerland's central bank, the Swiss National Bank (SNB) did something that was either quite extraordinary or inevitable, depending on how one thinks about risk. The Swiss decided to allow their currency, the franc, to float freely. For some years before that, the SNB had pegged the franc to the euro at 1.2 francs. Immediately after the franc was set free, it strengthened by 16 percent.

The SNB decision really should not have been that surprising. Those who followed the Swiss economy and local politics—especially those who knew who owns the Swiss National Bank—expected the exchange rate peg to break. It was not a matter of if but when the franc would be set free. The roots of the announcement grew when Switzerland's economy began outperforming its eurozone neighbors. Before the global crisis started in 2007 the euro was a success, a stable currency investors wanted. The crisis put paid to those thoughts: investors holding liquid funds and seeking safety began looking for new destinations. But there are not that many stable, well-run countries in the world. Switzerland is one of the few. Unsurprisingly, money poured into Switzerland, and, as in any market, when there are more buyers than sellers prices go up.

The first time the franc and euro traded in January 1999 the exchange rate was 1.6 francs to the euro, and it was almost in the same place when the global crisis started in June 2007. From that day on, the euro steadily fell, reaching a low of 1.05 francs in August 2011. Though nice for Swiss consumers, the fall was not all that good for Swiss exporters, and the SNB did what so many other central banks like to do in that situation: fix the exchange rate, in their case at 1.2.

It is easy, at least in principle, to prevent a currency from rising. Just print money and use it to buy foreign currency on the open market. The problem is that when Switzerland prints money to buy euros, it is inflationary since the money supply is expanding. To prevent inflation, central banks like to counteract the inflationary forces by sterilization, soaking up the freshly printed money by selling bonds. That works because if the central bank buys one thousand euros' worth of foreign currency by printing twelve hundred francs and then sells a bond worth twelve hundred francs, the amount of money in circulation does not change. So far, so good. But the central bank eventually runs out of bonds to sell and can no longer sterilize. Meanwhile, it is piling up paper losses. Not only does it forgo interest payments on the bonds it sells, but also if the currency eventually floats, the central bank will incur a substantial loss on its foreign currency holdings.

Central banks are rarely structured as corporations, but the SNB is: 60 percent of its shares are owned by public institutions, like regional governments—the cantons—while the remaining 40 percent trade on the open market. The cantons depend on dividends from SNB, so they are naturally unhappy about the central bank running a big loss-making position. So, even though the SNB supposedly operates independently of its shareholders, that policy is not true in practice. The SNB has to meet two objectives simultaneously: make money for its shareholders while also helping the economy. A currency peg makes those two objectives mutually exclusive. On the last day before the announcement, the SNB held 471 billion francs' worth of foreign currency. The size of the Swiss economy, its GDP, was 565 billion francs. The SNB lost 78 billion francs on 16 January. If it had waited even longer to abandon the peg, the eventual losses would have been higher. What does any of this have to do with Basel or the risk theater? Suppose we had gone to bed on 14 January 2015 and used the main Basel-approved riskometers to forecast the likelihood of a 16 percent appreciation of the Swiss franc (Table 1).[1]

The first two riskometers, EWMA and GARCH, found the likelihood of that happening so low that it could not be calculated. For the third, MA, the likelihood was smaller than once in every universe. For the fourth riskometer, t-GARCH, it was once every 14 million years, and for the fifth, EVT, once every 109 years. The riskometers were quite inconsistent. But then, did these five riskometers pick up on what had happened and forecast risk better after the appreciation? For one, t-GARCH, the risk of another 16 percent appreciation increased 104 times, while for another (EVT) it went up only by 14 percent. Which of these two is more likely to be correct? Neither. After the currency had appreciated by 16 percent, it was implausible it would see another appreciation of the same magnitude. It is like a dam bursting: we don't expect it to burst again for some time. The risk went down, not up, as the riskometers had it. It is not like I specially picked lousy riskometers; on the contrary, these five are state-of-the-art, recommended by the authorities, and used by industry.

Table 1. Riskometers (VaR) and the likelihood of the Swiss currency appreciation

Riskometer	Frequency in years	Context
EWMA	Never	Too low to be calculated by a computer
GARCH	Never	Too low to be calculated by a computer
MA	2.7×10^{217}	Age of the universe is 1.4×10^{10} years
t-GARCH	1.4×10^{7}	Age of the earth is 4.5×10^{9} years
EVT	109	A bit less than one crisis in a typical lifetime

Source: Author's calculations

Two, t-GARCH and EVT, are especially lauded for their ability to pick up tail risk.

When I was drafting my blog on the riskometers and the Swiss announcement, I sent a copy to Robert Macrae, a friend who ran a hedge fund, and asked him to comment on it. He responded by saying that my findings were not all that interesting because to a currency trader using such riskometers to determine risk and nothing else was naive. Any market participant would use a hybrid approach, combining a riskometer with a detailed study of the Swiss economy. A comment I have heard many times: It is not fair to criticize riskometers merely because they failed to predict the likelihood of the Swiss currency appreciation. However, Robert ran his own fund, and the authorities had no say in how he managed risk, so he could pick any riskometer he wanted. A regulated bank does not have that luxury. The authorities push banks to use a riskometer and not just not any riskometer: banks can choose only among a few, and as time passes they are increasingly told precisely how to measure risk.

I have presented the Swiss currency appreciation case many times to audiences in both the private and public sectors. Those in the private sector tend to react by saying something like, "So what? We know this already." In other words, they know that the risk measurements used to regulate banks are very unreliable. I find it especially amusing to hear that from the very risk managers whose job it is to report on Basel to the authorities. They have to use the officially sanctioned riskometers, even though they have no faith in them.

The reaction from regulators is more interesting. They often respond by saying that while the example holds true, it is irrelevant. The riskometers in Basel III are designed for microprudential regulations, the management of day-to-day risk, not for extreme outcomes, so the Swiss currency appreciation is not a fair test of them. The regulators are expressing a nuance that is generally lost on the rest of the world. After all, there is more to microprudential regulations than day-to-day volatility; measuring the likelihood of banks failing is key to their mission, and their preferred riskometers don't capture such risk.

The use of riskometers in regulations can have curious consequences. The BBC *Panorama* program came out with a provocative episode in 2014 titled "Did the Bank Wreck My Business?" about how two banks bailed out by the government, RBS and Lloyds, were unfairly destroying small companies. What the BBC missed was why the banks behaved this way. They were merely doing what they were supposed to do under the post-2008-crisis Basel regulations—derisk. The risk theater is to blame for the destruction of the small companies, not the capricious bankers, as *Panorama* argued.

The reason is because the global crisis in 2008 showed that the global financial regulations in place at the time, Basel II, were not up to the task. It was just too easy for banks to manipulate their capital—exploit capital structure arbitrage. The Basel committee wasted little time in coming up with its successor, Basel III, mostly in place by now. It happened with lightning speed, taking only a decade—yes, ten years is super fast by international regulation standards. That haste meant the committee did not have time to make any fundamental reforms. Basel III is only an incremental improvement on its predecessor, chipping away some of the most glaring deficiencies while leaving the underlying philosophy in place—Basel II on steroids, if you will. There is much talk about "Basel IV" addressing all the difficult issues, but I suspect regulatory fatigue may get in the way.[2] Basel III remains microprudential for most parts, leaving the system's stability to the newly established macroprudential regulators.

The primary focus of Basel III, like that of its predecessors, is capital. The 2008 crisis showed that the way capital was calculated was problematic because many banks with supposedly high levels of capital failed. Basel III's main thrust is in increasing both the amount and the quality of banks' minimum capital: the reason the banks discussed in the BBC *Panorama* program had supposedly been wrecking businesses. Because the banks have to hold much more capital for the riskiest types of loans, the inevitable consequence is that the availability of loans to small- and medium-sized enterprises sharply decreased while the interest rates on those loans increased significantly.

The regulators are proud of their creation. Banks now hold more capital, have more stable funding and robust systems for managing risk, promising a more resilient banking system, one that stimulates economic growth. All these reforms left the banks in much better shape for dealing with the Covid-19 crisis in 2020. The banks complain, but they complain surprisingly little and are much happier with Basel III than is often assumed. Compared with the very loud protests made by insurance companies and asset managers over being designated as systemically important, the banks appear to be outright acquiescent. In and by itself, worrying.

There is much to like in Basel III. Still, I have reservations. To begin with, Basel III still assumes the stability of the financial system is ensured if each bank is a prudent Volvo. Furthermore, Basel III not only fails to address procyclicality adequately, but also makes the problem worse. Alright, the standard response is "Basel III has a new type of capital buffer that is adjusted countercyclically according to the financial cycle." Not quite, as the adjustment buffers are small, and a temporary relaxation may not encourage them to lend more. The Covid-19 lowering of the capital ratios did not stimulate lending. More fundamentally, Basel III implements its predecessor more intensively but does not ask the critical question, What do we need from financial regulations? Yes, it does address things like financial stability and the provision of services. Still, it does not position itself properly within the context of what we want from the financial system and its regulations. So, yet again, risk theater. Perhaps worst of all, it mostly ignores the SIFIs.

The SIFIs are those systemically important financial institutions whose failure will cause a systemic crisis. Before 2008 nobody worried about the SIFIs; on the contrary, the prevailing wisdom maintained they were the safest of institutions. Globally diversified financial institutions that could offset losses in one area with profits in all the others. Well, that turned out to be wrong. The largest banks did fail. Worse still, they failed with catastrophic consequences, like the world's biggest bank at the time, RBS-ABN AMRO, not to mention Lehman Brothers.

One might ask why we allow financial institutions that are so dangerous. The answer is simple: politics. Even if the financial authorities preferred no SIFIs, their political masters overrule them. In other words, SIFIs exist only because politicians want them to exist. Why do politicians like SIFIs? The straightforward reason is that they are quite handy. A single financial institution that can provide financial services wherever your country's companies operate is beneficial. If a German company based in Düsseldorf has businesses in America, Brazil, and Korea, it helps to have a single bank that can service it in all these places. The other reason SIFIs exist is prestige. If your bank has your country's name on it—think Deutsche Bank—of course you want your bank to be big and powerful. Besides, having global banks in your jurisdiction allows you to project power. Austria gains power and prestige by having the regional SIFIs in its jurisdiction. The reason there are so many SIFIs in insecure midsize European countries (Figure 30).

So, how dangerous are the SIFIs? To answer that, I need to go back to bank capital. The numbers reveal that the SIFI problem is much worse for smaller countries (see Figure 30). The total assets of the largest American bank, JP Morgan, are only 13 percent of the GDP of the United States, while the total assets of the Swiss UBS bank exceed its GDP at 136 percent. One can use many ways to look at how vulnerable these SIFI banks are. The most obvious is the leverage ratio, the ratio of capital to total bank assets. The lowest ratio is Deutsche Bank's at 4 percent, while JP Morgan's exceeds 6 percent, and the Chinese ICBC's is almost 8 percent. No wonder Deutsche is always in the news, and not in a good way. It is the SIFI bank the pundits think will fail next.

The Basel III financial regulations say that a bank has to have a leverage ratio of at least 3 percent. So, by subtracting three from the leverage ratio

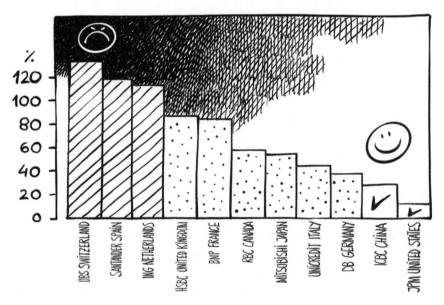

Figure 30. SIFI size and GDP. Credit: Copyright © Ricardo Galvão.

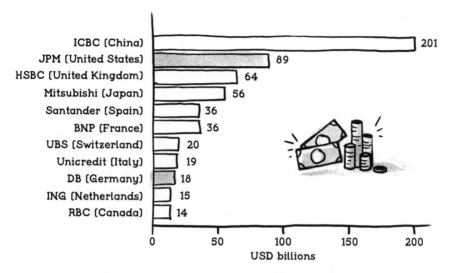

Figure 31. Distance to default. Credit: Lukas Bischoff/IllustrationX.

and multiplying it into total assets, we can see how big a loss the bank would have to suffer in order to be forced into bankruptcy—the distance from default (Figure 31). It would take a loss of only $14 billion for the Royal Bank of Canada to be shut down and $15 billion for the Dutch ING bank. Meanwhile, it would take $89 billion for JP Morgan and over $200 billion for the Chinese ICBC bank.

The failure of any bank whose assets are a significant portion of GDP will be tough to resolve. Of these banks, the United States could easily absorb even the largest losses arising from JP Morgan's failure, and China would not find it too hard to handle ICBC's default. However, it would be challenging for other countries, especially Switzerland, the Netherlands, and Spain, where the largest bank's assets exceed GDP. It is much better to try to prevent failure by containing the size of the largest banks.

PreCrime Macropru to the Rescue

We are all macroprudentialists now.
—*Claudio Borio*

While the Basel Accords are microprudential, focused on each bank's behavior individually, systemic risk is left to the macroprudential (macropru) authorities: the PreCrime police of the finance world. While the label macropru is new, it has always been one of the four central planks of the governments' financial policy, now just sporting a new name.

I suspect that Walter Bagehot and his nineteenth- and early twentieth-century counterparts would not have been the least surprised by the crisis in 2008. It was not so different from the crises they knew, like those in 1763, 1866, 1907, and 1914. What would have shocked them was how complacent and unprepared their twenty-first-century successors had become. Just as many policy makers in developing countries, like those affected by the Asian crisis of 1998 and the various Latin American crises, watched events unfold in 2008 with a wry weariness, if not schadenfreude. After being lectured by the developed countries for so many years, the shoe was now on the other foot. Still, to their credit the financial authorities quickly dusted off the history books in 2008, responding appropriately by applying past lessons. What is especially impressive is that the policy mistakes that led the financial turmoil in 1929 to become the Great Depression were deliberately avoided. The necessary liquidity was applied, trade was not restricted, and the banks kept alive. But not without a cost. Never again. The cost of responding to the 2008 crisis was so high that something had to be done to make the financial system more resilient. In response, we got the doctrine of macropru. The central banks set up financial stability divisions. An army of people, a vast amount of resources, and considerable powers have been given to the PreCrime macropru regulators. It quickly became a truism that macropru was the way forward, as Claudio Borio's quote above indicates.

So what is the objective of macropru? There is no single definition. That said, distilling the various notions out there, I find two. Prevent excessive risk from accumulating in the financial system, and if and when a crisis happens, contain it in the most efficient manner possible. While these objectives are sensible, if not complete, they are high level and need to be translated into specific policies. And that is precisely where there is no consensus: not between countries, not inside countries, not even within particular policy organizations. I find it amusing that a central bank can provide different and conflicting views on macropru without seemingly being concerned with the inconsistency or, worse still, not even realizing it. It is difficult to create effective macropru, and we are still finding our way. I often hear words to the effect that macropru at present is how monetary policy was in 1950—give it fifty years and it will become as sophisticated. One can do a lot of damage in fifty years, and those who know their monetary history will recall that the stagflation of the 1970s was in no small part due to the poor monetary policy of the era. The failure to hit inflation targets since 2008 shows that monetary policy is still far from perfect.

There are many directions the macropru authorities can take. Most are passive, focusing on fixed rules that hold through the financial cycle. Many such macropru implementations have been very successful in preventing crises—my favorite is the ban on buying stocks on margin in the United States in 1934. (Should I be worried about having a favorite macropru rule?) The alternative is active macropru, leaning against the wind in a discretionary manner. If risk is building up, tighten capital and liquidity standards. Relax when risk and growth are low, as we did following the Covid-19 crisis. If the market is too risk averse, follow Keynes and encourage it to take more risk. Such discretionary macropru policies are designed to be countercyclical, dampening out the financial cycle. Active macropru demands much more of the financial authorities than passive macropru. They need estimates of systemic risk and its impact on the real economy, from the early signs of a buildup of stress all the way to the post-crisis economic and financial resolution. They need tools to implement effective policy remedies in response to changes in risk. And the authorities need legitimacy, a reputation for impartiality, and political support.

To start with, systemic risk needs to be measured, not an easy job. There are many indicators of systemic risk out there, such as the European Central Bank's CISS. Most are prone to what statisticians call type I and type II errors: falsely finding something that is not there or failing to detect something that is. Not a problem with an easy solution. Systemic crises are infrequent, less than once every forty-three years on average, giving the statisticians little to work with. To complicate matters, the financial system's structure will be very different from one crisis to the next. Having identified that systemic risk is increasing, the authorities have to respond with one of the tools at their disposal. There are many tools in the macropru tool kit. Some are meant to limit procyclicality— lean against the wind—some shield the real economy, yet others are used to respond to imminent threats. Some tools are surgical and specific, like loan-to-value ratios aiming to limit the amount of money people can borrow when buying a house. Others are blunt—sledgehammers—like bank capital ratios which affect all bank activities. The blunt instruments may kill the patient, while the surgical ones may not work.

Frustrating the job of the macropru designers is the continuing evolution of the financial system. The past informs the tools, but the threats come from the future, like driving by looking into the rearview mirror. Meanwhile, the impacts and side effects of the tools are poorly understood. The most visible macropru problem, and politically the most important, is real estate, a common cause of financial crises. The macropru policy makers are always on the lookout for real estate bubbles. Simple things, bubbles. We borrow from banks to buy homes, and in response prices go up and the economy blossoms, encouraging more people to borrow to buy homes. Everyone feels happy in the short run, but over time fault lines emerge and a crash becomes increasingly likely. Both the bubble itself and the eventual crash create problems. Rising housing prices directly affect inequality. Homeowners get richer, and the rest are left out, with political consequences. Governments can be forced to implement policies that further stimulate housing prices—like the various policies helping first-time buyers and high-risk borrowers. The political desire to help poor households acquire property in the United States was the main reason for the emergence of the subprime mortgage market, a leading cause of the crisis in 2008. Real estate is one of the most common causes of banking crises. Elementary. Has to be solved, right?

Unsurprisingly, the macropru authorities have identified real estate as a significant priority. So what are they to do? One of the main tools in use today is the loan-to-value ratio, whereby one can borrow only a certain percentage (say, 80 percent) of the value of a house. However, while real estate is undoubtedly a macropru concern, the remedies deal only with the symptoms, not the causes. House prices are directly affected by economic growth and various government policies, like zoning laws, help-to-buy, tax deductible mortgage interest, ultralow interest rates, and subsidized mortgages for high-risk borrowers. Macropru has no impact on any of those, and all the macropru authority can do is to mop up after the other policy domains. Meanwhile, just using the macropru tools will expose the authority to considerable public hostility. Worse still, if the said authority is the central bank, being responsible for macropru may undermine the central bank's ability to effectively execute monetary policy. Real estate shows how difficult macropru is. Other parts of the government are responsible for causing the problem, and all the macropru authorities can do is clean up. However, the worst challenge for them is politics.

Covid-19, and how the authorities responded to it, also demonstrates the procyclicality of macropru. The authorities decided in March and April 2020 to relax capital constraints on banks in the hope that they would lend to Covid-stricken small- and medium-sized enterprises. But banks by and large did not respond the way the authorities wanted them to. They didn't want to lend, both because they saw these companies as bad credit but also out of precaution, not knowing how the Covid economic crisis would end. But these capital relaxations remain in place. And if the Covid economic crisis is V-shaped or K-shaped, the relaxation of capital may finally be used by banks to stimulate the economy at a time it is already overstimulated. Yet another example of procyclical macropru.

Politics Gets in the Way

While the hope is that the credibility of monetary policy rubs off on macroprudential policy, it is more likely that the fuzziness of financial stability and the interplay of political pressures will instead undermine monetary policy.
—*Jeff Chwieroth and Jón Daníelsson*

The most powerful bureaucrat in the world is the chair of the Federal Reserve System in the United States, currently Jerome Powell. He has more power than General Joseph Dunford, the head of the Joint Chiefs of Staff, even though the latter has nuclear weapons in his tool kit. The reason is that General Dunford reports to the president, while Chairman Powell reports to nobody. Paul Tucker, the former deputy governor of the Bank of England, in his book *Unelected Power,* questioned why a democratic society gives a bureaucrat like Powell such remarkable powers.

The reason is monetary policy, whereby the wisdom of independent central banks is backed up by decades of research, including the work of multiple Nobel Prize winners. Politicians cannot be trusted with interest rates—for that, we need an independent professional body. In the bad old days, when politicians ran monetary policy, they used interest rates to enhance their electoral prospects. Reduce interest rates a few months before elections to stimulate the economy. Some countries still do this, like Turkey. Politicians don't want to delegate their power to the central bank: witness President Trump's criticism of the Fed and President Erdogan's repeated firings of Turkey's central bank governors.

It is easy to hand monetary policy to an independent central bank because the policy is well defined. There is one unambiguous measurement (inflation), the objective is clear (perhaps 2 percent inflation), and there are two tools (the price and quantity of money). If the central bank fails in its job, it is clear for all to see. It is acceptable to have an independent central bank if its actions and outcomes are clearly monitored.

Some countries and central banks took independence and monetary policy to an extreme. The importance of the mission implied purity, so financial regulations and financial stability belonged elsewhere. The key reason the United Kingdom created the Financial Services Authority in 1997 and why many countries followed suit. Now the pendulum has swung the other way, and we want to house financial stability in the central bank. For two reasons. First, the hope is that the reputation and the power of the central banks as guardians of money will rub off on financial stability. Second, the central bank is the only institution that can create money on demand and therefore has to be at the center of fighting financial crises.

Will it work as hoped? No. The central bank in charge of financial stability faces a complex, ill-defined policy domain for which there is no clear consensus on either the problem or the objective. The indicators at their disposal are imprecise and conflicting. The surgical tools are ineffective, and the powerful tools blunt. Worse, and even more so than monetary policy, macroprudential policies result in clearly identifiable winners and losers, subjecting the policy authorities to intensive lobbying and political pressure. The ultimate decisions of anything that affects economic policy in a direct and personal way should fall under political oversight. It would be undemocratic if it did not.

Nowhere has the conflict between politics and independent regulations become more evident than in macropru's real estate policy. In 2013

Norwegian Parliament members threatened to withdraw the regulatory agency's ability to determine the loan-to-value ratio when the regulator planned to lower it. Similar debates have happened in many countries. The reason is apparent. If we cannot borrow to buy houses, we do not enjoy the benefit of wealth creation and security that comes with owning a property. The policy creates clearly identifiable losers. This is why less democratic countries like Malaysia, Singapore, Thailand, and Hong Kong find it easier to implement macroprudential policies. One example is Hong Kong's 60 percent loan-to-value ratio limits for first-time buyers and a maximum debt-service ratio of 40 percent for borrowers acquiring a second property. Singapore is another excellent example of what is possible when democracy does not get too much in the way, as it has implemented multiple rounds of real estate interventions and can do so without too many political considerations. It would be unthinkable for European countries and especially the United States to deploy such intrusive macropru tools. Democratic opposition and industry lobbying would get in the way.

Indeed, the biggest problem for the macropru policy makers is that they have to ignore political risk, as I discussed in a blog piece cowritten with Robert Macrae, "The Fatal Flaw in Macropru: It Ignores Political Risk." Very few major stress events are caused purely by excessive risk-taking, the target of macropru. Most have politics as a primary driver. War or the transition between political systems, as in Russia in 1919, Germany in 1923, Japan in 1945, and China in 1949. Houses for the poor, as in the United States in 2008. Covid-19 in 2020. Today, politics is the sole cause of the severe financial and economic crises in Venezuela and Zimbabwe.

Take Brexit. During the referendum campaign the Bank of England warned of serious economic consequences from Brexit, putting itself on the losing side of an acrimonious political debate. As a result, the bank came under repeated attacks from the new political leadership—the bank has had to affirm its independence and request support from the new government in a way we are not used to seeing. The new governor of the bank now loudly proclaims his support for the government's Brexit policies. The post-Brexit politicization of the Bank of England highlights the dangers facing central banks when they include politics in their considerations. Politics drive systemic risk. How deeply can or should a civil servant working in the European Central Bank venture into populism? While the election of President Trump heralded a dramatic change in US economic priorities, it was hard to see how the Fed could react.

In practice, and despite whatever may be said about their independence, the financial authorities are authorized by, controlled by, and gain their legitimacy from the political leadership. Unsurprisingly, the mandate from political leadership stipulates that the central banks look at financial and economic risk, not the risk emanating from the politicians themselves. Making it risky for the financial authorities to incorporate political risk as a determinant of systemic risk, despite its importance.

As a result, political risk is mostly missing from the macroprudential debate despite having always been the primary cause of systemic risk. It is not only institutionally challenging for the financial authorities to publicly anticipate crises with predominantly political causes, but also makes it difficult for them to contain such crises once they happen. That is why I think those who hope the quality of monetary policy will help macropru are misguided. Independent monetary policy is possible only because of the clarity of the mission. The messiness and politicization of macropru are much more likely to undermine the central banks' legitimacy and their reputation for impartiality, making it much harder to mobilize support for difficult policies.

Of Hammers and Nails

A few years ago I was invited to a conference at a European insurance regulator to discuss the impact of risk measurements on the efficacy of insurance regulations. The reason for the invitation is not that I'm an expert in insurance regulations, which I am not, but rather because a couple of years earlier I had coauthored three blog pieces on the European Solvency 2 regulations, focused on the systemic risk arising from valuing the reserves of insurance companies at market values.[3] The subtext to the event was that the Financial Stability Board (FSB), a policy body working at the behest of the G20 group of countries, was worried about the systemic consequences of insurance companies and asset managers. The reason it was so concerned was the pivotal role of the insurance company AIG in the global crisis in 2008, when AIG was the world's most active seller of CDSs via its London-based and France-regulated bank, the risk of which was missed by its New York State regulators.

The financial authorities now focus on the systemic threats emanating from insurance companies and asset managers, institutions that control trillions of dollars of assets with relatively little oversight and, as AIG showed, can make business decisions that threaten global financial stability. Both industries are fragmented, with nothing akin to globally coordinated banking regulations, and, until 2008, nobody thought either industry was systemic.[4] While insurance companies and asset managers may pose systemic threats, the nature of the threat is poorly understood, and until very recently there had been no studies of how these two industries interact with the rest of the financial system and the threats that poses to global stability. We have studied the systemic fragility of banks for over a century. There is no comparable research on insurance companies or asset managers. When all you have is a hammer, everything looks like a nail, and when the FSB started looking at the systemic risk in the nonbanking parts of the financial system, all they had was analysis of banking stability. The type of work I have discussed extensively in this book: bank runs, fire sales, liquidity dry-ups, and, most important, capital.

That was the reason I was invited to the conference at the insurance regulator. The FSB opted to analyze the fragility of insurance companies and asset managers by looking through the lens of banking fragility, which meant capital. But their risks are quite different. What kills insurance companies is writing insurance contracts too cheaply so they can't meet their eventual obligations. There is nothing systemic about that because most insurance payouts are uncorrelated with systemic financial risk. The AIG crisis happened because it decided to become a bank, and the relevant authorities did not pay attention. Asset managers use neither much leverage nor derivatives. They are systemic consequences of asset managers, but they are in exchange traded funds with illiquid assets like small company bonds. Capital has nothing to do with that.

So, when applying bank fragility analysis to asset managers and insurance companies, the financial authorities just end up saddling them with unnecessary burdens which the clients—us—pay. We might get the perception of safety but not actual safety: risk theater. The more fundamental danger is that if we increasingly harmonize regulations around a

Basel-type philosophy, including not only banks but also other activities in the financial system, like insurance, asset management, and nonbank banking, we get monoculture.

I recently gave a presentation at a central bank conference and made a throwaway remark that macropru could be procyclical. That is, it could perversely amplify the financial cycle instead of dampening it. To the audience, that was heresy, and some senior staff members got cross with me. After all, the fundamental promise of macropru is that it is countercyclical, dampening out the natural cycles in the financial system. So, could macropru be procyclical? Well, yes. I eventually cowrote a blog on this, "Why Macropru Can End Up Being Procyclical," arguing that discretionary macropru—leaning against the wind—has considerable scope for amplifying the financial cycle. Suppose the macropru authorities were successful in smoothing out the financial cycle. Would market participants respond to this gratefully and say, "What a great job the central bank is doing?" No, the market would see the resulting low risk as an invitation to take more risk: the Minsky effect. We have seen many examples in the past, like the Greenspan put.

Another reason macropru may be procyclical is the difficulty in measuring risk—riskometers aren't exactly reliable. Figure 32 shows a hypothetical time path of risk over one year. The target risk is three. In the first month the risk is too high at five, but nobody realizes it yet. A couple of months later the riskometers pick up on risk having been high, alerting the authorities, who start planning their reaction and, a few months later, decide on what to do. Eventually, in month twelve, the policy response is implemented. Meanwhile, risk has been steadily falling and is already below the target by the middle of the year. By the time the policy intervention takes place in month twelve, risk is too low. Instead of bursting a bubble, it exacerbates the derisking already taking place, and risk crashes to one, way below the target level of three. A problem caused by reacting with a time lag to indicators of risk that are themselves measured with a time lag: the policy response can come too late and be procyclical.

By the end of the year the appropriate policy response would have been to increase risk to stimulate economic activity, not to decrease risk. Such a procyclical policy response is common. A recent example was Japan in

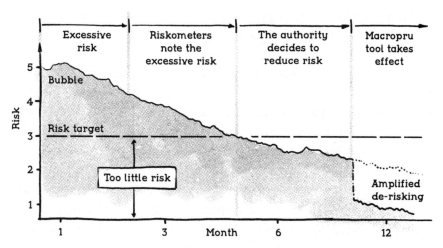

Figure 32. Procyclical macropru. Credit: Lukas Bischoff/IllustrationX.

2007, when the authorities issued guidance restricting bank lending to real estate developers just when foreign lenders were also withdrawing from this market, thereby leading to a severe credit crunch. And there is a real danger that all the Covid-19 stimulus may simply end up inflating the postvirus bubble. Political pressures and lobbying further amplify the policy procyclicality. We sometimes hear complaints like "The banks are failing because they have already overextended credit" or "Helping Wall Street to increase lending leads to even bigger moral hazard" or "Macropru is discredited because it was supposed to have prevented this credit event in the first place—why should it do better this time?" All of these objections call for a procyclical policy response.

I don't think the potential for procyclical macropru would have surprised Friedrich Hayek. His argument against central planning was that economic information is created locally—by the farmer, the mechanic, and all the companies making up the economy. As decisions are taken on higher and higher levels, the decision makers necessarily have to aggregate information. Unfortunately, when we take an almost infinite amount of local knowledge and summarize it in a few key macropru indicators, quite a lot is lost along the way. It is much better for the farmer than the ministry of agriculture to decide what to grow and when. The macropru authorities wield enormous power, just like the planning ministries of the Soviet Union, but may not be any better at getting the result they desire.

Mark Carney's confident proclamation (see chapter epigraph above) that the problem of crises has been fixed sounds promising but hard to verify in practice. Financial crises are not frequent. The typical OECD country can expect such crises less than once every forty-three years. Mark Carney will be long retired before we can validate his statement. I am not as optimistic. There are many good things in the new financial regulations, such as the dual requirement for the leverage- and the risk-weighted capital ratios and the emphasis on the type of capital that is hardest to manipulate. Capital was too low before the 2008 crisis, and the banks depended too much on short-term funding. However, some aspects of the new financial regulations are not useful and even down-right dangerous, like the continuing focus on individual prudence and dependence on riskometers; antidiversity and the neglect of the system are the worst. Central bank research has given us so much evidence on the importance of diversity and the system for financial stability. It is unfortunate that so little of that work is reflected in actual policy. The overall thrust of financial policy is moving in the wrong direction, with too much risk theater. I would much rather the focus of financial regulations be on diversity.

11

The Uniformity, Efficiency, and Stability Trilemma

Common beliefs and action are the enemy of financial stability. The best way to get stability is diversity, both in regulations and financial institutions.

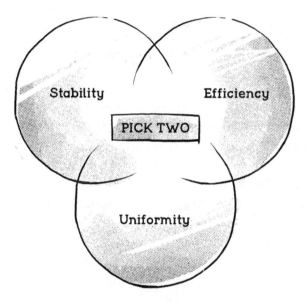

Figure 33. Credit: Lukas Bischoff/IllustrationX.

The most popular banana in the nineteenth century was the Gros Michel. It tasted good, came in big bunches, and had a bruise-resistant peel. Ideal for export. But the Gros Michel banana had a vulnerability. Each banana was a clone of every other, so they were all genetically identical. It came as no surprise when the fungus *Fusarium oxysporum,* nicknamed the Panama disease because of the extensive banana plantations in Panama, came calling at the end of the nineteenth century. It managed to wipe out almost every Gros Michel. Evolution did not provide resistance because the Gros Michels were clones. If one banana was vulnerable, so was each and every other one. Genetic diversity protects. When the Spanish flu hit in 1918 tens of millions of people died, but our genetic variety protected us. If humans had all been clones, we could have become extinct.

Bananas show monoculture at its best and worst. Monoculture reduces uncertainty so growers can optimize their plantations to achieve maximum efficiency. The trade-off is stability, in this case the vulnerability to disease. When choosing among stability, efficiency, and uniformity, we can pick only two (Figure 33). What does any of this have to do with finance? After all, the financial system is not full of clones, and banks are not bananas, even though I do get the impression that monkeys run some of them. The forces of creative destruction are as powerful as ever, with plenty of new ideas and new businesses pushing diversity, not uniformity. Unfortunately, strong forces oppose diversity. Decision makers tend to opt for efficiency and uniformity, rejecting stability. Of course, that is not how they would put it, and I am sure many will be offended by my words here. All say they want stability, adding that they prefer diversity, not uniformity. Those are words. Actions say otherwise.

The consequence of choosing uniformity and efficiency is lower volatility and fatter tails, the successful smoothing out of day-to-day price fluctuations at the expense of large future crashes—tail risk (Figure 34). The light gray line is the natural fluctuations of some hypothetical returns. The fat black one is where we successfully squeeze out short-term risk but then, by 2028, end up with a crisis.

The private institutions in the financial system are becoming more similar every day. The reasons are subtle. Not many call for less diversity, at least not explicitly; the antidiversity preference instead tends to show up indirectly. As when calling for best practices. It is hard to oppose best practices. After all, why would anyone ever want to have second-best practice? But there can only be one best practice, so if all pick the best practice, they all have the same practice: monoculture. Fairness and level playing fields are also drivers of uniformity, as they demand the same

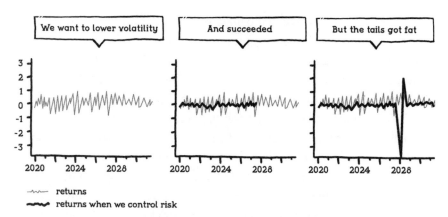

Figure 34. Lowering volatility and fattening the tails. Credit: Lukas Bischoff/IllustrationX.

rules for everybody. And if the rules are about specific conduct, like all the micro risks the microprudential regulators concern themselves with, we get harmonization of action. The financial industry also pushes for monoculture. Almost every financial institution has the same objective: maximizing profits subject to constraints. That takes them closer to other institutions' optimal asset mix, leading to more crowded trades and procyclicality.

While there are not many solid measurements of diversity, one metric points in that direction: the number of banks is steadily falling. Half a century ago we had a wide variety of financial institutions. Every country had its own financial regulations, and they were all different. Each country had many types of banks, regulated and operated differently, all driving diversity and stability. The most diverse of all was the United States. It used to leave banking regulations to the states, and, of course, they were all different. Banks in Arkansas operated under rules that were different from those of banks in New York, resulting in herd immunity. Per the Glass–Steagall Act banks were not allowed to operate across state borders. Then the rules were relaxed, banks *could* operate across state lines, they were increasingly federally regulated, and state regulations became harmonized. One consequence of these changes is that the number of banks has fallen sharply. The federal reserve bank in St. Louis has collected data on the number of banks in the United States from 1984, when there were 14,400 commercial banks. By 2020 the number had fallen to 4,404, a reduction of 3.3 percent a year.[1]

Sam Peltzman, an economics professor at the University of Chicago, came up with a radical idea in 1975: risk compensation. When regulations are enacted to improve safety, the unintended consequence is more risk. Take American football. At the beginning of the twentieth century football players started to demand helmets to protect themselves against injuries. In the beginning, helmets reduced injuries, but over time, as the helmets became better and better, the way of playing changed. Players started using their heads as ramrods, running headfirst into the opposition. Because helmets improved, the shocks to the head became more violent, and injuries increased—the players compensated for being protected by taking on more risk. The vicious feedback between better helmets, more aggressive playing, and injuries showed how the laudable objective of protecting players by making them use helmets could perversely harm them. In the sister sport of rugby, heads are unprotected, but because the players don't use them as ramrods, head injuries are much rarer than in American football.

Risk compensation is particularly pernicious in the financial system, driven by common beliefs, that is, everyone observing the world in the same way. Blame the riskometers. If everybody uses the same one, we all end up seeing the world in the same way. Financial institutions obviously don't all use the same riskometer, as they are a part of the secret sauce that makes some better than others. There is, however, a limit to how different the riskometers can be, especially in banks. Industry trends directly influence even the largest banks. Their modelers studied in the same universities and read the same academic papers. They go to the same conferences and move freely between banks. Not to mention regulations, which also make risk management practices more homogeneous. All pushing banks toward similar ways of modeling risk, so they increasingly see the world the same way.

Beliefs are only half the picture. The other half is common action, also driven by riskometers. Half a century ago, before the widespread use of statistics and risk management and regulations and best practices, every financial institution was quite free to do what it wanted. They were primarily partnerships and allowed to make the dumbest decisions. Not today. We have a myriad of controls from regulators, media, shareholders, accountants, stakeholders, and politicians, all wanting to constrain what financial institutions can get up to. All pushing toward reacting the same way to shocks.

Common beliefs and actions are the enemy of stability. Instability arises from a lack of diversity, when we move as a herd. Like the Millennium Bridge wobbling when all the pedestrians behaved as one (see chapter 7). When the ~~wisdom~~ lunacy of the crowds tells us risk is low, more risk makes perfect sense: Minsky, yet again. Everybody tells us that—the risk takers, the risk controllers, the regulators, the journalists, the academics, and the pundits. We then all pile into the same risky assets. Then a shock comes along. It could be any of the ones I discussed earlier, like Archduke Ferdinand's assassination in 1914 or the realization in 2008 that CDOs full of subprime mortgages were not as clever as assumed, or a virus like Covid-19. It all goes pear-shaped. The same people now tell us risk is too high, that we must derisk. Harmonization of belief and action is pro-cyclical, amplifying the boom-and-bust cycle up and down. It doesn't take much to set these processes of coordinated buying and selling in motion. Figure 35 shows an *Economist* cartoon that is more realistic than we would want it to be.

The Kaizen Revolution in Finance

The largest antihunger charity in the United States is the Food Bank for New York City, which feeds about 1.5 million people every year. The Food Bank is financed by donations, most of which take the form of money or food. But when the charity approached Toyota, it got *Kaizen*, Japanese for "continuous improvement," the key to Toyota's success.[2] It worked wonders for the Food Bank. In one soup kitchen in Harlem, Toyota's engineers reduced the wait for dinner from ninety minutes to eighteen. Volunteers packing supplies for the victims of Hurricane Sandy used Kaizen to shorten the time it took to pack a box from three minutes to eleven seconds.

Finance went through its own Kaizen-type revolution, in three phases. The first commenced in 1950, when Harry Markowitz defended his doc-toral thesis in economics at the University of Chicago, later published

Figure 35. The *Economist* on procyclicality. Credit: Kevin KAL Kallaugher, *Baltimore Sun,* Kaltoons.com.

under the title "Portfolio Selection." His critical insight was that investors should focus on two variables: expected returns and the variance of asset returns, and it has been known as the mean–variance model ever since. Markowitz's thesis was controversial from the very beginning, and he almost did not graduate. Milton Friedman felt that the mean–variance model contained too much statistics and not enough economics and therefore did not deserve a PhD in economics. Even so, it earned Markowitz the Nobel Prize in Economics in 1990, as his work was by then the cornerstone of financial economics.

Markowitz formalized an ancient idea: the more risk we take, the higher the return we demand. His insight was to reduce a complicated decision-making problem to a simple choice between only two variables and, in the process, sidestepping four complex issues. The first issue is that in the real world, everybody has different objectives—or utility functions, in the language of economics. Earlier I discussed how Paul, Ann, and Mary all have the same portfolio and technology but need different risk measurements. Well, Markowitz assumed they are all identical, and hence all prefer the same riskometer. The second problem he avoided is the distinction between risk and uncertainty by simply ignoring uncertainty. He assumed we know variance of asset returns, that variance is risk, and there is no uncertainty. Third, he assumed ergodicity, that the statistical laws governing the financial markets are constant over time. In practice, that means both the expected returns and variances never change, so once you know them you have what you need to make investment decisions until the end of time. Finally, he surmised that every market participant is tiny (atomistic) and has no impact on the evolution of prices—all risk is exogenous. His implicit assumption of atomistic market participants is crucial because otherwise trading will change prices, undermining his other assumptions.

Even though the technology behind investment decisions has come a long way since Markowitz, I suspect quite a lot of fund managers still use his technique, mostly unmodified. And even when his model is augmented, most improvements are still based on the same four assumptions: identical investors, where uncertainty doesn't matter, along with ergodicity and exogenous risk.

Markowitz's mean–variance framework was theoretical—supposing we know the vital statistics. They are not known in the real world and have to be estimated, the bit of the puzzle supplied by the second phase of the Kaizen finance revolution. Many researchers and institutions contributed, but two deserve special mention: Robert Engle's ARCH model in 1982 and JP Morgan's Value-at-Risk method in 1994. Yet it wasn't until 1996 that the second Kaizen phase got the official stamp of approval, when the Basel committee updated Basel I with the Amendment to the Capital Accord to Incorporate Market Risks, heralding the birth of scientific financial risk management. The regulators thought until then that risk belonged in buckets. Money lent to the government in the risk-free bucket. Most loans to corporations are low risk, while those to hot dog stands are high risk. The 1996 amendment upended all of this, introducing the internal ratings-based (IRB) approach. IRB meant that the most sophisticated banks got to use a riskometer to identify the risk of each of its activities, like determining bank capital, what JP Morgan wanted when it proposed Value-at-Risk two years earlier. The timing of the 1996 amendment is not coincidental.

Practically every financial institution followed the lead. Academics started churning out papers on risk management, universities created courses in risk management and risk forecasting, and risk consultants pushed into every financial institution. A wave of optimism hit the financial risk management community. It looked as if financial risk had been successfully reduced to an engineering problem, Kaizen-style—financial risk management became scientific. Just like structural engineers design safe bridges, financial engineers create safe banks and financial systems.

I am as guilty as anybody. I paid for my house in London by teaching executive education courses on implementing Value-at-Risk techniques. And have written a book called *Financial Risk Forecasting*. One of my LSE masters courses is called Quantitative Methods for Finance and Risk Analysis, all about implementing the techniques in my risk-forecasting book.

While the first phase of financial engineering was about theory and the second statistics, a significant problem was left unaddressed. Riskometers are complicated beasts. They want to be fed with a lot of complex financial data, and although there is a lot of data in finance, it is not easy to work with. Databases are inconsistent, full of errors, and much of the data is incredibly complicated, with arcane, inconsistent conventions. There can be multiple standards for measuring the same thing. To this day there is no single surefire way to identify a particular financial institution in this sea of data. Suppose two financial institutions trade with each other. Even if both report the trade to the authorities, it may be impossible for the authority to match the trades because of the lack of uniform trade identifiers.

We need a central place where financial institutions can access all the data they need, cleaned and synchronized. They can feed in their positions, run ready-made models on the data, or, even better, have artificial intelligence manage it all. The financial system version of Amazon Web Services (AWS). I am a huge fan of AWS. Before I started using it I was always looking for computational resources, building expensive machines in my office, and trying to get accounts on high-performance computers. Then I discovered AWS, and it was a revelation. Instead of doing difficult things in-house, having to be an expert in hardware and operating systems and high-performance software, I could outsource it all. The complexity and costs went down and efficiency went up. I use AWS every day.

The financial system version of the Amazon cloud is Aladdin and Risk-Metrics, products of BlackRock and MSCI, respectively. There are other vendors, but as cloud computing is a business with increasing returns to scale, those two are dominant, especially Aladdin. But I have a soft spot for RiskMetrics. It is the name given by JP Morgan to the model they recommended for estimating Value-at-Risk when they proposed it in 1994, the EWMA model. JP Morgan then realized that the name RiskMetrics was too valuable to be given to a mere statistical model and assigned it to the risk management division, which they eventually spun off. To this day, you run into people referring to the EWMA model as RiskMetrics. While I understand JP Morgan's sensible commercial decision to repurpose the name, I wish I could still use it instead of the unpronounceable EWMA. Aladdin's and RiskMetric's promise is that users won't have to buy and maintain expensive, inconsistent databases and hire an army of systems engineers and programmers and financial engineers to run the models. They can outsource it to the cloud. Let artificial intelligence take care of all the gory details.

So What Does the Kaizen Revolution Do to Risk?

The three phases of financial engineering—that is, the theory of Markowitz, the empirics of Robert Engle and JP Morgan, and the riskometers to the cloud—make it much easier to manage financial risk. All good, right? Not so fast. All that technology has not overcome the more fundamental problems about the reliability and inconsistency of the riskometers.

Demonstrating how riskometers disagree is easy. The Swiss currency appreciation discussed in chapter 10 is one example. Suppose I take a common concept of risk, one that is embedded in Basel III—Expected Shortfall—and apply it to returns on the S&P 500 index and Amazon

Table 2. Expected shortfall on a $1,000 portfolio, 1 September 2020

Asset	HS	EWMA	GARCH	t-GARCH	EVT
S&P 500	$64.7	$20.2	$18.4	$34.2	$67.8
AMZN	$66.2	$53.0	$43.8	$107.0	$70.9

Source: Author's calculations

stock prices. I then estimate the Expected Shortfall with six of the most common techniques and show the results in Table 2. The highest risk reading is more than three times that of the lowest. Similar results would obtain for other assets and times. For a lot more examples you can go to my website, extremerisk.org, where I estimate risk every day.

Does it matter that the riskometers are so inconsistent? In theory it shouldn't. A good risk manager knows riskometers are imprecise. They know the strengths and weaknesses of each, treating them as a portfolio of methods, picking the best one for the problem at hand. For example, among the six in Table 2, EWMA is really simple, and nothing can go wrong when it's implemented. It reacts quickly to changing information. However, just like an overeager teenager, it can respond way too strongly. HS is the opposite, calm and stable: like a seasoned bureaucrat, it never gets ruffled. Which do you prefer? It depends. HS's conservativeness is an asset for day-to-day operations, but when a shock hits, you need a quick reaction, and that is when EWMA can be invaluable. Then, there is the dark horse of EVT, short for extreme value theory. Like a wise man who has nothing to say about day-to-day occurrences but tells us what we need to know about the extremes when everything goes wrong.

All the riskometers have their good sides, and a *good* risk manager will be guided by her intuition and experience. Seeing EWMA is $20.2 and GARCH $18.4, while HS is $64.7, tells her that short-term risk not only has fallen quite a bit recently but also is still relatively low by historical standards. EVT says long-term risk is not affected very much by Covid-19. The risk manager knows each number tells a different part of the story, and by using all of them she gets a much more complete picture.

The problem is that such subjective judgment may not be acceptable. Where the professional risk manager draws important lessons from the diversity of measurements, the uninitiated see a problem. It is the same asset. How can risk be so different? You know, they are all measuring the same true process—risk—and if they disagree, one must be accurate and the rest wrong. And that is precisely the conclusion the Basel committee and the European Banking Authority reached when they saw the inconsistency in risk measurements. The solution then is to pick one riskometer—of course, the best of breed—and mandate its use. So does that matter? Yes, if every bank has to use the same riskometer, they always see the risk in the same way—their beliefs get harmonized. The regulators would respond by saying that the banks can choose their own riskometers; yes, to some extent, but the wiggle room is really small.

There is an interesting consequence of mandating all banks to use the same riskometer. Under current financial regulations, banks have to measure risk from proprietary trading by 97.5 percent Expected Shortfall. In plain English that means risk is the amount of money they expect to lose on the worst day in every two months. So, if a bank holds $1 million worth of Amazon stock and uses the EWMA riskometer (see Table 2), then the risk on the day I did the measurement was $53,000, that is, the bank was expected to lose $53,000 one day every two months.

The law of the land is 97.5 percent Expected Shortfall. Does it matter? Yes, for two reasons. The first is the question of whether the 97.5 percent Expected Shortfall is the correct risk to measure. After all, it captures the worst day every two months and says little about any other type of event. Earlier, I gave the example of Mary, Ann, and Paul, who all invest in Google but all have different objectives for their investment. Paul cares about short-term fluctuations, Ann is concerned about big losses in the next half-year, and Mary worries about the pension she will start drawing in half a century. The 97.5 percent Expected Shortfall risk measure provides no valuable information for Mary and her pension problem and little for Paul and Ann. It would be unfortunate if Mary lived in one of the countries mandating the use of Expected Shortfall for pension funds. The more interesting question is what the 97.5 percent Expected Shortfall does to the market.

Imagine the total amount of risk is a balloon and that the balloon covers all possible outcomes. We first squeeze the balloon in one place (Figure 36). What happens? The obvious. The place where we squeeze narrows, and the risk pops out everywhere else. In the second figure, three hands squeeze in different places, so risk is much more uniformly

Figure 36. Squeezing risk. Credit: Lukas Bischoff/IllustrationX.

managed and never balloons out. Because we target the same part of the risk universe—the 97.5 percent Expected Shortfall—that type of risk falls. But like a balloon, it ends up getting squeezed out elsewhere. And one part that will get squeezed is the extreme left tail, the big, nasty events that blow up banks and cause banking crises. Perversely, by mandating the 97.5 percent Expected Shortfall, the financial authorities increase the most dangerous types of risk. The law of unintended consequences. Yet another example of lowering volatility and fattening the tails.

When the Basel committee and the European Banking Authority acknowledged that riskometers give very inconsistent measurements, the interesting thing is how they saw the problem and what they proposed. They could have said, "Okay, this is a known problem, and we want to incorporate best practices in risk management into the regulation process." That means running multiple riskometers on the same assets and using the strengths of each in meeting the objectives of the regulations. How good risk managers work in practice. No. That is not what the authorities said. They expressed concern and concluded that the inconsistency meant that some banks were using low-quality riskometers. It was essential to require banks to use only the best. In other words, we need to find the best riskometer and force all banks to use that and only that riskometer. Why would the authorities have come to that conclusion? It is not that they don't know better. Having talked to a lot of regulators, I have concluded the answer has to do with philosophy. If regulation is risk-based, we must measure risk accurately, meaning models should give the same assessment of the risk of a particular exposure. Otherwise, risk-based regulations, like the Basel Accords, are fundamentally unsound. As the regulators see it, their mission depends on the one true model, even if few would admit to that.

The risk philosophy has further interesting consequences because of bank lobbying. If we make regulations risk sensitive—that is, set risk targets for banks and specify the methodological approaches as we do in the Basel Accords—then the output of the riskometers has a material impact on banks. Suppose we have two banks, call them A and B, with an identical portfolio, perhaps $1 million in Amazon. If A uses the t-GARCH riskometer and B GARCH, then A has a risk of $107,000 and B only $43,800. Because minimum capital is three times the risk, just imagine how loudly A will scream, doing everything in its power to switch riskometers.

It all ends with a race to the bottom, whereby every bank wants to use the riskometer that gives the lowest risk readings. The only way to prevent that is for the authorities to decide on which riskometers are acceptable. We then get an iterative process between banks wanting to measure risk as low as possible and the regulators reducing the banks' freedom to measure risk as they see fit. The resulting ratcheting between the risk philosophy and bank interests can end only one way: the regulators end up dictating how banks should measure risk. Convergence to the "one true model."

I think a lot of people would react to this by saying, "So what!" We are adopting best practices, the best riskometer, which means we will measure risk in the best possible way. That might be correct if we look at each bank in isolation and if they are small. However, for larger banks and especially for the financial system in its entirety, there are at least three serious consequences: procyclicality, transfer of responsibilities, and ossification.

Start with procyclicality. I've spilled a lot of ink on it in this book and so will be brief. If everybody ends up using similar or identical riskometers, we harmonize beliefs and action. Everybody reacts in the same way to shocks, all buying and selling the same assets, amplifying the cycles: procyclicality and systemic risk.

The second problem is more insidious. The more we transfer responsibility to the financial authorities, the more obligation they have for ensuring things go well. Suppose the authority is in charge of how risk is measured; then, when the next crisis comes along, the critics will say, "Why did the authorities pick such a stupid way to measure risk?" The banks will say, "We did nothing wrong. We followed the guidelines coming from the authority. Give us a bailout." So, because the regulators end up being the risk modeler for the banking system, they are also responsible for its well-being, and hence to blame for large losses.

The final problem is that even if the authority manages to pick the best riskometer of all possible worlds—the one riskometer that will not fail—it will still end up ossifying. The technical issue is both the pace and the process of designing regulations. Financial regulations, especially global rules, change slowly. Basel I took effect in 1992. The Basel II's design process started in the mid-1990s, and it was partially implemented only in 2007. As for the postcrisis regulations, Basel III has been in discussion since 2008. One and a half decades pass between each iteration of the global banking regulations. Throughout the process the regulators are bombarded by lobbying from industry and governments. They have to be seen as fair and transparent. The rules need to be as technically undemanding as possible.

Even if the designers of financial regulations manage to pick the very best riskometer today, it will be put into practice years in the future and used for decades thereafter. Over that time the riskometer will become increasingly out of date—ossified—capturing irrelevant risks and neglecting important ones, giving banks ample scope for manipulation. Supervisory-mandated riskometers are much more likely to stagnate than riskometers developed internally in a competitive environment, Kaizen style.

When I read the Basel committee's and the European Banking Authority's reports on risk, I wrote a blog piece on the implications, "Towards a More Procyclical Financial System," arguing that it was inevitable for the authorities to coalesce around a single riskometer. A few weeks later I did a presentation at a central bank event, and a few of the people criticized me, saying words to the effect of "We are not stupid. Everybody knows harmonizing riskometers is procyclical. The reports you cited are just expressing that for political reasons; we don't really mean it." Okay, having participated in the drafting of such reports, I know the writing process is intensely political. A lot of people and entities want to shape the results. So every line is the result of fraught negotiations. Maybe neither the Basel committee nor the European Banking Authority meant to imply that they prefer riskometer harmonization. Maybe they tried so hard to paper over disagreements that a misunderstanding slipped out. But I have more evidence. Harmonizing riskometers is precisely what the authorities do in practice.

Finance and Scientific Socialism

One of the things I find so fascinating in finance is that while so many of the people who work in the financial system proclaim a belief in free markets—indeed, many see themselves as libertarians—they go about their business in a very socialistic way, with no apparent irony. Bailouts are the obvious example: privatize profits and socialize losses. Just about every bank in the United States got a bailout in 2008.

More relevant here is that the way we measure and manage risk has its roots in an old idea called scientific socialism, a concept proposed by Friedrich Engels in his book *Socialism: Utopian and Scientific*. We don't hear much about scientific socialism anymore, but it used to be quite familiar. The idea is that we can avoid all the worst aspects of capitalism by scientifically creating a better socialist society. Scientific socialism gives us testable theories based on empirical observations. When reality does not happen as predicted by theory, ad hoc assumptions are added to make theory fit the facts.

The idea that theory can be made to fit the facts is why Karl Popper, in his book *The Open Society and Its Enemies*, described scientific socialism as a pseudoscience. Theory can be incompatible with all observations and still be scientific, but the opposite is not true. A theory that is compatible with all possible outcomes precisely because it has been modified to accommodate a particular observation is not scientific. Popper argued that science is founded on testable theories based on empirical observations; theories are accepted, changed, or refuted on the basis of actual outcomes. Since one cannot test the claims of scientific socialism, and hence not prove it or disprove it, it is pseudoscientific.

What does that have to do with the management of financial risk? Quite a lot, actually. No measurement of risk can be properly validated because risk is latent. Risk is not directly observable, so there is nothing concrete a risk forecast can be related to. We have to compare it to some other model's output, one that has its own set of untestable assumptions and can create an infinite number of statements about what is essential, most of which are mutually inconsistent. In Karl Popper's language, since we can't falsify a risk forecast, it is not scientific.

The riskometer is pseudoscientific in the same way scientific socialism is, but it doesn't present itself as such. It is the objective, scientific way to measure risk. By using the riskometer, we supposedly move away from subjectivity, incompetence, and even corruption. But we don't. The edifice on which we build our control of the financial system, the riskometer, is no more scientific than scientific socialism. And all the free market supporters working in finance have adopted one of the most fundamental tenets of Marxism in their day-to-day work.

The definition of the term "trilemma" is that when faced with three choices we can only pick two. When it comes to managing a risky financial system, we have three options: uniformity, efficiency, or stability. Which do we pick? So far, all the incumbent powers in the financial system, the private institutions, and the regulators favor uniformity and efficiency. The commercial institutions because it reduces competition and makes money for them, and the regulators because it makes their job easier. There are two lessons one can take from this: either we need better technology or we do something different.

12

All about BoB:
Robots and the Future of Risk

I'm sorry, Dave, I'm afraid I can't do that.
—2001: A Space Odyssey

Figure 37. Credit: Copyright © Ricardo Galvão.

I was recently at a conference on financial regulation where one of the speakers gave a presentation on how artificial intelligence, AI, would change the world for the better. I got into a debate with him. What follows is a fictionalized account of the conversation, taking into account other, similar discussions:

SPEAKER, EXCITED TECHNOLOGY ENTHUSIAST.
AI is changing the world. Computers double in speed every eighteen

months. We now have self-driving cars and robo-advisors and all sorts of fantastic technology that is rapidly improving society. AI will revolutionize the financial system and give us fantastic financial regulations.

ME, OLD FOGEY/CLUELESS SKEPTIC. What about all the recent AI failures, like Facebook's and YouTube's inability to eliminate scams, hate speech, antivaccination propaganda, and advertisements for fake products?

SPEAKER. Give it time. Ten years ago nobody thought cars could drive themselves. Remember Moore's law.

ME. So is there anything you can't see computers doing better than humans?

SPEAKER. There are many things AI cannot do today, but technology is advancing rapidly, and AI can do new things every day. There is nothing AI will not be able to do, and it will all be wonderful. Just keep your mind open.

ME. But the financial system is very complex, and it is surely beyond the ability of any computer algorithm to keep it under control.

SPEAKER. No. That is precisely why AI will be so valuable. Put it in charge, and it will master all the complexity human beings can't. Financial crises will be a thing of the past, and the financial system will be superefficient. Just wait and see.

I walked away intrigued but skeptical. The next thing I did was to sit down and investigate whether my interlocutor was right. I ended up writing a series of articles on the subject.

We might think the financial system is the ideal application for AI. After all, it generates almost infinite amounts of data, plenty for AI to train on. Every minute decision is recorded, trades are stamped to the microsecond. Emails, messages, and phone calls are recorded. But data does not equal information, and making sense of all this data flow is like drinking from a fire hose. Even worse, the information about the next crisis event might not even be in this sea of data. I've concluded that the speaker was mostly wrong.

What Is Artificial Intelligence?

The computer says no.
—*Carol Beer*

A lot has been written about AI, and there is no need to repeat that here. I highly recommend Stuart Russel's book *Human Compatible*. But I need to establish where I'm coming from, so bear with me. The idea behind AI is that a computer learns about the world so it can make decisions by itself. It can be something as simple as playing a game, as complex as driving cars, and it can even regulate the financial system. Describing AI is not straightforward; not even the experts agree. Let's start with machine learning, a computer algorithm that uses available data to learn about the world that created that data. The algorithm studies all the patterns and complicated causal relationships. What is magical is that it can do so without human intervention: unsupervised learning. That is different from the way we usually do science, where we start with some idea of how the world might work—a theory—and see if data is compatible with that theory.

A supermarket might use machine learning to figure out where best to place Coca-Cola cans to maximize sales. The data scientist takes all the historical observations on Coca-Cola sales, the weather, and demographics. She runs the data through her machine-learning algorithm and then tells the supermarket where best to place the cans on the shelf. That is a lot of data. For a chain like Walmart it can easily be quadrillions of observations. Precisely what is called big data. The critical thing is that the machine-learning algorithm doing this doesn't need to know anything about Coca-Cola or supermarkets—it just gets data and finds the patterns.

There is no such thing as a free lunch, and there is a trade-off. Machine learning needs a lot of data, much more than most other statistical applications. It needs big data. The reason is that it knows nothing about the world and so has to learn everything from the data. Human beings know the world and bring prior information—cultural, economic, historical, and so on—to bear on a problem and thus need a lot less data. They know theory, allowing traditional statistics to work with small datasets.

While machine learning is all about extracting information from a data set, the objective of AI is to make decisions based on that data. AI is used to make a lot of decisions today. In the 2000s British comedy show *Little Britain,* a recurring sketch featured a bank loan officer named Carol Beer, who responded to every customer query by typing into her computer and then answering, "The computer says no," even to the most reasonable of requests.

The term AI is a bit of a misnomer, though. The AI of today isn't intelligent in the sense a human being is intelligent. It merely knows a lot about what-if rules. If the traffic light flashes red, stop. If it flashes green, look at the traffic and then go. AI replicates the human brain, sort of. The average human brain has eighty-six billion neurons, all interconnected by synapses to form neural networks. A computer with a large enough number of artificial neurons wired in the same way could become intelligent—in theory. We haven't reached that stage yet. We are still competing with the average insect. Take cockroaches. They are among the smartest of insects and can learn and adapt to their environment, not to mention being the only animal that supposedly will survive a nuclear war. They are not the most social of animals but do exhibit complex social behavior. AI has not caught up with cockroaches. In the words of the theoretical physicist Michio Kaku, "At the present time, our most advanced robots . . . have the collective intelligence and wisdom of a cockroach; a mentally challenged cockroach; a lobotomized, mentally challenged cockroach."[1]

Moore's law, named after Gordon Moore, the cofounder of Intel, observed that the number of transistors in a microchip doubles every eighteen months. Will that help? That was exactly what the technology enthusiast I debated with argued. When I did my PhD, I ran my computer code on a $27 million Cray Y-MP supercomputer. Time on the Cray was carefully rationed, and the computing jobs of an economics PhD student did not get first priority. I learned that the queue of jobs tended to finish early over the weekend, so by waking up at four on Sunday mornings and going to the office I could have the Cray all to myself. I did this way too often. When I was in Paris recently, I saw a Cray Y-MP in the Science Museum. The iPhone in my pocket is many times faster. The speed of computation has increased exponentially since before I was born, and it shows little sign of slowing down.

Will Moore's law help AI catch up with human intelligence? The short answer is no. Moore's law is about the speed of computations, and the problem with AI catching up with humans is not about speed. It is about concepts. The quality of today's AI algorithms simply cannot take us very far, regardless of how fast computers are. Yet breakthroughs can happen overnight, and someone may already have thought of a completely new algorithm, one that allows AI to surpass humans. Or it may never happen.

The pundits call that eventuality the technological singularity, and some think it is not too far away. In the words of Ray Kurzweil, Google's director of engineering, "2029 is the consistent date I have predicted for when an AI will pass a valid Turing test and therefore achieve human levels of intelligence. I have set the date 2045 for the 'Singularity' which is when we will multiply our effective intelligence a billion fold by merging with the intelligence we have created."[2]

However, we don't need the singularity for AI to be useful; it doesn't need human intelligence and not even that of a cockroach or an ant to be useful. The more confined a problem is, the better AI performs, which is why it excels at playing games with a known set of rules and clear objectives. A celebrated recent AI is Google's AlphaGo Zero, which, being instructed only with the rules of the game of Go, was able to learn over the span of three days how to conquer its predecessor AlphaGo, which had earlier defeated the Go world champion.

Does being good at playing complicated games mean that one is good at other things? A lot of people think so. The Soviet Union venerated its chess players, believing that if one could master the complexities of chess strategy, one should also be able to manage a centrally planned economy or fight a war. Lenin was a serious chess player, and Stalin even more so. However, AI that is good at chess is much more likely to be an idiot savant, like the main character in the movie *Rain Man*. Being good at chess says nothing about the ability to do other things, such as regulating the financial system or driving a car. Games like chess have a predefined number of actions a player can take, and all the information about the state of the game is visible to the players. In the language of game theorists, information is complete, and the action space is finite.

This is also why AI can, sort of, drive cars. There is a lot of information to learn from, the rules are well understood, and they don't change much. Even then, AI can drive only on highways, and then only if the weather is not too bad. It is far from being able to drive in cities, not to mention in deep snow, where all the signs are hidden. Perhaps the worst challenge for a car-driving AI is human beings. We are unpredictable and can behave in a way that upsets self-driving cars. In response, some AI designers have proposed reprogramming humans.[3]

The more we move away from the confined space of board games and driving on the highway, the worse AI performs. It is not good at playing games in which information is incomplete and the action space ill-defined. I suspect it would not do well in my favorite game, Diplomacy. I once played Diplomacy over the internet with a few friends, one of whom is a politician. He beat us hands down, showing deviousness and strategy that none of the other players had. I find it hard to believe AI will beat him any time soon. It is especially challenging for AI if the rules evolve during play, as happens in most human endeavors.

I have my own personal test for robots and artificial intelligence. Today, I can pay someone who has never been to my house $100 to do my laundry. He comes to my university office, and I give him money, keys, and my home address. He finds his way to my house, gets in, finds my laundry baskets and washing machine, figures out how to operate it and where to find the detergent. He manages to do the laundry and put it into my closet and cupboards, and then he slides my keys through the mail slot on my door when done. All without any explanation or instruction. The technology involved is older than I am. When I find AI that can do that, I will be impressed.

The Bank of England Bot: BoB

A few years ago the chief economist of the Bank of England, Andy Haldane, envisioned a new way to control the financial system, one in which the regulator will track "the global flow of funds in close to real time (from a *Star Trek* chair, using a bank of monitors), in much the same way as happens with global weather systems and global internet traffic. Its centerpiece would be a global map of financial flows."[4] Let's give him a name, BoB, short for the Bank of England bot (see Figure 37). BoB is the future AI who oversees the British financial system. BoB will take all the data and human behavior and use that to figure out all the contingencies and identify fragilities, inefficiencies, and systemic risk. Suppose further that other major financial centers also develop their version of BoB, like Fran and Edith, and all AI are friendly and cooperating with each other. The financial institutions will also have their AI: Gus, Mary, and Betty. Is this a pie-in-the-sky futuristic vision doomed to failure, like the flying cars of the 1970s? No. While BoB and friends don't exist yet, the technology to create them is already here. Well, most of it. We just lack the will.

Roboregulators already exist in microprudential regulatory agencies. The latest buzzword is RegTech, short for regulation technology. Its chief cheerleader, the UK's Financial Conduct Authority (FCA), defines RegTech as the "adoption of new technologies to facilitate the delivery of regulatory requirements." I was involved with RegTech research over the past few years because of a joint research program conducted by the FCA, my research center, and other interested parties.

The starting point is the rulebook, all the rules and regulations which, if printed out, create a stack of paper two meters high. The FCA has translated the rulebook into an AI engine so it can check it for inconsistencies and give faster and better advice. Financial institutions corresponding with the FCA bot find that it answers much better than its human colleagues. AI is also revolutionizing risk management in banks. The first step in creating a risk management AI is to develop and manage riskometers, an easy task for AI. It quickly learns all the approved models, the data is readily accessible, and it is easy for it to create riskometers. A lot of financial institutions have AI engines today that do precisely that. The AI then needs to learn about all a bank's investments, the individuals who made them, and, voilà, we have a functioning risk management AI. The necessary information is already inside banks' information technology infrastructure, and there are no insurmountable technological hurdles along the way. And if there are, just use Aladdin or RiskMetrics. The cost savings will be enormous. The bank can replace most risk modelers, risk managers, and compliance officers with AI. The technology is already here. All that remains to be done is to inform the AI of a bank's high-level objectives. The machine can then automatically manage risk, recommend who gets fired or gets a bonus, and advise on how to invest.

Risk management and microprudential supervision are the ideal uses for AI—they enforce compliance with clearly defined rules and processes based on vast amounts of structured data. They have access to closely monitored human behavior, are guided by precise, high-level objectives, and produce directly observed outcomes. Just as in games, information is mostly complete and the action space finite. There is still some way to go, but it is eminently conceivable for AI to take over many current functions given the trajectory of technological advancement. The main hindrance is not technology but legal, political, and social considerations.

The macroprudential problem is different because all the preconditions for AI to perform well are absent. Data is scarce. The events being controlled are mostly unique and very infrequent. After all, the typical OECD country suffers a systemic crisis only one year out of every forty-three, giving AI precious little to train on. Even worse, when the authorities and the private institutions learn from past crises, they tend not to repeat mistakes, instead creating new ones, frustrating AI. I looked into the main issues facing AI doing macroprudential policy in a recent paper with two of my collaborators, Robert Macrae and Andreas Uthemann, titled "Artificial Intelligence and Systemic Risk" (the remainder of this chapter is based on that work). There are four areas we identify as being of particular concern: procyclicality, unknown unknowns, need for trust, and optimization against the system.

Banking is inherently procyclical. Banks lend freely in good times, amplifying booms, then in turn they contract-lend when things turn sour, causing a credit crunch. Modern financial regulations and risk management practices further exacerbate procyclicality because of their dependence on riskometers and risk dashboards. Riskometers work by looking at recent history, and if that recent history seems stable the riskometers tell us risk is low. The problem is that price data tends to be more calm in upturns than in downturns, and any backward-looking, data-driven process, including the machine learning that feeds AI, will identify risk as being low in quiet times and high after a crisis—the measurement process itself is procyclical. The way we use the output of riskometers is also procyclical. They feed risk-control systems and regulations so that the portfolio managers and loan officers and the traders who make decisions on risky investments also amplify the financial cycle. Of course, there is nothing inherently AI about that. But my contention is that AI makes the problem worse because of the particular way it interacts with risk measurement and management.

The AI engines at financial institutions and regulators all have access to the same data and machine-learning techniques, all have significant computational resources. The various AI engines will inevitably converge to the same riskometer much more rapidly than human risk modelers, thus harmonizing knowledge. AI will also harmonize action, how the financial institutions react to new information. It has a much better understanding of best practices than any human being does. It knows what should be done and what prevented. The AI will push banks to manage risk in the same way.

All of this is procyclical because of how it interacts with the banks' objective functions, maximizing profits subject to constraints. The more similar information is, the closer the various banks' solutions become to each other. That means crowded trades so the financial cycle gets amplified. Ultimately, AI is procyclical because it favors monoculture. Because it has more information than human risk managers, the solutions it recommends become increasingly similar across the industry. Even then, the AI would not necessarily be all that procyclical if it were not for all the external constraints, most important, regulations. The feedback between regulations and AI is the most dangerous driver of monoculture and systemic risk.

If we ask AI to manage financial stability, where will it look for danger? With the benefit of hindsight there are plenty of warning signals for the 2008 crisis, and many have criticized the human regulators for missing all of them. Could AI have done any better? Unlikely. Suppose there are no observations of the consequences of subprime mortgages being put into structured credit products with hidden liquidity guarantees, crossing multiple jurisdictions, institutional categories, and countries. Then there is nothing for AI to learn from. It is conceivable that an appropriately instructed AI engine might, in 2008, have noticed the connections between house prices, mortgage defaults, and default correlations, the factors that determine the prices of CDOs. It could also have realized the fragility of the structured credit products when liquidity evaporates. Even if AI identified each individual step, the likelihood that it would put all the pieces together is quite remote, necessary for the chain of vulnerabilities to be discovered. We are asking a lot, not only of AI but also of the banks and the national financial authorities who would have to allow such intrusive data-driven international supervision.

The ability to successfully scan the financial system for systemic risk hinges on where the vulnerability lies. Everyday factors, well founded in economic theory, drive financial crises. Yet the underlying details are usually unique to each event. After each crisis, regulators and financial institutions learn, adapt processes, and tend not to repeat the same mistakes.

I suspect that BoB will focus on the least important types of risk, the exogenous risk that is readily measured while missing the more dangerous endogenous risk. It will automate and reinforce the adoption of mistaken assumptions that are already a central element of current crises. In doing so, it will make the resulting complacency even stronger. In other words, BoB will be what the Soviet central planner Hayek warned us against in his article "The Use of Knowledge in Society." The problem is one of how information aggregates, and BoB will have all the individual pieces but will not know how to connect the dots. BoB measures all the minute details of how a financial institution operates so he can understand all the risks. He then aggregates the results to quantify not only the risk of an individual institution but also systemic risk. Quadrillions of bits of tiny risks that end up as simple summary measures. The risk-weighted assets of a bank and the European Central Bank's systemic-risk dashboard. How well does that work? About as well as it did for Gosplan, the State Planning Committee of the USSR: almost all the relevant information is lost. Okay, you may retort. The current human-centered setup is no better. Nothing in this tells us AI makes it worse, and it could certainly do better because it will be much better at solving the aggregation problem. Perhaps, if it were not for trust.

I have presented the work discussed here many times, and the most frequent pushback I get is on the question of trust: "Jón, I may buy your conclusions, but it doesn't matter because we will never put AI in charge of anything important." I disagree because trust has a sneaky way of creeping up on us. Twenty years ago almost nobody trusted internet banking. Then, seeing that it works, almost everybody today uses online banking. Very few people would have trusted computers to fly aircraft or drive cars a quarter of a century ago, and now we mostly do. We are happy for AI to control surgical robots. AI is proving its worth in critical day-to-day applications, and that creates trust. The more we see AI outperforming human beings, the more we prefer AI decision makers to humans.

The guardians of financial stability, the central banks, are already us-ing AI. I recently gave a talk on AI at a central bank, where the audience assured me AI made no decisions. Well, that day I could not easily enter the central bank because the AI controlling the security system didn't like me. When I told that to the audience, they responded by saying, "We meant AI controls nothing important." They got it wrong. The central banks already employ AI in a variety of places, doing a good job today, building trust. And there are plenty of cost savings to be had. The staff might not like it, but the board sees the benefits of replacing an army of PhD-level economists with computers.

And herein lies the problem. In the 1980s AI called EURISKO used a cute trick to defeat all of its human competitors in a naval wargame: it sank its slowest ships to achieve better maneuverability than its human competitors. An example of what is known as reward hacking, something human beings are, of course, expert in.[5] EURISKO's creator, Douglas Lenat, notes that "what EURISKO found were not fundamental rules for fleet and ship design; rather, it uncovered anomalies, fortuitous inter-actions among rules, unrealistic loopholes that hadn't been foreseen by the designers of the TCS simulation system." Each of EURISKO's three successive victories resulted in rules changes intended to prevent a repeat. The only thing that proved effective in the end was to disinvite Lenat and his AI.

And that is the problem with AI. How do we know it will do the right thing? Human admirals don't have to be told they can't sink their own ships. They just know. AI has to be told. But the world is complex, and it is impossible to create a rule covering every eventuality. BoB will eventually run into cases in which he makes critical decisions in a way no human would. And that is where humans have the advantage over AI. Of course, human decision makers mess up more often than BoB. But there is a crucial difference. The former also come with a lifetime of experience and knowledge of relevant fields, like philosophy, history, and ethics, al-lowing them to react to unforeseen circumstances and make decisions subject to political and ethical standards without it being necessary to spell them out.

Before putting humans in charge, we can ask them how they would make decisions in hypothetical scenarios and, crucially, ask them to justify their decisions. They can be held to account and be required to testify to Senate committees. If they mess up, they can be fired, punished, incarcerated, lose their reputation and even their lives. You can't do any of that with AI. Nobody knows how it reasons or decides, and it cannot explain itself. You can hold the AI to account, but it will not care. But AI has some advantages. The human might be incompetent, callous, or corrupt, unlike AI, which, paradoxically, can behave more humanely than humans. Judges sentence people more harshly when they come up in front of them an hour before lunch as opposed to an hour after. AI has no such biases.

How important, then, is the question of trust? It depends on what we ask of AI. Trust is not all that important for microprudential regulations because the existing rulebook already specifies the objectives and rules. There is little danger of AI making seriously wrong decisions. If it does, the short reporting timescales, the large number of repeated observations, and the relative unimportance of decisions mean we realize the problem quickly, allowing us to react in time. It is different with macroprudential regulations, macropru. The problem is unbounded, the system is infinitely complex, the events under control are very infrequent, and almost all are unique. There is little to train the machine on, and the wrong decisions will be catastrophic. If we let a machine with fixed objectives interact with an infinitely complex environment, the outcome is unexpected behavior. AI will run into cases in which it makes critical decisions in a way no human would—the financial version of sinking its own ships. The chance of a catastrophic outcome increases over time when the machine is forced to reason about unforeseen contingencies. The consequences could be disastrous, perhaps a Minsky moment.

Optimization against the System

> Any observed statistical regularity will tend to collapse once pressure is placed upon it for control purposes.
> —*Goodhart's Law*

Every time we try to control people's behavior, they evade. It's in our human nature. Why the Panopticon exists. We have to continually guard against those who seek to undermine the controls. For the lack of a better phrase, I will call these people hostile agents, those intent on exploiting the system for private gain by optimizing against the system. People do this all the time, and there is nothing uniquely AI about it. But AI has inherent weaknesses that make optimization against the system particularly dangerous.

The starting point is that the very fact we exercise control changes the system—exactly why the epigraph above is so prescient. The world looks different with and without the control. In most applications, optimization against the system is not very important. Human drivers exploit self-driving cars for their own advantage. They know the self-driving car follows the rules and drives conservatively and predictably. It is easy for the human to gain an advantage when it comes to merging traffic, at four-way stops, and in any situation in which drivers are competing. However, such optimization against the system is quite limited. The cost of failure is local and small, and, most important, the drivers do not influence the rules of the game.

And that is the crucial difference between most AI applications and the regulation of the financial system. While human drivers taking advantage of a Tesla on the freeway cannot build new roads to disadvantage the Tesla or change the traffic rules or even move signs around, their counterparts in the financial system can do all of that. Because the rules and the structure of the financial system are mutable, the financial system is a particularly fertile ground for optimization against the system. There is a lot of money to be made, the adversaries are smart and well resourced, the system is infinitely complex, and there are plenty of places to misbehave. Ultimately, the financial system's controllers are forever doomed to be on the losing end of a cat and mouse game.

The complexity of finance offers many ways for economic agents to bypass regulations, perhaps by creating new financial instruments that mimic controlled instruments but are regulated differently, the driver of much financial innovation. A good example is high-frequency trading. The SEC in the United States has repeatedly changed the rules, but the high-frequency trading firms are still quite able to exploit regular investors, as noted in Michael Lewis's book *Flash Boys*.

Most hostile agents don't deliberately break the law. Most, but not all. Rogue traders have always been around. Take Nick Leeson and Kweku

Adoboli. Leeson was trading futures contracts for the Barings bank in Singapore and exploited the "error account," numbered 88888—meaning super lucky in Chinese. It was supposed to be used to correct mistakes in trading, but Leeson used it to hide his trading losses, which amounted to $1.4 billion. Adoboli, trading on behalf of UBS, was making unauthorized trades, entering false information into the bank's computers to hide his actions. His eventual losses amounted to $2 billion. Leeson and Adoboli were just individuals who illegally manipulated the control systems, and, though materially important to their employer, their impact on society was negligible.

A more insidious example of optimizing against the system is when an entire bank or a group of financial institutions join forces in destabilizing the system. There may be nothing illegal about what they are doing. It is quite possible they don't even know that they are destabilizing, and those in charge may be blissfully unaware of the consequences of what is going on. A good example is all the dangerous financial instruments created before the crisis in 2008. Nobody had an overview of all the CDOs and conduits and all the other nefarious instruments that proved so damaging. They were all optimizing against the system in their own little parts of it, where everything looked okay. It was damaging only in the aggregate. We don't need a single big entity. The consequences are just as serious if optimization against the system involves many small, hostile agents. Their profit may be maximized if they coordinate their hostile actions. Acting as a wolf pack, sharing information, outwitting the controllers.

Even worse is a hostile agent intent on causing damage, a terrorist or a rogue nation. It is even harder to detect such agents because they don't play by the standard rules. The rogue trader is motivated by profit and a desire not to be caught, limiting what he gets up to. If someone doesn't care about making a profit, it is much easier to cause damage. Can AI solve these problems? After all, BoB can patrol the financial system much more extensively than any human being can and use machine learning to find all the hidden connections. He knows everything that has happened and is a much better enforcer than humans. The microprudential AI will have the advantage over hostile agents. The stakes are small. There is ample information about repeated events, plenty of data for the AI to train on and learn all the hostiles' nefarious tricks. And that is why AI will be so valuable for both microprudential regulations and internal risk management and control, why we will be able to outsource to AI the vast majority of jobs in these functions.

Yet again, it is different for macroprudential regulations, where the hostile agents, intent on profiting or even causing damage, have the advantage over BoB. The macroprudential problem is a much bigger game than the microprudential. There will be hostile agents optimizing against the macro authorities, and while the AI might catch most, even almost all, it takes only one slipping through the cracks to cause a systemic crisis. Since the financial system is infinitely complex, there is only a small area for the controllers to patrol, so the hostiles just have to find another one that is not monitored. Often the boundaries between jurisdictions.

The Standard Defenses Won't Work

When someone hacks financial regulations, the regulator cannot respond within hours or days. It might have to wait decades.

When I have discussed optimization against the system with AI experts, they all recognize the problem but also add that defenses do exist. A self-driving car faced with hostile humans intent on taking advantage can respond by mimicking the human drivers' aggressiveness and irrationality. The AI selectively obeys the rules, even making its own rules. Except such a defense strategy does not work well in financial regulations. The reason is the need for transparency, fairness, simple rules, slow decision-making, and silos. Financial regulations must be transparent and enforced fairly. Randomized responses have to be programmed into the macroprudential AI, but it would be unacceptable for the AI to decide by itself which rules to enforce, not to mention being allowed to make new rules. Meanwhile, even if permissible, randomized responses will require the AI designers to specify the statistical distribution for how it will respond. Given time, that distribution can be reverse engineered.

The need for fairness and transparency also implies that the rules have to be simple and easily implemented. When I read financial regulations, it is remarkable how basic the models are, much simpler than those taught in university courses. But that very simplicity frustrates the standard defenses. It is hard to randomize responses when the rules are simple and crystal clear. And the rules don't change very often. The Basel rules are updated every couple of decades or so. Even at the local level, the relevant laws have to be passed by Parliament and then implemented by the supervisory agency. A process that is slow, transparent, with plenty of lobbying. When someone hacks financial regulations, the regulator cannot respond within hours or days. It might have to wait decades.

Then we have the silos. When the Icelandic banks failed in 2008, I talked to a senior European regulator about why the problems and misbehavior were not detected. He said, "Simple. The banks did not misbehave in any single jurisdiction. It was only in aggregate that they were causing serious damage." While the European authorities have now plugged that particular loophole, the problem remains. Even individual countries have multiple regulators, controlling ill-defined and ever-changing domains. When the German bank Wirecard failed due to fraud in 2020, the relevant regulator, Bafin, disclaimed any responsibility because it said it had decided it did not need to regulate Wirecard. Apparently nobody had responsibility for one of the largest German banks. The regulators vigorously patrol the boundaries of their domains. It's even worse internationally, where regulators are jealous of their data and powers, refusing to share and cooperate across borders. All helping the hostile agents to operate across jurisdictions without hindrance and frustrating AI. Ultimately, the AI engine's innate rationality, coupled with demands for transparency and fair play, puts it at a disadvantage over human regulators.

BoB might still have a fighting chance against the hostile agents if the financial system's structure remained static. If the system never changes, BoB learns more about the system every day and one day might be able do a perfect job. The problem is that the financial system isn't static. Not only is it infinitely complex for all practical purposes, it is endogenously infinitely complex, meaning the complexity is continually evolving in response to what everybody in the system is up to. The worst outcomes happen when seemingly unconnected parts of the financial system reveal previously hidden connections. The vulnerabilities spread and amplify through opaque channels, the dark areas nobody thought to be worried about. Competition makes the system adversarial, and any rules aiming to contain risk-taking become obstacles to be overcome.

The hostiles take full advantage. They are like cockroaches, scurrying out of the lit areas the authorities monitor into the shadows, and in an infinitely complex system find plenty of dark areas to feed on. The hostiles, like everybody working in the financial system, have an incentive to increase its complexity in a way that is very hard to detect. There are many ways to do so, perhaps by creating new types of financial instruments that have the potential to amplify risk across apparently distinct parts of the system.

All of these factors frustrate BoB's mission, but the ultimate problem is that BoB isn't smart enough to ensure financial stability and never will be. His computational problem is harder than that of his adversaries. BoB has to patrol the entire financial system, searching for the hidden corners inhabited by the hostile agents where instability thrives. The hostiles have to find only one vulnerability, one dark corner where they can feed. And that is a much simpler problem. The hostiles always have a computational advantage over BoB. Moore's law or technological developments do not help. The more we use AI in the financial system, the more the advantage tilts toward the hostile agents.

The Need for a Kill Switch

OK, computer, I want full manual control now.
—*Douglas Adams,* Hitchhiker's Guide to the Galaxy

Suppose BoB is put in charge of financial stability, where he talks to his counterparts in the private sector, perhaps Gus, Mary, and Betty. Those three are grandmasters in portfolio construction and risk management, trained in the entire corpus of historical asset price movements. They know everything that has ever happened and have a sensible structure permitting extensive extrapolation.

Suppose a new type of instability emerges. Being the most aggressive of the bunch, Gus smells a profit opportunity and goes on the attack, realizing that by attacking Mary and Betty he will make lots of money. And so he does. It may even dawn on him that attacking BoB is profitable. What prevents such an eventuality? Either Gus has to be told to desist or the profit-maximizing masters of Gus will have to foresee that eventuality.

But it is impossible to predict everything. The alternative is to have a kill switch. Will it be possible to turn BoB and the other AI off? The longer we leave them in charge, the harder it will be. BoB's knowledge of the financial system and his internal representation of data will be unintelligible to humans, and turning him off will disrupt the system in unforeseen ways. Even in a crisis, as when BoB is clearly making the wrong decisions, the side effects of turning him off might be worse.

And then there is a question of whether BoB will actually allow us to. That is precisely what Dave was trying to do in the quote from *2001: A Space Odyssey*. The AI engine has a purpose programmed into it, and being turned off prevents the AI from meeting its objectives, and therefore it may not allow us to do so.

Artificial intelligence will become increasingly helpful to the financial authorities—financial logic makes it certain, the cost savings are just so great. But not overnight. BoB will first have to earn our trust, but he will. That is fine for some purposes. BoB will do a fantastic job with microprudential regulations, allowing the authorities to dispense with expensive, slow, inconsistent humans. Replacing them with AI that performs cheaper and better on all levels. Not a problem because the microprudential problems are contained and involve repeated outcomes and precisely identified regulations, all playing to BoB's strength.

It is different with macropru. The events under control are very infrequent, and each is unique. The cost of failure is high. To perform well BoB will have to exercise control across borders and silos, randomize his responses, and create rules in a nontransparent manner. He has to understand causality and unforeseen cases and reason on a global rather than local basis. Meanwhile, he has to identify threats that have not yet culminated in bad outcomes. These are either unacceptable, beyond current capabilities, or both.

The cost of AI making the wrong decision can be catastrophic. Once we realize we can't live without AI, it will be too late to do anything about it. We might want to have a kill switch to turn BoB off if he starts misbehaving, but we will not get one. If AI will not save us, how best to regulate?

13

The Path Not to Take

The past informs the tools, but the threats come from the future.

Figure 38. Credit: Copyright © Ricardo Galvão.

It is devilishly difficult to bend the financial system to our will. We want the impossible: fat investment returns and high economic growth without too much risk. Not easy. The financial system is among the most elaborate of human constructs, so how does one make something infinitely complex do what we want? There are many ideas out there. Perhaps the best we can do is the setup we have now, what I call the modern philosophy of financial regulations. Some think technology will save us, maybe cryptocurrencies or central bank digital currencies. Others favor political solutions, like the libertarians, who think it best if the government stays away from finance, or the socialists, who want tough regulations to bend it to the will of society. And then there is the way forward I will propose in chapter 14, putting the inherent stabilizing forces of the financial system to good use.

What Is the Point of the Financial System and Financial Regulations?

The financial system is necessary, bringing financial intermediation: the channeling of funds from one person to another across time and space. It reallocates resources, diversifies risk, allows us to build pensions for old age, and helps companies make multidecade investments. Finance is also dangerous. Financial institutions exploit their clients. Banks fail and cause crises. The bankers lack empathy and are arrogant while having no qualms about demanding bailouts when they mess up—privatize profits and socialize losses. Finance is not popular except with some of those who make a living from it. It is needed, and hence tolerated, but not accepted, and society's response is to enjoy the benefits of the financial system while also regulating it heavily. Not an easy task, and there certainly is no consensus as to how to do it.

So what do we want to achieve from the financial system? Plenty of answers out there. But supposing one dispenses with all the politics and special interests and asks a typical person, I think we would get a simple answer: high economic growth without too many costly recessions and crises. In other words, maximize long-term economic growth and minimize the cost of crises and recessions:

$$\text{Maximize} \frac{\text{cumulative long-run economic growth}}{\text{cumulative cost of crises and recessions}}$$

It is hard to translate such a general objective into actionable policy, as so many special interests push for what works best for them. The bankers hope to eliminate competition and be given free rein otherwise. The regulators want to demonstrate they have done their job. The anticapitalist activists aim to eliminate all speculation and even close down privately owned banks. The politicians desire quick growth before the next election. The pundits crave attention. So how to go about meeting the ob-

jective and overcoming all the objections from the special interests? Start
with learning from history, the last financial crisis, 2008, with a detour
to Voltaire. In his book *Candide, ou l'Optimisme* (1759), Voltaire tells
the story of a young man, Candide, who lives a sheltered life in a supposed paradise on earth. His mentor is Professor Pangloss, who likes to
proclaim "All is for the best in the best of all possible worlds." We get
from him the word "Panglossian," an excessively optimistic view of the
world.

The global crisis in 2008 should not have happened. The years before
2008 were the great moderation, evoking the 1920's permanent era of
stability. The financial engineers had tamed risk. Yes, there were losses
here and there, even large ones like Enron or WorldCom, and developing
countries did have their crises, like Korea in 1998. But even then it was
the accountants and lawyers and politicians who failed, not the financial
engineers. Crises were a thing of the past, at least in the developed world.
Even in the developing world crises happened only when the good advice
of the IMF was rejected. By 2007 we were so safe that the IMF itself was
on the verge of being drastically downsized because there were no crises
and nothing for it to do.

It was the best of all possible worlds. The rules and institutional structure, founded on the rigor of scientific risk management, protected us.
The riskometers told us we had never been as safe as in 2007. For good
reasons. We have used statistical analysis to manage risk ever since Blaise
Pascal in the sixteenth century. The three waves of Kaizen took financial
engineering to the pinnacle of its success. The financial industry collects
vast amounts of data, which it processes with sophisticated models on
superfast computers, all overseen by highly educated financial engineers,
graduates of the world's best universities. How can that not make the
financial system do what we want? Elementary. While the financial engineers focus on all the micro risks—the grains of sand being examined
above (Figure 38)—new and dangerous forms of risk emerge where nobody is looking—the endogenous risk monster that had been hiding all
along. Why did we miss it? Because the financial system is infinitely complex, the financial engineers can only patrol a tiny part of it, while the
monster hides where they are not looking. The Panglossian great moderation, meanwhile, encouraged even more risk-taking, à la Minsky. And

we did not know because the riskometers measure only exogenous risk, not endogenous risk.

Then—boom!—2008 happened. Northern Rock, Bear Stearns, AIG, and finally Lehman. We had a full-blown global crisis on our hands. The exogenous risk indicators shot up. The authorities reacted quickly, initially with improvised responses and eventually the doctrine of macropru. Are we protected? I don't think so. Regulations are backward looking, aiming to prevent the mistakes of the past. The rules that would have prevented a repeat of 2008 ossify, while the world continually changes. The market participants become increasingly good at evading the rules—new risks get taken where nobody is looking, and the cycle repeats (Figure 39). When you start hearing the world described in terms of a permanent era of stability or the great moderation or growth and safety being ensured by financial engineers or your country's prosperity being due to cultural

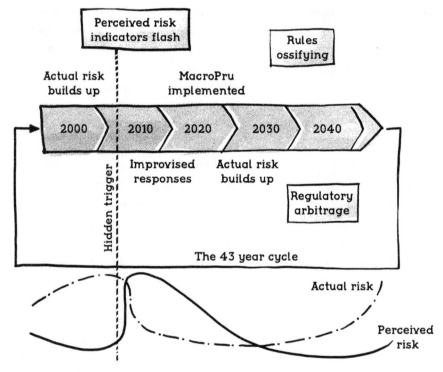

Figure 39. The forty-three-year cycle of financial crises. Credit: Lukas Bischoff/IllustrationX.

superiority, or the central banks proclaiming all is fine, it is time to run. When Professor Pangloss discussed the best of all possible worlds, he was only protecting Candide from seeing it.

Cognitive Failures

The CIA had a lot of information on Al Qaeda in early 2001 and much forewarning of the 9/11 attack. In his book *Rebel Ideas: The Power of Diverse Thinking,* Matthew Syed clearly illustrates the cognitive failures that led the CIA to dismiss the threat. The CIA staff was predominantly upper-middle-class, white, Ivy-League-educated men, and when all the intelligence on Al Qaeda was filtered through their cultural lens an attack was inconceivable. Like the CIA in 2001, so many fund managers, bankers, and regulators have enormous power and resources. What frustrates their mission is four cognitive failures that blind them to the threats and opportunities. They make facts fit their biases, and when they don't, find other facts.

The first cognitive failure is a fallacy of composition, whereby we infer that something must be true if all, or even some, parts of it are true: "Hydrogen (H) is not wet. Oxygen (O) is not wet. Therefore, water (H_2O) is not wet." The fallacy of composition in financial regulations is that if all the individual micro risks are kept under control, the entire financial system is safe, implying that the financial system is the simple sum of all the individual activities within it, so all the scientist has to do is study the grains of sand on the beach (see Figure 38).

Suppose each and every bank is prudent—they are all Volvos, as I called them earlier. They all do what they are supposed to do, with none taking crazy risks. Still, they have to make risky investments like mortgages and loans to small- and medium-sized enterprises; otherwise, they would not be a bank. Some of those risky investments have a market price, but the value of the majority can be determined only by a model, while risk in all is measured by riskometers. The fallacy of composition means that even if all the banks are prudent, the system is not safe.

Blame it on shock absorption, or rather the inability of prudent banks to absorb shocks. Suppose some external shock arrives—Brexit or a tsunami or Ukraine or Trump or an earthquake or China or Covid-19, or just anything—so that the price of some assets held by the Volvo banks falls. The consequence is that exogenous risk shoots up, inevitable by design since the riskometers are based on short-term historical fluctuations. What is our Volvo supposed to do? Dispose of its riskiest assets and hoard liquidity, of course, because that is prudent. But such selling will just make the prices fall more, which makes exogenous risk increase further. Cue more selling and a vicious feedback between falling prices, evaporation of liquidity, and higher risk. If there is no buyer (because all possible buyers are prudent), it can end only in tears (crisis). Nobody does anything wrong. It is like passing a hot potato from one person to another: they all pass it on in order to not get burned by it (Figure 40). Financial stability is not achieved by making all the financial institutions prudent.

The second cognitive failure is invariance, the view that the financial system does not change when observed and controlled. After all, the world of physics is invariant, so why not the financial system? There is, though, a crucial difference: endogenous risk. Anybody who interacts with the financial system changes it, whether as asset managers, salespeople, regulators, journalists, investment bankers, university professors, or finance ministers. Some significantly, others not so much. But while their impact can be tiny, it is never zero. That may not matter much, and most of us can safely behave as if risk were exogenous. But for the guardians of financial stability and those worried about tail risk, like pension funds, the

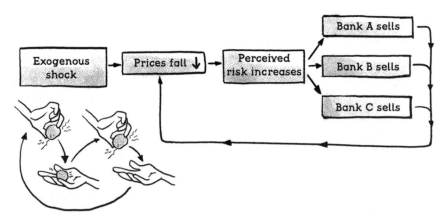

Figure 40. The hot potato feedback. Credit: Lukas Bischoff/IllustrationX.

distinction is crucial. Accepting invariance means underestimating the forces of large losses and instability.

The third cognitive failure is believing riskometers measure true risk. I likened that in my earlier discussion of the myth of the riskometer to seeing the riskometer as a device akin to the thermometer. That we can somehow plunge a riskometer deep into the financial system and get an accurate reading of risk. The problem is that the riskometers capture merely a small part of the vast domain that risk is. They promise to summarize all that risk into one number, and invariably a lot is lost in the process. When employed to capture a bank's risk or the risk of an entire financial system, the measurements are essentially content-free. The riskometer is comfortable to those in charge. They get a feeling that because the risk dashboard only shines green, all is good. The riskometer misdirects them to look only at the numbers that tell them what they want to hear.

The final cognitive failure is taking financial stability as an objective in itself. It is not. Stability is only an instrument. The objective is sustainable economic growth with not too many costly crises. The financial system is a tool, and financial stability is important only insofar as it takes us toward our objective. Policy makers who focus excessively on stability and see it as the be-all and end-all of their mission are doing a disservice to the society they are supposed to serve.

The four cognitive failures blind decision makers to what really matters. And that has many real world consequences. To begin with, when we, with the best of intentions, aim to reduce or even annihilate risk, we may just end up displacing it. It is possible to eliminate financial risk, as Cuba and North Korea have shown: don't have a financial system. But that is an all-or-nothing approach, and we don't like that, preferring growth, which means risk. And because the financial system is so complex there are plenty of places for taking said risk. Risk is like a balloon. By reducing one type of risk, we may just displace it elsewhere, often into the more shadowy parts of the system, where the controllers have less oversight. Out of sight, out of mind.

The cognitive failures also make us neglect the network that links everybody in the financial system together. Okay, the regulators and bankers will tell you that everybody is connected to everybody else, that the network not only exists but also is of utmost importance. However, while

Figure 41. The silos. Credit: Copyright © Ricardo Galvão.

it is easy to acknowledge the network's importance, it is much harder to incorporate it into standard practices. I once heard a deputy governor of a central bank complain about network analysis, saying that all such work ever shows is that everybody is connected to everybody else, which he already knew.

The reason the network gets ignored is all the silos. Everybody working in the financial system lives inside a silo (Figure 41). The financial engineers are experts in their personal subareas, foreign exchange, loans to southern European small- and medium-sized enterprises, American subprime mortgages, treasury management, and all the myriad business areas of the modern financial institution. Even the largest banks operate solely within particular parts of the system. And the financial authorities all live in silos. They are tasked with regulating insurance in a US state or market conduct in Germany. There is no authority in charge of the systemic risk of a single country, and certainly not the whole world. Because nobody has the mandate to control the network, nobody does. All we have is a patchwork of government agencies regulating a small part of it—their own silo—and they don't like to collaborate with other silos. If you think this can't be true, ask the regulators about sharing data across jurisdictions, and they will all tell you how much resistance data-sharing meets. While ignoring the network helps the decision makers to sleep well, the problem is that the network both dampens and amplifies shocks.

Some of the most powerful and destructive forces in the financial system not only lie on the boundaries of the silos but also actively exploit them.

The most damaging consequence of the cognitive failures is short termism—the dissonance of the short and long run. Almost every economic outcome we care about is long term. Pensions, the environment, house prices, education, you name it, all are about what happens years and decades hence. The short run isn't all that important. Day-to-day fluctuations in stock prices or real estate values or loan portfolios or interest rates don't matter much to most of us. So, does the way we measure and manage financial risk reflect the importance of the long run? By and large, no. We proclaim we care about the long term but actually just end up managing short-term risk.

The reason is simple. It is really hard to measure long-term risk because, after all, extreme infrequent events are, by definition, very scarce. The problem of measuring long-term risk is entwined with that of standard risk management practices. Consider a sovereign wealth fund that cares about very long-term risk, decades into the future, where such a time perspective is written into its laws and mandates. However, the fund is monitored quarterly, and if it performs poorly over a few quarters, questions are raised, bonuses may not be granted, the head of the fund could be summoned to appear in front of a parliamentary committee, and some people may be fired. That makes the managers of the sovereign wealth fund care about quarterly, not the decennial, performance regardless of what the legal mandate says.

And the implications are unfortunate. If the short-term risk dashboards are reassuring, as they were in 2006, we may easily take on undesirable levels of risk, oblivious to the dangers. The impact on financial markets will be lower volatility and fatter tails—day-to-day fluctuations become smaller, while the chance of catastrophic long-term outcomes increases.

There are real world consequences to all of that. Economic growth suffers. Growth has been slowing in the developed world over the past few decades, a phenomenon called secular decline (Figure 42).[1] "Hold on, Jón," I suspect many of you will think when reading this. "There are many causes of secular decline, it is poorly understood, and to blame the cognitive failures is a bit far-fetched." Fair enough, they are not the only cause, but do make it worse. For the economy to grow, we need risk:

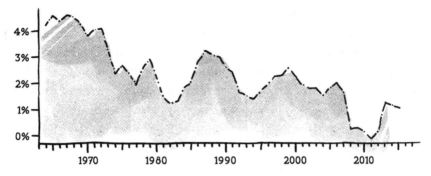

Figure 42. Secular decline in economic growth. Credit: Lukas Bischoff/
IllustrationX.

entrepreneurs who have easy access to capital at each level of a company's growth, from the very first incubation state all the way up to the IPOs and beyond. Because loans to start-ups have high short-term risk, they attract high capital charges, making it doubly costly for banks and other financial institutions to finance the new companies that will drive future growth. Meanwhile, the large, established corporations have high credit ratings, good relations with banks, and easy access to financing. But they are not growing very much. The very sectors that reliably deliver economic growth are starved of funding. Earlier I gave an example of such deprivation when discussing a BBC *Panorama* program on how banks were hurting the all-important small- and medium-sized enterprises, SMEs, so vital to growth. While the program makers blamed predatory bank behavior, the actual impact was caused by the Basel III capital regulations that make it much more expensive to lend to the SMEs.

The Covid-19 Lesson in How the Financial Authorities See Their Mission

What are policymakers to do? First and foremost, reduce uncertainty.
Do so by removing tail risks, and the perception of tail risks.
—*Olivier Blanchard (2009)*

The Covid-19 crisis in 2020 and the global crisis in 2008 are a lens for looking at how the financial authorities think the financial system should be controlled. While there is no single term or phrase that captures how they see their mission, I would like to propose "the modern

philosophy of financial regulations." As far as I can tell, no policy authority has expressed any view on what the purpose of regulations is beyond
the most vacuous. The single exception is the Bank of England, whose
senior policy makers manage fairly consistent views. Perhaps the financial
authorities don't want to tell us what the modern philosophy is. After all,
they are masters of constructive ambiguity, trying very carefully to say as
little as possible in a lot of words. The official reason is, of course, that
constructive ambiguity is a necessary evil because of moral hazard: coordinating the markets while keeping them guessing. I think the real reason
is more prosaic. The lack of clarity helps them to get the job done and paper over differences of opinion. I have read many official documents, and
the deliberate lack of transparency shows up everywhere, even in places
where it shouldn't. A few years ago I read the Basel III market risk regulations, trying to understand how the main component of market risk was
meant to be calculated. It is a simple calculation and should be easy to
explain. The document was quite unclear despite spending many words
on the explanations, and I could not figure out how to do the calculation.

I would love for everybody to ask their central bankers and regulators how
they see financial regulations benefiting their country. Please let me know
if you get an answer. In the absence of clarity, I will use deduction. Having
read enough speeches and policy reports, participated in plenty of conferences, and had many talks with regulators, I have arrived at the following
definition of how the financial authorities see the modern philosophy.

> Definition: The modern philosophy of financial regulations as
> indirectly expressed by the policy authorities:

1. Calm markets in distress with whatever it takes, in order to reduce
   uncertainty
2. Afterward, identify those parts of the financial system that were at
   the heart of the distress, and figure out what happened—lessons
   learned. Aim to impose corrective regulations so as not to get a
   repeat
3. By ensuring every financial institution behaves prudently, meaning
   each individual risk is kept under control, the system is safe.

When I asked some friends working for the regulatory agencies what
they thought of my definition, they all agreed with the first two parts.

The third is more controversial and not how many people working for the macroprudential authorities see it. (The microprudential regulators would agree with my third part.) But my interlocutors agreed that was only words and personal opinions. Actions were consistent with all three. One of them added that the annual Risk Monitoring Exercise epitomized the problem.

Covid-19 nicely demonstrates the modern philosophy in practice. The initial Covid-19 shock was purely exogenous, so the virus was akin to Archduke Ferdinand's assassination, which set in motion the systemic crisis of 1914. What happened after the virus hit was the typical endogenous response. The epidemiological, social, and economic outcomes were all the result of the interaction of the human beings who make all the decisions—endogenous risk.

Covid did not cause a financial crisis. At best, we suffered turbulence. Why? There are two schools of thought. The authorities maintain it is thanks to both the post-2008 regulations leaving the financial system highly resilient and also the swift policy responses in March and April 2020 (system bailout). In the words of the head of the Basel committee, Pablo Hernández de Cos, in 2021, "The global banking system has remained broadly resilient. . . . The initial Basel III reforms, alongside an unprecedented range of public support measures, are the main explanations for this outcome." Since the initial shock was purely exogenous, I suspect the financial system would have had little trouble absorbing the virus shock even without the bailout and Basel III. The FSB, with input from all the leading financial authorities, published a report in November 2020 on what went wrong, how they responded, and lessons learned. The document is called the *Holistic Review of the March Market Turmoil* and sheds light on how the policy authorities see their mission:

> The policy response was speedy, sizeable and sweeping. . . . Absent central bank intervention, it is highly likely that the stress in the financial system would have worsened significantly.
>
> Some parts of the system, particularly banks and financial market infrastructures, were able to absorb rather than amplify the macroeconomic shock, supported by the post crisis reforms.
>
> The March turmoil has underscored the need to strengthen resilience in the NBFI [nonbank financial intermediation] sector.[2]

In other words:

1. There was excessive market turmoil
2. Our job is to reduce uncertainty, and we did so successfully
3. The part of the system we regulated after the last crisis in 2008 did well (a great job: we turned the banks into Volvos)
4. Unfortunately, we had to provide liquidity to the NBFIs to calm the markets
5. So we will regulate the NBFIs to prevent a recurrence.

Left unsaid, but implied, is that the template for the regulations of the NBFIs is bank regulations. So did it all work as well as the FSB suggests in its *Holistic Review*? My collaborators and I have been looking at that very question. Two days after the worst day in the equity markets in March 2020, we published a paper, "The Coronavirus Crisis Is No 2008," on how the Covid-19 crisis differed from the 2008 crisis. We concluded that as the Covid-19 turmoil was not the same as that in 2008, a new policy response was called for. In particular, liquidity injections would not be very effective this time around.

Our subsequent research has continued to support these conclusions in a paper titled "The Calming of Short-Term Market Fears and Its Long-Term Consequences: The Central Banks' Dilemma." We took advantage of a unique data set on option markets that allowed us to identify how the financial markets' fear of large losses changed owing to all the central bank interventions.[3] As the data is rich in time and space, spanning a large number of stocks and countries and maturities from one week all the way up to thirty years into the future, we have a comprehensive picture of how the markets reacted to the Covid interventions.

The primary objective of the policy interventions in March and April 2020 was the immediate calming of market fear, but only in the short run. Long-term fear would ideally not fall since that signals moral hazard. But that is precisely what happened. The impact on long-term market fear, even ten years into the future, was larger than at the short term. The lesson the financial markets took from the interventions was that the central banks stand ready to do what it takes. The market will be less vigilant and take on more risk—moral hazard.

I can demonstrate that in more detail by taking one example out of our paper: the Fed relaxed bank capital requirements under which the world's largest bank, JP Morgan, works. Fear in JPM's stock price fell significantly in response, both in the long and the short run. As the lowering of bank capital requirements is explicitly designed to make banks take more risk, one would have expected long-term fear to increase. However, the markets took it the other way, long-term fear fell—moral hazard increased.

That result, and others in our paper, lead me to conclude that the modern philosophy is destabilizing. Why? History provides guidance. The economic profession went off the rails in the 1950s and 1960s, after John Maynard Keynes died and before the pathbreaking work of Robert Lucas. The prevailing view in those lost years was that one could control the economy with a static framework, what I have termed Excelonomics. Achieve policy objectives—high growth, low unemployment, low inflation—by tweaking the parameters of a static economic model. The financial authorities and the governments loved it, as this way of doing economics made them feel powerful, even omnipotent. Except it didn't work. The Lucas critique showed us why. Expectations matter, and economic agents react to policies in a way that undermines the policy objective. All we got was the word of the 1970s "stagflation"—inflation and stagnation.

Expectations also matter when it comes to macroprudential policy. Banks were strongly affected by the 2008 crisis, so the policy authorities sharply increased the intensity of regulations and the required levels of bank capital. When Covid came, it all seemed to work splendidly since the banks were hardly affected by the virus. But the risk now had spilled over to the shadow banking system. You see, the economic agents that comprise the financial system do not take regulations lying down. They react to them, changing the financial system in the process. Once the regulations take effect, they apply to a system that no longer exists: the Lucas critique.

The authorities now ask the right question: "What can we do to prevent a repeat?" but come to the wrong answer: "More regulations and more control." Fair enough, that might be the political outcome you desire, but there are consequences. The first is that diversity suffers since the lesson learned is that the nonbank sector needs to be brought under official control that is similar to that of the banking sector. Financial institutions will become more like each other and the financial system more procyclical. Systemic risk will increase.

Furthermore, the financial authorities gain even more power. But that power comes at a cost. To begin with, the more power a state agency has, the more democratic oversight it needs. We can't have unelected bureaucrats making decisions of fundamental importance to society when they have no direct democratic legitimacy. But even worse, it makes the financial authorities even more responsible for stability. They have all the information and the power, and hence get blamed when things go pear-shaped. And then it is much harder to resist bailing out private institutions.

Then we have the very high cost of the new regulations, and who pays the cost? The banks' clients—us. Not necessarily a big problem in the United States, where only a third of financial intermediation comes via the banks. But in Spain, the home country of the head of the Basel committee (Governor Pablo Hernández de Cos), 96 percent of company financing is provided by the banks. Spain is not exactly doing well economically and might think that the worst policy would be to further increase the cost and reduce the availability of company loans.

And finally the political consequences. Bailouts are dangerous things, and nobody likes them except the recipients. They drive populism and moral hazard and undermine the credibility of the state. If the financial authorities can do no better than design a setup requiring a bailout every decade, neither the authorities nor the governments that empower them appear to be competent or honest. Fortunately for the authorities, all the Covid-19 bailouts passed unseen, lost in all the virus hoopla, unlike what occurred in 2008.

The ultimate consequence of the modern philosophy of financial regulations is to make us question the private financial system. Why not bring it under direct state control?

The Magical Solutions

While the modern philosophy of financial regulations is the way we control the financial system today, there is no shortage of alternative proposals for how to fix the financial system. Start with cryptocurrencies. While the crypto advocates are a broad church, a common view is that the established institutions of the state and the private sector are corrupt

and cannot be trusted. Repeated crises with their bailouts and quantitative easing mean it would be much better to replace the central banks
with algorithms—mathematics can be trusted. In steps bitcoin. It is a
complicated subject, meriting much more space than I have here, and
I have written extensively on it elsewhere.[4] The specific form of money,
whether the fiat money we use today or cryptocurrencies, is not all that
important for the objectives of financial policy; what matters is the power
the financial authorities have and how they exercise it. So, cryptocurrencies are not the solution.

What, then, about their cousin, central-bank digital currencies, or
CBDCs. The idea is that the central banks create a new digital form of
the fiat money every country uses today. Perhaps as a token on a blockchain. There was a lot of enthusiasm about CBDCs a few years ago. They
promised to solve so many of the problems we have with the financial
system, allowing targeted bailouts, the fine-tuning of the money supply,
and provision of ample information about what financial institutions are
up to, especially all the liquidity flows. The central bank governor can
then manage everything with their AI—BoB. Then the disadvantages became clear. In their purest form, CBDCs mean the central bank controls
all the money in the economy because it controls the blockchain. Every
transaction is visible to it, so the central bank not only closely monitors
what citizens are up to but also makes all the loans. We don't want that,
so today's CBDC proposals aim merely to improve the payments system.
Here, the authorities are haunted by PayPal, which came out of nowhere
two decades ago, and by the time they woke up it was too late to do anything about PayPal. So, the primary motivation for CBDCs today is to
forestall alternative payment systems, especially those under the control
of foreign companies. Certainly a worthwhile goal, but does nothing to
solve the problems I am discussing here.

If technology is not the solution, then what about politics? On the
libertarian wing of the political spectrum, the root of the problem is the
state, especially its regulations, bailouts, and currency mismanagement.
By forswearing regulations and bailouts, we will see crises, but not nearly
as many as now, since the reason we need bailouts is that the government promises them. That is true, but the laissez-faire position makes
sense only in theory, not in practice, because in a democratic society we

demand the governments help us and politicians respond. It is simply not credible to expect the politicians not to regulate and bail out the financial system when needed. We need a solution that recognizes that reality.

And that brings me to socialism. If the state has to bail the financial system out every time things go wrong, in 2008 and 2020 and 20??, why not just have the state run the banks? Many commentators call for heavy regulations, perhaps pointing to the golden era of Bretton Woods, when the financial system was nailed down and there were no financial crises. Impose very high capital requirements along with strict limits on activities and risk. Even just nationalize the whole system and let the government run it. Certainly doable, but only at a cost. Finance is, after all, a service. The safer the service becomes, the more costly it is. The more the state gets involved with the provision of finance, the more political, bureaucratic, and corrupt it becomes. Who pays for all that? We do, in lower economic growth. I don't think the socialist solution is viable either.

We need a balanced financial policy that protects us from the financial system's excesses and ensures that we are given good services and innovation at a reasonable cost. Society wants the financial authorities to find a balance between safety and growth and for money managers to focus on long-term performance and risk. That is not what we get now. There is too much focus on short-term risk, not enough on long-term risk, and certainly not enough on economic growth. We rely too much on risk measurements that provide a veneer of scientific management of risk. There are too many risk dashboards and excessive control of day-to-day activities, and not enough thought given to long-term risk and performance. The financial engineers who optimize the investment portfolios and design modern regulations and risk management systems have created this superpowerful microscope to look at all the individual risks. They are like the scientist who is an expert at studying the grains of sand on a beach but misses the incoming tsunami (see Figure 38).

14

What to Do?

Diversity stabilizes.

Figure 43. Credit: Copyright © Ricardo Galvão.

What to do about the financial system? Plenty of pundits tell us
they know how to make it deliver for us, with no crises, great investment
returns, and robust economic growth. Good luck with that. We may wish
to have our cake and eat it too, but there is always a trade-off between
safety and risk. All the easy solutions target the most visible exogenous
risk, ignoring the hidden dark forces behind tail risk and crises. All is not
lost, as there are sensible ways to get what we want. I have discussed the
issues in detail throughout this book and below distill them into five principles for getting the best out of the financial system.

Focus on Endogenous Risk

The first principle is to recognize that the real threat comes from endogenous risk, the dark forces that hide until it is too late. We too often ignore endogenous risk and focus our efforts on the visible exogenous risk that leads us down the garden path (Figure 43). Endogenous risk captures the fundamental forces of instability and losses. Excessive leverage. The belief that liquidity is infinite in an interconnected financial system that depends for its very existence on that infinite liquidity. Prudent desires to protect oneself. The promise of government bailouts. Focus on the visible while ignoring the hidden. Good control inside the silos and willful disregard of the world outside. The hope that good times will last forever. Low risk that encourages risk-taking, Minsky style.

Every crisis has some of these fundamentals at its core, like De Neufville's in 1763, John Pierpont Morgan's in 1907, and Covid in 2020. The problem for anybody concerned with risk is that these fundamental causes of losses and instability are difficult to grapple with. It is hard, to the point of impossible, to measure such endogenous risk. Nobody knew about the dangers from subprime mortgages put into structured credit products in the years before 2008 until it was too late to do anything about them. The temptation then is to control the system by what we can measure, not by what matters.

Endogenous risk lies dormant for years and decades until it is brought to life by some exogenous shock. The Covid-19 virus triggered three fundamentals: liquidity, the precautionary principle, and bailout promises. The system had operated as if liquidity were infinite, but then the virus made the liquidity providers cautious—poof, a liquidity crisis. The same precautionary principle that made the Millennium Bridge wobble in 2000 and investors to go on strike in 2007. Add to that the promise of bailouts; the risk takers knew the financial authorities stood ready with an open checkbook, so they took much more risk than they would have otherwise. The Covid financial turmoil was inevitable. If the virus had not triggered it, something else would have.

While only a few well-understood fundamental causes of crises exist, the number of triggers is infinite. Assassination of an archduke in 1914, virus in 1918 and 2020, sour bets on shipping technology as in 1866, a small price drop in 1987 and 2007, end of war in 1763, etc., etc. The triggers are as varied as they are numerous. The key difference between the triggers and the fundamentals is visibility—the triggers are simple and for all to see, while the fundamentals are obscure. And that very visibility leads us down the wrong path, a trigger that causes a crisis today may whimper out into nothing tomorrow. It would be much better to ignore the triggers and focus on the fundamental driver of crises and bad performance—endogenous risk.

Beware of the Riskometer and False Resilience

The second principle is to be wary of false resilience. It is easy to set up some framework that tells us what we want to hear. All is fine because that is what the risk dashboard tells us. Meanwhile the endogenous risk monster is laughing at us (Figure 44). If the risk dashboard tells us risk is low, we want to take more risk. But that is false resilience. The crisis in 2008 did not happen because all the bankers went risk mad that year. No. It was all the crazy risk they took in the go-go years of the early 2000s, and when 2008 came along there was nothing to do except

Figure 44. Monster under the bed. Credit: Copyright © Ricardo Galvão.

mitigate the worst. We were already in a crisis. And then, once something bad happens, we like to learn the lessons. Figure out what went wrong so it can never happen again—closing the barn door after the horse escapes. That also brings false resilience. The forces of instability congregate in the dark areas where no one is looking, so by its very definition, the danger will emerge somewhere else next time.

The main driver of false resilience is that the risk we measure, all the micro risks, tends not to be the type of risk we most care about. The reason is the riskometer, the magical device that pops out measurements of financial risk when plunged deep into the bowels of the financial system. Financial regulations, risk control, and portfolio management depend on the riskometer, more and more every day. Why? Because it is seen as scientific and objective, helping decision makers collapse a complicated problem into a small set of precise numbers on a risk dashboard.

And that is where things go wrong. The riskometer is not nearly as scientific and objective as its proponents think. They have been waylaid by precise scientific instruments, like the thermometer, which allows us to measure temperature as accurately as we want, in real time. There is only a single unambiguous notion of what temperature is, and it is easy to use the thermometer to control temperature with real-time feedback techniques. When the temperature is too high, turn down the thermostats; that's why the problem of keeping the risk manager's office at a steady 72°F or 22°C is easy. We can't implement such feedback mechanisms with most financial risk, even if plenty have tried to. Why? To begin with, there is no uniform view of what is important and hence what risk to target. Is it day-to-day volatility? Tail risk, the hefty price-drops that cause sudden big losses, bankruptcies, and crises? Or the slow drip-drip-drip movements of prices downward, with no significant fluctuations and no discernible tail risk, but prices that only go south? Is it the chance of a pension not delivering on that comfortable retirement fifty years hence? The likelihood our country will suffer a systemic crisis next year?

Each concern calls for a different concept of risk—what is risk depends on what we care about. It is unfortunate that the easiest risk to measure, and hence the one most widely used, is short-term, day-to-day events—volatility or its close cousins Value-at-Risk and Expected Shortfall. These have little or nothing to say about tail risk or crises or the solvency of your pension fund. Astonishingly, the very financial regulations and risk management practices that are meant to keep banks safe, protect our pensions, and prevent crises are so often based on nothing more than day-to-day price fluctuations.

Even after picking a concept of risk, we are left with the problem of measurement. There are dozens of competing techniques out there that deliver widely different measurements of the same risk, with no clear way to discriminate among them. All purporting to be state-of-the-art, and each with its own groupies. And even then we have measured only the risk in a single asset, perhaps a stock, a loan, or a derivative. The next step is even harder, the aggregation of risk across time and space. How to go from all the micro risks to the portfolio, department, bank, and the system, today and years and decades into the future. The more we aggregate risk, the less accurate the result is. There is a subtle point at work here. While it is obviously true that systemic risk is the aggregate of all the individual micro risks, that conceptual notion does not mean we know how to do the calculations. It is a common problem in science. You can know everything about a human being's physiology and biology and know nothing about them as a person. We can't easily aggregate risk because of the complex interactions between all the individual risks. In real life, outside of the universe of the risk modeler, the strongest connections between risk factors manifest themselves only in times of extreme stress. They are simply not seen otherwise.

Why? Liquidity is the most obvious reason. Liquidity is ample most of the time, even seemingly infinite. But it is by and large not measurable and has the annoying tendency of evaporating when most needed, in times of stress. Becoming the common crisis factor that affects all assets and liabilities, exposing all the hidden connections we never knew existed, until its too late. If we measure risk in normal times, we underestimate each asset's risk and especially how it relates to other assets, because the very factor that makes them strongly related—liquidity—is not visible. So while it is easy to come up with a number for the aggregate risk of a bank or a country or even the entire world, the calculations' accuracy is very low. I think many readers will disagree since it is standard practice in finance to do precisely that. Yes, it is easy to come up with a number for aggregate risk. It is not so straightforward to do it accurately. Those who propose doing so might be confused by physical systems. Math captures all in physics and not in finance. I saw the problems with such aggregate risk measures firsthand a few years ago when I joined forces with three co-authors, Kevin James, Marcela Valenzuela, and Ilknur Zer, in studying the accuracy of measures of systemic risk. We wrote two papers, "Model Risk of Risk Models" and "Can We Prove a Bank Guilty of Creating Systemic Risk? A Minority Report," and, by looking at all the leading indicators of systemic risk, concluded that they were very inaccurate, and could not be recommended for use.

Like so many other tools, the riskometer is helpful when used appropriately, like controlling risk on the trading floor. It is dangerous when in the hands of someone who either does not know about its limitations or, what I think is much more common, willfully ignores all the warning signs because it helps them do their job. They might argue "We have to control the amount of risk. The riskometer gives us usable measurements. It is not perfect but allows us to exercise some control." But by doing so only reinforces the illusion of control.

Ultimately, the riskometer drives false resilience, the view that because the risk dashboard flashes green, we have risk under control. The consequences of false resilience are unfortunate. Investment management that focuses excessively on short-term risk, like daily fluctuations or quarterly performance. Investors get deceived. Perhaps when their portfolio managers tell them the portfolio risk is $15,000 or there is a 25 percent chance of a loss over the coming year. Misleading, since the accuracy of such assertions depends on the reliability of the risk calculations and the relevance of that risk to the investor. Furthermore, because the asset managers calculate the risk measurements, they have the incentive to choose a riskometer that presents their promises in the best possible light. Which often means one based on short-term exogenous risk.

While money managers may care only about the short run, most investors don't. Pension funds, sovereign wealth funds, family offices, insurance reserves are all concerned with losses spanning years or even decades. The problem is that these investors rely on outsiders to manage their investments, which means performance monitoring. And that monitoring is more often than not done with risk dashboards populated by the output of riskometers that emphasize the short term. Investors may then look for false diversification. Perhaps buying private equity funds, which do not exhibit much short-term volatility even though they are cointegrated with equity markets in the long term.

The macroprudential regulators are similarly waylaid by false resilience. By the very definition of their existence, they are meant to concern themselves only with long-run risk, act countercyclically, slow the system down in good times, and stimulate it when hit by shocks. There is much more to macropru than the measurement of risk, but if your job is to think about bad outcomes years and decades into the future, you need some way to measure long-term resilience. And the go-to tool for that is the riskometer. Combine recent fluctuations in the financial markets with accounting information, where the relevant variables are chosen by how well they forecast past stress events. Hope that informs the future. The regulators might think they are doing a splendid job when they ensure all the micro risks are low—the fallacy of composition. And when they measure aggregate financial-system risk—like ECB's CISS—measurement error is very high. The systemic risk dashboards may flash green when the actual systemic risk is high, giving oxygen to the forces of instability, or just as likely do the opposite, making the authorities clamp down when systemic risk is low, the economy suffering, so a stimulus is called for.

Beware of false resilience. True resilience focuses on the fundamental drivers of losses and instability, not on measures of risk or fixing what went wrong last time.

Remember the Objectives

The third principle is to always keep your objectives in mind. Maximum return with acceptable risk for investors and economic growth with reasonable financial stability for the regulators. Consider the entirety of the problem together: think globally, not locally.

It is easier for investors to do so, as profit maximization is at the front of everybody's thoughts. The concern here is the dissonance of the short and long term, since it is all too common to focus excessively on the short term, by using risk measurements that capture short-term fluctuations, while ignoring the tail risks that can be so damaging to long-term investment returns. The objectives of investors can end up being sacrificed for scientific risk management techniques that only mitigate short-term threats to investment performance, statistical techniques that promise accuracy, sold by spurious precision—expected return on this portfolio is 25.234 percent over the next two years while risk is 12.228 percent. Most risk calculations use a riskometer based on some model the vendor has created, one that is tailor-designed to signal what most benefits the vendor, not the client. Those investors who are concerned with long-run risk, which means most of them, should dispense with performance controls that push to the short term and insist that money managers also care about long-run risk and the risk that matters to them.

It is much harder for the regulators to keep the objectives in mind, because they don't even agree on what they are. As I argued earlier, the objective of financial policy should be to maximize long-term economic growth and minimize the cost of crisis:

$$\text{Maximize} \ \frac{\text{cumulative long-run economic growth}}{\text{cumulative cost of crises and recessions}}$$

The policy authorities should clearly express what their objectives are, why they are regulating, and what they aim to accomplish. High-level statements are welcome, like those made by Chairman Powell, emphasizing low, steady inflation and high employment, but such clarity is mostly absent in the actual documents that outline policy actions.

And straying firmly into controversy, unlike so many other commentators, I think a key purpose of central banks and other financial authorities is to help the financial system operate at higher risk levels than it otherwise would do. As a general rule, more risk means more economic growth, and by helping the system to operate at higher levels of risk than it otherwise could safely do, we all benefit.

Blow Up the Silos

The fourth principle is that the authorities should focus their efforts on both maximizing growth and minimizing the cost of crises. We don't do that today because the policy makers live in silos. They care deeply about their own corner of the world but are instructed to ignore the rest of the universe. A few years ago I gave a presentation at a central bank and had the privilege of sitting next to the governor over dinner. We got to discussing the topic of silos, and I asked him about how central bank policy since the crisis in 2008 affects inequality. He told me that on a personal level he was deeply concerned about inequality, but from his central bank's point of view it was irrelevant because inequality was not in its legal mandate.

Policy makers optimize locally, not globally. Researchers of financial stability are usually no better, even though they should be unencumbered by the silos. I have heard a lot of conference presenters claim that "the financial system is dangerous, I have identified the most important risks, and this is how you measure and control them. If you follow my suggestion, we meet our objective." Derisking the very part of the system they have spent years studying.

The silos can lead to strange outcomes. The Bank of England decided in June 2017 to tighten capital constraints on commercial banks because it thought they were taking on too much risk. That month it also opted to keep interest rates low to encourage banks to make more risky loans to small- and medium-sized enterprises in order to stimulate the economy. These policy decisions are obviously contradictory. While I have no idea how the bank came to this point, I can think of only two reasons: Either it wanted to please two separate political interests and was cynical enough to recognize that nobody would spot the contradiction. Or the decisions were made by two distinct parts of the bank—the financial stability and monetary policy divisions—and they didn't coordinate with each other.

Overcoming the silo mentality requires that financial policy be done in a more holistic way, and the only authority able to make that happen is the government. It can mandate the necessary interagency and inter-silo cooperation, force the various policy authorities to optimize globally and not locally. I can hear the objections: "Government agencies should focus on a single objective; if they have multiple mandates, one will lose out." "It will politicize the central banks." "It will lead to muddled and confusing policy-making." "We will get inflation." Every agency will find a host of reasons for why this is both a horrible idea and practically impossible. Balderdash. It is certainly doable, and one country, Singapore, leads the way.[1] The Monetary Authority of Singapore collaborates closely with both the Ministry of Finance on fiscal policies and the Ministry of National Development (land supply policies). Singapore has been quite successful in meeting my objective, high long-run growth and a stable financial system. There is no inherent reason such global optimization cannot be done elsewhere. All it takes is will.

Diversity to the Rescue

The enemy of stability and good investment performance is uniformity.

The final principle for getting the best out of the financial system is to embrace diversity, the most potent force of financial stability and good investment performance. Suppose some shock hits the markets, perhaps a virus like Covid-19 or the fight between the Reddit investors and the short-selling hedge funds in January 2021. If I react to a shock by buying and my buddy Ann by selling, our reactions cancel each other out—together, we create countercyclical random noise. If, instead, we both buy or sell, we procyclically amplify the price movements. We are procyclical when we see and react to the world in the same way, and countercyclical when we don't. The reason why Baron Rothschild was so prescient when he wrote two and half centuries ago that the best time to buy property was in the middle of a Civil War—buying in crises stabilizes. We need the Rothschilds, the Soroses and Buffetts, all the sovereign wealth funds, someone who sees buying opportunities during turmoil. For such individuals and entities to exist, they have to be unencumbered and free to invest the way they see best.

The enemy of financial stability and good, stable, long-term investment returns is uniformity. The more similar financial institutions are, the higher systemic risk becomes, because they will amplify the same shocks and inflate the same bubbles. The Millennium Bridge wobbled because the pedestrians on the bridge acted like a troop of soldiers, not like civilians. And that is what always happens in times of turmoil. Market participants become much more uniform in outlook and action than they usually would be.

Not many disagree. The relationship between diversity and systemic risk is well understood. But that is theory. Practice is different, and the incentives of the banker and the regulator push toward uniformity. There are good and bad reasons for this. The most apparent is best practices.

Nothing wrong with that. Nobody likes to use the second best. But there is a problem when it comes to risk. Because best practices mean using the one state-of-the-art riskometer and risk management technique, all will see and react to risk in the same way—uniformity, not diversity.

Increasing returns to scale also erode diversity. Banking favors the large because the fixed costs of financial services are so huge. The bigger the banks become, the cheaper it is to service all the complex needs of their large clients. Competitive forces drive mergers. While sometimes bemoaning the falling number of banks, the financial authorities encourage it in practice, happy to use mergers when resolving crises and failing banks.

Financial regulations further favor uniformity. There are two costs a bank has to pay when complying with regulations, variable and fixed costs—understanding how the regulatory apparatus works, knowing the legal environment, and the like. While well meaning and generally useful, there is a dark side. Because the fixed cost is substantial, the bigger the bank, the cheaper it is, per unit of size, to comply—increasing returns to scale (Figure 45).

The problem of antidiversity regulations is especially pernicious in Europe because the financial authorities there have to deal with transnational regulations of national banks and the politics of managing unruly countries on a European level. That means they need to be seen as providing a level playing field—why Basel III applies to all banks instead of

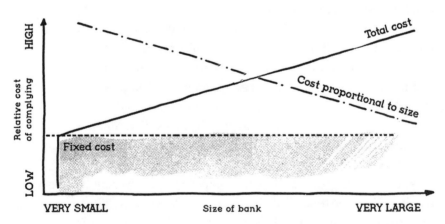

Figure 45. The fixed and variable cost of regulations. Credit: Lukas Bischoff/IllustrationX.

only to the largest, which would be much more appropriate and what the rest of the world wanted. The result is uniform rules that treat all banks, large and small, in the same way. Since we need complex rules for the largest, the cost of complying favors the large.

Bank-based financial systems also favor uniformity. In the United States only about one-third of lending to companies is done by banks; the rest happens via the bond markets and various other nonbank entities that intermediate funds from savers to companies. In the rest of the world about 90 percent of credit comes from banks, over 80 percent in the United Kingdom, 92 percent in Germany, and 96 percent in Spain. And even then the typical bank in the United States is much smaller relative to the size of the economy than banks in other countries. There are about 4,400 banks in the United States and only 200 in Japan, even though the Japanese economy is about half the size of the U.S. economy. The large number of banks in the United States plus their small share of overall credit make the US way of funding companies much more resilient, and much easier for the country to whip its banks into shape after a crisis, as it did following 2008. Bank-based financial systems provide less financing for innovative and risky companies, the cost of finance is high, and it is very hard to regulate the banks without imposing significant economic costs. The stillborn European Capital Markets Union was meant to help, but the power of the incumbent interests was just too great.

The financial authorities face a thorny way forward. They have to juggle a lot of issues and are subject to ferocious lobbying. But they should embrace diversity. Actively encourage new financial institutions, especially those whose business models are different from everybody else's. Regulate financial institutions for consumer protection, but don't control all the micro risks. Unfortunately, the financial authorities are not keen on diversity. Their rules actively get in the way of start-ups and new business models. The start-ups have to comply with regulations suited for the largest banks and, before getting licenses to practice, having to set up the myriad of functions that make up the modern financial institution; like the board, capital, management, IT system, and compliance. A slow, cumbersome, and very expensive process. And at the end of the day there is no guarantee they will get a license. The reason the regulatory process is so antidiversity and anti-start-up is that the regulators are worried about making a mistake; they are like the Chinese air traffic controllers I discussed earlier. Focused on risk to themselves, not on the benefits to society. That risk aversion means the licensing process favors uniformity and the incumbents.

What is lacking is risk culture. The financial authorities could do well by learning from their counterparts in other fields, like aviation. The airline industry is regulated with a view to simultaneously maximize the benefit to society and keep risk under control, and we see the outcome. The cost of flying is steadily falling while safety gets better every year. The central banks and regulators need such risk culture.

The financial authorities should be made to explain how the job they are doing benefits the rest of us. Telling us what the objective of what they are doing is, outlining how they are achieving that goal, and how it all fits in with what the other agencies are doing.

Diversify the regulators. If we put a single regulator in charge of everything—the super regulator so common today—we end up with a government agency that prefers uniformity, one that shares the goals of the incumbent interests and loathes what is different. We need competition between regulators, so we get agencies that both regulate and defend their part of the industry, protecting heterogeneity along the way.

While there are no silver bullets when it comes to the financial system, some ways of controlling it are better than others. The worst thing is to fight risk, the preferred option of the financial authorities. The financial system is like the Hydra, and though the authorities can cut off as many heads as they want, they will always grow back. It is much better not to try the impossible, instead just taking advantage of the inherent forces of stability and the five principles for how to deal with the system.

The first is to recognize that the real danger is endogenous risk, not the type of risk we usually measure. There are few fundamental reasons why the financial system does not do what we want it to do, and that is where our attention should be. It is all too easy to focus on the triggers of crises and bad investment performance, as they are there for all to see while the fundamental causes are hidden.

The second is to be aware of riskometers and false resilience. It is easy to convince oneself all is okay, that we are fully hedged against the worst tail events and comfortably safe since the financial authorities have systemic risk under control. It is another matter altogether to make it happen. Riskometers misdirect us away from the real threats, especially when we ask them to do the impossible, creating aggregated risk measures for a portfolio, bank, or the entire financial system. True resilience focuses on the fundamental drivers of losses and instability, not on measures of risk or fixing what went wrong last time.

The third principle is to remember the objectives. There is a reason why we regulate finance, it should not be regulation for regulation's sake, and the authorities should clearly show how what they are doing helps meeting their ultimate objectives, solid economic growth and financial stability. Fund managers should use risk management methods that reflect the needs of their clients, typically long-term tail risk, and not just measure and manage short-term risk.

The fourth principle is to blow up the silos, think globally, not locally. The financial system is a network connecting all, but most who work within it are instructed to ignore the network. Their job is invariably confined to a silo, and while they may care deeply about their silo, they don't pay much attention to the world outside them. We pay for that because the forces of bad investment performance and crises take advantage of the silos, operating on the boundaries where no one has oversight.

Finally, the best way to bend the financial system to one's will is to embrace diversity. We need a new risk culture like the one that works so well for the airline industry, so that the regulators are incentivized to allow new types of financial institutions to set up shop. The more different from each other the institutions of the financial system become and the more heterogeneous the regulations are, the more stable and diversified the system will be, and hence the better investment portfolios will perform. The only way to overcome the forces of uniformity is for the government to force the regulators to embrace diversity.

What gets in the way of us getting what we want out of the financial system is all the incumbent interests, the private firms that want to protect their franchises and the risk-averse regulators who want to demonstrate they are doing their job. The special interests are antidiversity, and that is where the government can step in. It can mandate the financial authorities to do what is necessary. All it takes is political will, and most of us will benefit.

Notes

1. Riding the Tiger

1. Box, "Science and Statistics," 791–99.
2. Goodhart, "Public Lecture at the Reserve Bank of Australia."

2. Systemic Risk

1. Schnabel and Shin, "Liquidity and Contagion: The Crisis of 1763," 929–68, and Quinn and Roberds, "Responding to a Shadow Banking Crisis: The Lessons of 1763," 1149–76.
2. International Monetary Fund, Bank for International Settlements, and Financial Stability Board, *Guidance to Assess the Systemic Importance of Financial Institutions, Markets and Instruments: Initial Considerations*, 2.
3. From Hans Christian Andersen's nineteenth-century tale "The Emperor's New Clothes."
4. Carville, television interview.
5. Black-Scholes refers to the statistical techniques for pricing options developed by Fischer Black and Myron Scholes in 1973, earning them the Nobel Prize in 1997.
6. Black, "Hedging, Speculation, and Systemic Risk," 6–8.
7. As quoted in Hoyt, *The Cyclopedia of Practical Quotations*.
8. Holder, Senate Judiciary Committee testimony.

3. Groundhog Day

1. Capra, *It's a Wonderful Life*.
2. The primary source of historical banking crises is Reinhart and Rogoff, *This Time It's Different*. I combine that with the IMF crisis database, Laeven and Valencia, "Systemic Banking Crises Revisited."
3. Prince, interview in the *Financial Times*.

4. Martin, "Address before the New York Group of the Investment Bankers Association of America."

5. As quoted in Day, *A Wonderful Life: S&L HELL: The People and the Politics behind the $1 Trillion Savings and Loan Scandal.*

4. The Risk Panopticon

1. Who watches the watchers?

2. Chapter 13 in www.globalfinancialsystems.org/slides.

3. Goodhart, "Risk, Uncertainty and Financial Stability."

4. *New York Times,* "Paul A. Volcker, Fed Chairman Who Waged War on Inflation, Is Dead at 92."

5. The Myth of the Riskometer

1. As he told Dunbar in "Value-at-Risk Inventor Longerstaey on the Perils of Oversimplification."

2. Ibid.

3. Greenspan, "Maintaining Financial Stability in a Global Economy."

4. Researchers have known about the fat tail problems for over half a century, at least since the work of the future Nobel Prize–winner Eugene Fama and his PhD advisor, Benoit B. Mandelbrot.

5. Jansen and de Vries, "On the Frequency of Large Stock Returns: Putting Booms and Busts into Perspective."

6. http://tylervigen.com/spurious-correlations.

7. Daníelsson, "The New Market-Risk Regulations."

6. Ideas Matter

1. Keynes, *The General Theory of Interest, Employment and Money.*

2. Mises, *The Ultimate Foundation of Economic Science.*

3. Hayek, "The Use of Knowledge in Society."

4. See Rosenzweig, "Robert S. McNamara and the Evolution of Modern Management."

5. Yankelovitch, *Corporate Priorities: A Continuing Study of the New Demands on Business.*

6. Rumsfeld, U.S. Department of Defense (DoD) news briefing.

7. Josiah Stamp is recounting a story from Harold Cox, who quotes an anonymous English judge.

8. Goodhart, "Risk, Uncertainty and Financial Stability"; Shackle, *Keynesian Kaleidics.*

9. Buffett, "Berkshire Hathaway 2011 Letter to Shareholders."

10. Minsky, "The Financial Instability Hypothesis: An Interpretation of Keynes and an Alternative to 'Standard' Theory."

11. Yellen, press conference.

12. Goodhart, "Public Lecture at the Reserve Bank of Australia."

13. Lucas, "Econometric Policy Evaluation: A Critique," in *The Phillips Curve and Labor Market.*

7. Endogenous Risk

1. Keynes, *The General Theory of Interest, Employment and Money.*
2. Crockett, *Marrying the Micro- and Macro-Prudential Dimensions of Financial Stability.*
3. The average return in excess of the risk-free rate divided by volatility.
4. For a lucid description of events, see Lowenstein, *When Genius Failed: The Rise and Fall of Long-Term Capital Management.*
5. Ibid.
6. Ibid.

8. If You Can't Take the Risk, Change Riskometers

1. Fitzpatrick, "J.P. Morgan to SEC: That Model Change Doesn't Count as Change"; Henry and LaCapra, "JP Morgan and Other Banks Tinker with Risk Models."
2. Flitter, "Emails Show JP Morgan Tried to Flout Basel Rules—U.S. Senate."
3. Suppose a bank buys a put option, that is, the right but not the obligation to sell an asset in the future at a price called the strike price, X1. The bank then writes a put option for a lower strike price called X2. The effect of the former is to provide risk against the price of the asset falling below X1, while the second exposes the bank to large losses if the price of the asset drops below X2.
4. CDO stands for collateralized debt obligations, a structured credit product used to house subprime mortgages.
5. If the likelihood of losses is below the Value-at-Risk probability, typically one day out of a hundred, then the risk is recorded as zero.
6. Comment on Daníelsson, "Risk and Crises."

9. The Goldilocks Challenge

1. Described in Elliot, *Overend & Gurney, A Financial Scandal in Victorian London.*
2. Real total return, including dividends and adjusting for inflation.

10. The Risk Theater

1. Details on the specifics can be found on my website at www.modelsandrisk.org/Swiss.
2. The Basel committee came out with some adjustments to Basel III in December 2017. While sometimes dubbed Basel IV, they do not have (or deserve) that formal moniker.
3. Daníelsson and Keating, "Valuing Insurers' Liabilities during Crises: What EU Policymakers Should Not Do"; Daníelsson et al., "A Prudential Regulatory Issue at the Heart of Solvency II"; Daníelsson et al., "Countercyclical Regulation in Solvency II: Merits and Flaws."

4. I discussed the systemic importance of asset managers in a blog piece, Daníelsson and Zigrand, "Are Asset Managers Systemically Important?"

11. The Uniformity, Efficiency, and Stability Trilemma

1. https://fred.stlouisfed.org/series/USNUM.
2. El-Naggar, "In Lieu of Money, Toyota Donates Efficiency to New York Charity."

12. All about BoB

1. Kaku, *The Future of Quantum Computing*.
2. Kurzweil, *Communication to Futurism*.
3. Kahn, "To Get Ready for Robot Driving, Some Want to Reprogram Pedestrians."
4. Haldane, "Maxwell Fry Annual Global Finance Lecture: Managing Global Finance as a System."
5. EURISKO is certainly not the only such example. For a list of similar examples, see Krakovna, "Specification Gaming Examples in AI."

13. The Path Not to Take

1. Moving average economic growth for high-income countries, those in which 2015 GNI per capita was $12,476 or more. Data source: World Bank, *World Development Indicators*.
2. Financial Stability Board, *Holistic Review of the March Market Turmoil*.
3. Kindly provided by the data vendor IHS Markit.
4. See modelsandrisk.org/cryptocurrencies.

14. What to Do?

1. Monetary Authority of Singapore, "Macroprudential Policies: A Singapore Case Study," 321–27.

Bibliography

Adams, Douglas. *The Hitchhiker's Guide to the Galaxy.* London: Pan Books, 1978.

Admati, Anat, and Martin Hellwig. *The Bankers' New Clothes: What's Wrong with Banking and What to Do about It.* Princeton: Princeton University Press, 2014.

Akerlof, George A. "What They Were Thinking Then: The Consequences for Macroeconomics during the Past 60 Years." *Journal of Economic Perspectives* 33, no. 4 (2019): 171–86.

Aliber, Robert Z., and Charles P. Kindleberger. *Manias, Panics, and Crashes: A History of Financial Crises.* New York: Palgrave Macmillan, 2015.

Bagehot, Walter. *Lombard Street: A Description of the Money Market.* London: H. S. King, 1873.

Bank for International Settlements. *Report on the Regulatory Consistency of Risk-Weighted Assets for Market Risk.* Basel: Bank for International Settlements, 2013.

Basel Committee on Banking Supervision. *Amendment to the Capital Accord to Incorporate Market Risks.* Basel: Basel Committee on Banking Supervision, 1996.

———. *Fundamental Review of the Trading Book: A Revised Market Risk Framework.* Basel: Basel Committee on Banking Supervision, 2013.

BBC. "Did the Bank Wreck My Business?" *Panorama*, 2014.

Bernstein, Peter L. *Against the Gods: The Remarkable Story of Risk.* New York: John Wiley, 1996.

Bevilacqua, Mattia, Lukas Brandl-Cheng, Jón Daníelsson, Lerby Ergun, Andreas Uthemann, and Jean-Pierre Zigrand. "The Calming of Short-Term Market Fears and Its Long-Term Consequences: The Central Banks' Dilemma." SSRN Electronic Journal, 2021.

Bitner, Richard. *Confessions of a Subprime Lender: An Insider's Tale of Greed, Fraud, and Ignorance.* New York: John Wiley, 2008.

Black, Fischer. "Hedging, Speculation, and Systemic Risk." *Journal of Derivatives* 2 (1995): 6–8.

————, and Myron Scholes. "The Valuation of Option Contracts and a Test of Market Efficiency." *Journal of Political Economy* 27 (1973): 399–418.

Blanchard, Olivier. "(Nearly) Nothing to Fear but Fear Itself." *The Economist,* 2009.

Borio, Claudio. "The Macroprudential Approach to Regulation and Supervision." VoxEU.org, 2009.

Box, George. "Science and Statistics." *Journal of the American Statistical Association* (1976): 791–99.

Buffett, Warren. "Berkshire Hathaway 2011 Letter to Shareholders." 2011.

————. "Why Stocks Beat Gold and Bonds." *Fortune,* 2012.

Calomiris, Charles W., and Stephen H. Haber. *Fragile by Design: The Political Origins of Banking Crises and Scarce Credit.* Princeton: Princeton University Press, 2014.

Capra, Frank, dir. *It's a Wonderful Life.* 1946.

Carney, Mark. "Ten Years On: Fixing the Fault Lines of the Global Financial Crisis." *Banque de France Financial Stability Review,* no. 21 (2017).

Carville, James. Television interview. 1992.

Chwieroth, Jeffrey M., and Jón Daníelsson. "Political Challenges of the Macroprudential Agenda." VoxEU.org, 2013.

Crockett, Andrew. *Marrying the Micro- and Macro-Prudential Dimensions of Financial Stability.* Basel: BIS, 2000.

Daníelsson, Jón. "The Emperor Has No Clothes: Limits to Risk Modelling." *Journal of Banking and Finance* 26 (2002): 1273–96.

————. "The Myth of the Riskometer." VoxEU.org, 2009.

————. *Financial Risk Forecasting.* New York: John Wiley, 2011.

————. "Risk and Crises." VoxEU.org, 2011.

————. *Global Financial Systems: Stability and Risk.* London: Pearson, 2013.

————. "The New Market-Risk Regulations." VoxEU.org, 2013.

————. "Towards a More Procyclical Financial System." VoxEU.org, 2013.

————. "What the Swiss FX Shock Says about Risk Models." VoxEU.org, 2015.

Daníelsson, Jón, Paul Embrechts, Charles A. E. Goodhart, Con Keating, Felix Muennich, Olivier Renault, and Hyun Song Shin. *An Academic Response to Basel II.* London: LSE Financial Markets Group, 2001.

Daníelsson, Jón, Kevin James, Marcela Valenzuela, and Ilknur Zer. "Model Risk of Risk Models." *Journal of Financial Stability* 23 (2016).

————. "Can We Prove a Bank Guilty of Creating Systemic Risk? A Minority Report." *Journal of Money Credit and Banking* 48 (2017).

Daníelsson, Jón, Frank de Jong, Roger Laeven, Christian Laux, Enrico Perotti, and Mario Wuthrich. "A Prudential Regulatory Issue at the Heart of Solvency II." VoxEU.org, 2011.

Daníelsson, Jón, and Con Keating. "Valuing Insurers' Liabilities during Crises: What EU Policymakers Should Not Do." VoxEU.org, 2011.

Daníelsson, Jón, Roger Laeven, Enrico Perotti, Mario Wuthrich, Rym Ayadi, and Antoon Pelsser. "Countercyclical Regulation in Solvency II: Merits and Flaws." VoxEU.org, 2012.

Daníelsson, Jón, and Robert Macrae. "The Appropriate Use of Risk Models: Part I." VoxEU.org, 2011.

———. "The Appropriate Use of Risk Models: Part II." VoxEU.org, 2011.

———. "The Fatal Flaw in Macropru: It Ignores Political Risk." VoxEU.org, 2016.

———. "The Dissonance of the Short and Long Term." VoxEU.org, 2019.

Daníelsson, Jón, Robert Macrae, Dimitri Tsomocos, and Jean-Pierre Zigrand. "Why Macropru Can End Up Being Procyclical." VoxEU.org, 2016.

Daníelsson, Jón, Robert Macrae, and Andreas Uthemann. "Artificial Intelligence and Systemic Risk." *Journal of Banking and Finance* (2021).

Daníelsson, Jón, Robert Macrae, Dimitri Vayanos, and Jean-Pierre Zigrand. "The Coronavirus Crisis Is No 2008." VoxEU.org, 2020.

Daníelsson, Jón, and Hyun Song Shin. "Endogenous Risk." In *Modern Risk Management: A History*. London: Risk Books, 2003.

Daníelsson, Jón, Hyun Shin, and Jean-Pierre Zigrand. "Endogenous Extreme Events and the Dual Role of Prices." *Annual Reviews* 4 (2012).

Daníelsson, Jón, Marcela Valenzuela, and Ilknur Zer. "Learning from History: Volatility and Financial Crises." *Review of Financial Studies* (2018).

Daníelsson, Jón, and Chen Zhou. "Why Risk Is So Hard to Measure." Amsterdam: De Nederlandsche Bank NV, 2016.

Daníelsson, Jón, and Jean-Pierre Zigrand. "Are Asset Managers Systemically Important?" VoxEU.org, 2015.

Day, Kathleen. *A Wonderful Life: S&L HELL: The People and the Politics behind the $1 Trillion Savings and Loan Scandal*. New York: W. W. Norton, 1993.

Diamond, Douglas W., and Philip H. Dybvig. "Bank Runs, Deposit Insurance, and Liquidity." *Journal of Political Economy* 91 (1983): 401–19.

Dunbar, Nicholas. "What JP Morgan's Release of VaR Has in Common with Sex and Computer Viruses." 2012. http://www.nickdunbar.net/articles/what-jp-morgans-release-of-var-has-in-common-with-sex-and-computer-viruses/.

———. "Value-at-Risk Inventor Longerstaey on the Perils of Oversimplification." Bloomberg Briefs, 2012.

Elliot, Geoffrey. *Overend & Gurney, a Financial Scandal in Victorian London*. London: Methuen, 2006.

El-Naggar, Mona. "In Lieu of Money, Toyota Donates Efficiency to New York Charity." *New York Times*, 2013.

Engle, Robert. "Autoregressive Conditional Heteroskedasticity with Estimates of the Variance of the United Kingdom Inflation." *Econometrica* 50 (1982): 987–1007.

Engels, Friedrich. *Socialism: Utopian and Scientific*. London: Swan Sonnenschein, 1880.

European Banking Authority. "EBA Interim Report on the Consistency of Risk-Weighted Assets in the Banking Book." 2013.

Fama, Eugene. "Mandelbrot and the Stable Paretian Hypothesis." *Journal of Business* 36, no. 4 (1963): 420–29.

———. "Are Markets Efficient?" Posted at https://review.chicagobooth.edu/economics/2016/video/are-markets-efficient, 2016.

Financial Stability Board. *Holistic Review of the March Market Turmoil*. Financial Stability Board, 2020.

Fitzpatrick, Dan. "J.P. Morgan to SEC: That Model Change Doesn't Count as 'Change.'" *Wall Street Journal*, 2013.

Flitter, Emily. "Emails Show JP Morgan Tried to Flout Basel Rules—U.S. Senate." Reuters, 2013.

Friedman, Milton, and Anna Jacobson Schwartz. *A Monetary History of the United States: 1867–1960*. Princeton: Princeton University Press, 1963.

Gissurarson, Hannes. *Twenty-Four Conservative-Liberal Thinkers, Part II*. Brussels: New Direction, 2021.

Goodhart, Charles A. E. "Public Lecture at the Reserve Bank of Australia." 1974.

———. *Risk, Uncertainty and Financial Stability*. London: Financial Markets Group, London School of Economics, 2008.

———. *The Basel Committee on Banking Supervision: A History of the Early Years 1974–1997*. Cambridge: Cambridge University Press, 2011.

Greenspan, Alan. *Discussion at Symposium: Maintaining Financial Stability in a Global Economy*, at the Federal Reserve Bank of Kansas City (1997): 54.

Haldane, Andy. "Managing Global Finance as a System. Maxwell Fry Annual Global Finance Lecture," Birmingham University, 2014.

Hayek, Friedrich von. "The Use of Knowledge in Society." *American Economic Review* 35, no. 4 (1945): 510–30.

Henry, David, and Lauren Tara LaCapra. "JP Morgan and Other Banks Tinker with Risk Models." Reuters, 2013.

Hernández de Cos, Pablo. "Basel III Implementation in the European Union." BCBS Speech, 2021.

Holder, Eric. US Senate Judiciary Committee testimony. 2013.

Honohan, Patrick, and Daniela Klingebiel. "The Fiscal Cost Implications of an Accommodating Approach to Banking Crises." *Journal of Banking and Finance* 26 (2003).

House of Commons library. "Financial Services: Contribution to the U.K. Economy." Briefing Paper Number 6193, 2017.

Hoyt, Jehiel Keeler. *The Cyclopedia of Practical Quotations*. London: Funk & Wagnalls, 1907.

International Monetary Fund, Bank for International Settlements, and Financial Stability Board. *Report to G20 Finance Ministers and Governors. Guidance to Assess the Systemic Importance of Financial Institutions, Markets and Instruments: Initial Considerations* (2009): 2.

Jansen, Dennis, and Casper G. de Vries. "On the Frequency of Large Stock Returns: Putting Booms and Busts into Perspective." *Restat* 73 (1991): 18–24.

Johnson, Rian, dir. *Star Wars: Episode VIII—The Last Jedi*. 2017.

Kahn, Jeremy. "To Get Ready for Robot Driving, Some Want to Reprogram Pedestrians." Bloomberg, 2018.

Kaku, Michio. *The Future of Quantum Computing*. At https://www.youtube.com/watch?v=YgFVzOksm4o (2011).

Keynes, John Maynard. *A Treatise on Probability.* London: Macmillan, 1921.

———. *The General Theory of Interest, Employment and Money.* London: Macmillan, 1936.

Kindleberger, Charles P. *Manias, Panics, and Crashes: A History of Financial Crises.* 3d ed. London: John Wiley, 1996.

King, Mervyn. "Inflation Report Press Conference." Bank of England, 2007.

Knight, Frank Hyneman. *Risk, Uncertainty and Profit.* New York: Houghton Mifflin, 1921.

Kohn, Meir. "Early Deposit Banking." Hanover, NH: Department of Economics, Dartmouth College, 1999.

Krakovna, Victoria. "Specification Gaming Examples in AI." https://vkrakovna .wordpress.com/2018/04/02/

Kubrick, Stanley, dir. *2001: A Space Odyssey.* 1968.

Kurzweil, Ray. *Communication to Futurism.* 2017.

Laeven, L., and F. Valencia. "Systemic Banking Crises Revisited." IMF Working Paper, 2018.

Lenat, Douglas B. "EURISKO: A Program That Learns New Heuristics and Domain Concepts: The Nature of Heuristics III: Program Design and Results." *Artificial Intelligence* 21, nos. 1, 2 (1983): 61–98.

Lewis, Michael. *The Big Short: Inside the Doomsday Machine.* Detroit: Gale Cengage Learning, 2010.

———. *Flash Boys.* New York: Penguin, 2015.

Lowenstein, Roger. *When Genius Failed: The Rise and Fall of Long-Term Capital Management.* New York: Random House, 2000.

Lucas, Robert. "Econometric Policy Evaluation: A Critique." In *The Phillips Curve and Labor Markets,* ed. K. Brunner and A. Meltzer, 19–46. 1976.

Magnus, George. *Red Flags: Why Xi's China Is in Jeopardy.* New Haven: Yale University Press, 2019.

Malkiel, Burton Gordon. *A Random Walk down Wall Street.* New York: W. W. Norton, 1973.

Mandelbrot, Benoit B. "The Variation of Certain Speculative Prices." *Journal of Business* 36 (1963): 392–417.

Markowitz, Harry. "Portfolio Selection." *Journal of Finance* 7 (1952): 77–91.

Martin, William McChesney, Jr. "Address before the New York Group of the Investment Bankers Association of America." 1955.

Marx, Karl. *Das Kapital: Kritik Der Politischen Oekonomie.* Verlag von Otto Meissner, 1867.

Merler, Silvia, and Jean Pisani-Ferry. "Who's Afraid of Sovereign Bonds?" Bruegel Policy Contribution, 2012.

Minsky, Hyman. "The Financial Instability Hypothesis: An Interpretation of Keynes and an Alternative to 'Standard' Theory." *Nebraska Journal of Economics and Business* 16 (1977): 5–16.

———. *Stabilizing an Unstable Economy.* New Haven: Yale University Press, 1986.

———. *The Financial Instability Hypothesis*. Annandale-on-Hudson, NY: Jerome Levy Economics Institute, 1992.

Mises, Ludwig von. *The Ultimate Foundation of Economic Science*. Princeton: Van Nostrand, 1962.

Monetary Authority of Singapore. "Macroprudential Policies: A Singapore Case Study." *BIS Papers,* no. 94 (2017): 321–27.

New York Times. "Paul A. Volcker, Fed Chairman Who Waged War on Inflation, Is Dead at 92." 2019.

OECD. *G20/OECD INFE Report on Adult Financial Literacy in G20 Countries*. OECD, 2017.

Orlik, Thomas. *China: The Bubble That Never Pops*. Oxford: Oxford University Press, 2020.

Popper, Karl. *The Open Society and Its Enemies*. London: Routledge, 1945.

Prince, Charles ("Chuck"). Interview in the *Financial Times*, 2007.

Quinn, Stephen, and William Roberds. "Responding to a Shadow Banking Crisis: The Lessons of 1763." *Journal of Money, Credit and Banking* 47, no. 62 (2015): 1149–76.

Reinhart, Carmen, and Kenneth Rogoff. *This Time Is Different: Eight Centuries of Financial Folly*. Princeton: Princeton University Press, 2009.

Rodgers, Kevin. *Why Aren't They Shouting?* London: Penguin, 2016.

Rosenzweig, Phil. *Robert S. McNamara and the Evolution of Modern Management*. Cambridge: Harvard Business Review, 2010.

Rossi, Hugo. "Mathematics Is an Edifice, Not a Toolbox." *Notices of the AMS* 43, no. 10 (1996).

Rumsfeld, Donald. U.S. Department of Defense (DoD) news briefing, 2002.

Russel, Stuart. *Human Compatible*. London: Allen Lane, 2019.

Santayana, George. "Reason in Common Sense." In *The Life of Reason*, 1:284. New York: Scribners, 1921.

Schlosser, Eric. *Fast Food Nation: What the All-American Meal Is Doing to the World*. Boston: Houghton Mifflin, 2001.

Schnabel, Isabel, and Hyun Song Shin. "Liquidity and Contagion: The Crisis of 1763." *Journal of the European Economic Association* 2, no. 6 (2004): 929–68.

Schneier, Bruce. "Beyond Security Theater." *New Internationalist,* 2009.

Schumpeter, Joseph. *Capitalism, Socialism and Democracy*. London: Harper & Brothers, 1942.

Shackle, George L. S. *Keynesian Kaleidics*. Edinburgh: Edinburgh University Press, 1974.

Shapiro, Fred R. *The Yale Book of Quotations*. New Haven: Yale University Press, 2006.

Silver, David, Julian Schrittwieser, Karen Simonyan, Ioannis Antonoglou, Aja Huang, Arthur Guez, Thomas Hubert, et al. "Mastering the Game of Go without Human Knowledge." *Nature* (2017).

Skalweit, Stephan. *Die Getreidehandelspolitik und Kriegsmagazinverwaltung Preußens 1756–1806*. Berlin: Acta Borussia, 1931.

Smith, Adam. *An Inquiry into the Nature and Causes of the Wealth of Nations.* London: W. Strahan, T. Cadell, 1776.

Soto, Hernando de. *The Mystery of Capital.* New York: Basic Books, 2000.

Syed, Matthew. *Rebel Ideas: The Power of Diverse Thinking.* New York: Flatiron Books, 2019.

Triana, Pablo. *The Number That Killed Us.* London: John Wiley, 2011.

Tukey, John W. "The Future of Data Analysis." *Annals of Mathematical Statistics* 33 (1962): 1–67.

UBS. *Shareholder Report on UBS's Write-Downs.* UBS, 2008.

Viniar, David. "Goldman Pays the Price of Being Big." *Financial Times* interview, 2007.

Whitehouse, Kaja. "One 'Quant' Sees Shakeout for the Ages—'10,000 Years.'" *Wall Street Journal,* 2007.

Yankelovich, David. *Corporate Priorities: A Continuing Study of the New Demands on Business.* D. Yankelovich Inc., 1972.

Yellen, Janet. Press conference. Federal Reserve Board, 2014.

Index

Page numbers in italics refer to illustrations.

Adams, Douglas, 221
Admati, Anat, 59
Adoboli, Kweku, 217–18
Against the Gods (Bernstein), 51
AIG (American International Group), 184–85, 226
airlines, risk culture of, 252, 253
Akerlof, George A., 96–97
Aladdin (risk management system), 197, 211
alchemy, 139
Aliber, Robert, 153
AlphaGo Zero, 209
Al Qaeda, 227
Amazon, 154
Amazon Web Services (AWS), 196–97
Amsterdam, 6, 12, 35
Andropov, Yuri, 2
arbitrage, 68, 123, 126, 135–36, 174
ARCH (autoregressive conditional heteroskedasticity), 86–87, 143, 195
Archegos Capital, 144
Argentina, 149, 166
artificial intelligence (AI), 5, 159, 196, 197, 205–22

Arup Engineering, 110, 111–12
Asian debt crisis (1998), 8, 37, 178
asset management, 185–86
asteroids, 4
Austria, 38–39

backtesting, 89
Bagehot, Walter, 151–52, 178
bailouts, 13, 44, 48, 147, 224, 238; during Covid-19 pandemic, 47, 162, 234, 237, 241; in Greece, 43, 47, 95; for Long Term Capital Management, 125; as middle-class benefit, 166; as moral hazard, 162, 163; popular resentment of, 237; as socialistic practice, 203
Banca Monte dei Paschi, 166
Banco Ambrosiano, 62–63
Banco de México, 69
Banco Popular, 165
bank capital, 58–60, 176, 180
Bank for Commerce and Credit International (BCCI), 63–64
Bank for International Settlements, 8, 65, 113
bank–government doom loop, 45

Bankhaus Herstatt, 61–62

Banking Act (1933), 38

Bank of England, 13–14, 20, 39, 40–41, 45, 210, 233; contradictory policies of, 248; crisis of 2008 bungled by, 158; establishment of, 55; in panic of 1866, 151–52; politicizing of, 183; as regulator, 63–64, 248

Bank of Ireland, 47

Bank of Italy, 62

Bank of Japan, 65

Bank of United States, 31–32

bankruptcy, 17, 27, 31, 33, 163

banks: fragility of, 29; government debt held by, 44; necessity of, 28, 55; number of, in U.S. vs. Japan, 251; as political target, 27; retail clients of, 39; runs on, 29–30; wholesale funding of, 39

Barcelona, 56

Barings, 218

Basel Capital Accords, 90, 195, 201; cost of complying with, 250–51; delays in implementing, 66, 202, 220; entrepreneurship impeded by, 232; Expected Shortfall incorporated in, 135; leverage ratio prescribed by, 176; limitations of, 65–67, 173–75; opacity of, 233; traffic-light rule in, 134; Value-at-Risk incorporated in, 76, 81

Basel Committee on Banking Supervision, 64–67, 169, 199, 200, 202–3

Bear Stearns, 226

behavioral economics, 102

bell curve, 82

Bentham, Jeremy, 3, 53

Berkshire Hathaway, 137

Berlin, 7–8, 36

Berlin airlift, 99l

Bernstein, Peter, 51

big data, 207

The Big Short (Lewis), 20, 127

Bitner, Richard, 142

Black, Fischer, 16

Black Death, 12

Black Monday (1987), 9, 118–19

BlackRock, 54, 197

Blanchard, Olivier, 232

Bohr, Nils, 72

Borio, Claudio, 177, 178

Box, George, 3, 74, 90

Bretton Woods system, 28, 60, 61, 170, 239

Brexit, 15, 78, 183

bubbles, 32, 103, 104, 116, 121–22, 152–54, 180

Buffett, Warren, 78, 102, 137

Burrows, Jonathan, 54

Bush, George H. W., 15

Calomiris, Charles, 161–62

Calvi, Roberto, 62

Candide (Voltaire), 225

Das Capital (Marx), 58

capital conservation buffer, 60

capital ratio, 59, 65, 135

capital structure arbitrage, 68, 135–36, 174

Capone, Al, 23

Carney, Mark, 168, 188

Castello, Francesch, 56, 160

central bank digital currencies (CBDCs), 238

chess, 209

Chicago Board Options Exchange, 123

China, 154, 183; air traffic control in, 160; stock market closure in, 14

China: The Bubble That Never Pops (Orlik), 153

Chinese walls, 143

Chwieroth, Jeff, 166, 181

CIA (Central Intelligence Agency), 227

circuit breakers, in markets, 14

CISS (Composite Indicator of Systemic Stress), 79, 179, 246

clawbacks, 57

clearing, 11
climate change, 85
Clinton, Bill, 15
Coca-Cola, 154
cognitive failure, 227–32
collateral debt obligations (CDOs), 70, 133, 134, 139–42, 193, 212, 218
conduits, 70–71
Confessions of a Subprime Lender (Bitner), 142
confidence intervals, 79
confirmation bias, 2
convergence trading, 123
corporate finance, 237, 251
countercyclical capital buffer, 60
Covid-19 pandemic, 8–12, 113, 114, 179, 183, 193, 232; bailouts during, 47, 162, 234, 237, 241; banking regulation and, 29, 174–75; Chinese response to, 14; financial crisis of 2008 compared with, 21, 235; financial markets during, 153, 234; Icelandic economy buffeted by, 156; macroprudential policy during, 181, 187; modeling of, 91–92, 100; political response to, 15; safety vs. growth epitomized by, 21
Credit-Anstalt, 39
credit default swaps (CDSs), 141–42, 184–85
credit rating, 44, 67, 140
Credit Suisse, 144
crisis, crises: causes of, 31–34; corruption linked to, 33–34; costs of, 45–47; frequency of, 9, 32, 33, 50; IMF database of, 9, 46; textbook example of, 10; types of, 8
Crockett, Andrew, 121
cryptocurrency, 223, 237–38
Cuban Missile Crisis (1962), 2
Cyprus, 36, 42–43, 45, 66

data snooping, 88
de Cos, Pablo Hernández, 234, 236

deflation, 31
Deloitte & Touche, 63
Delta Works, 85
de Neufville, Leendert Pieter, 6–7, 10, 241
deposit insurance, 37, 38, 39, 41–42
Depository Trust and Clearance Corporation (DTCC), 115
Deutsche Bank, 176
devaluation, 106
developing countries, 17–18
de Vres, Casper, 85
Diamond, Douglas, 39
dinosaur extinction, 4, 113
diversity, in financial system: forces opposing, 190–91, 249–50, 251; measurement of, 191; stability linked to, 5, 188, 190, 193, 249, 253
divorce-and-margarine fallacy, 89–90
Dominican Republic, 34
Dondelinger, Albert, 64
dot-com bubble (1990s), 154
Dunford, Joseph, 181
Dybvig, Philip, 39
dynamic replication, 119

"Early Deposit Banking" (Kohn), 56
"Econometric Policy Evaluation" (Lucas), 107
econometrics, 96
elasticity of demand, 118
Engels, Friedrich, 203
Engle, Robert, 86–87, 195, 197
Enron, 225
Erdogan, Recep, 182
ergodicity, 95, 101, 145, 195
Ernst & Young, 63, 133
EURISKO (artificial intelligence system), 215
Eurodollars, 69
European Banking Authority, 199, 200, 202–3
European Capital Markets Union, 251

European Central Bank, 22, 31, 42; quantitative easing by, 45; risk dashboard of, 78, 88, 92, 127, 214; signals missed by, 79–80, 88

European Commission, 42, 43

European Union, 66

evergreening, 49

EVT (riskometer), 172–73

exchange rates, 77, 170–71

exchange traded funds, 185

expected shortfall, 75, 135, 197–200, 243

exponentially weighted moving average (EWMA, riskometer), 131–32, 172, 197, 198

externalities, 163

extreme value theory (EVT), 85, 198

fallacy of composition, 4–5, 227, 246

false resilience, 242–43, 245–46, 252

Fama, Eugene, 256n4 (chapter 5)

Fast Food Nation (Schlosser), 130

fat-tail risk, 82–85, 231

Federal Aviation Administration (FAA), 161

Federal Deposit Insurance Corporation (FDIC), 38, 39

Federal Reserve, 16, 32, 125, 149–50; during Great Depression, 148–49, 152

fiat money, 30, 238

Financial Conduct Authority (FCA), 54, 64, 159, 211

financial crisis of 2008, 1, 4, 8, 9, 15, 127, 152, 203, 213, 225, 232; causes of, 67, 133, 153, 188; Covid-19 pandemic compared with, 76, 81; credit default swaps linked to, 184–85; European Central Bank's blundering linked to, 79–80, 88; government policies linked to, 16–17; Lehman Brothers bailout and, 47; liquidity during, 32, 149, 170, 178; regulatory shift following, 29; subprime mortgages linked to, 16, 19–20, 88, 133, 141, 153, 180, 183, 241

financial liberalization, 35–36

financial repression, 66

Financial Risk Forecasting (Daníelsson), 196

Financial Services Authority (FSA), 40, 41, 64, 182

Financial Stability Board (FSB), 8, 169, 184, 185, 234

financing, types of, 102–3

Finland, 46, 47

Flash Boys (Lewis), 217

flooding, 84–85

Food Bank for New York City, 193

Food Standards Agency (UK), 161

football, 192

Foster, Norman, 110

Fragile by Design (Calomiris and Haber), 161–62

France, 38–39, 49

Franz Ferdinand, archduke of Austria, 10–11, 120, 193, 234

French, Fama, 154

French and Indian War, 6–7, 120

Friedman, Milton, 32, 148–49, 194

Friedrich II, king of Prussia, 7–8

Fusarium Oxysporum, 189–90

Galvão, Ricardo, 128

gambling, 55

Gamestop crisis (2021), 11, 115

GARCH (riskometer), 143, 172, 198, 201

Gauss, Johann Carl Friedrich, 82

General Motors, 163

General Theory of Interest, Employment and Money (Keynes), 96, 98, 101, 112–13, 158

Georgiou, Andreas, 120, 149

Germany, 49, 61–62, 183, 251

Giffen, Robert, 118

Giffen gods, 118

gilts, 45, 151

Gissurarson, Hannes, 98–99

Glass-Steagall Act (1935), 148, 191

Global Alpha fund, 137–38

Global Financial Systems (Daníelsson), 135, 164

Goldman Sachs, 23, 137

Goodhart, Charles, 3, 20, 60, 64, 66, 101, 105, 107–8

Goodhart's law, 3, 105–8, 216

Goodwin, Rupert, 129

Google, 154, 209

Great Depression, 1, 8, 28, 178; bank regulation during, 143; bank runs during, 31, 38, 41; Federal Reserve's passivity during, 148–49, 152; margin buying linked to, 116; market failure linked to, 97, 98; money supply collapse during, 32; volatility during, 86

Great Moderation, 16, 69–70, 103, 139, 225

Greece, 42–43, 47, 66

Greensill Capital, 144

Greenspan, Alan, 16, 82, 186

Gros Michel banana, 189–90

Groundhog Day (film), 26

G20 group, 49, 53, 65, 169, 184

Haber, Stephen, 161–62

Hagan, Patrick, 130

Haldane, Andy, 210

Hamburg, 7, 36

Hayek, Friedrich August von, 94, 97–99, 101, 114, 187, 214

hedge financing, 102–3

hedge funds, 122–23, 127

Hellwig, Martin, 59

Henderson, James, 101

Herstatt, Jowan David, 61

Herzberg, Elaine, 169

high-frequency trading, 217

Holder, Eric, 25

Hong Kong, 183

Honohan, Patrick, 46–47

HSBC, 25, 159

Human Compatible (Russel), 207

hurricanes, 82

Hurricane Sandy, 193

ICBC (Industrial and Commercial Bank of China), 176–77

Iceland, 36, 44; financial crisis in (2008), 22–23, 24, 37, 42, 149, 153, 155–56, 220

IKB Bank, 70–71

Iksil, Bruno, 139

India, 52–53

Indonesia, 46

inflation: bailouts linked to, 164; central banks' focus on, 182; excessive preoccupation with, 4, 157–58; intractability of, 31; misconceptions surrounding, 69; in 1970s, 38, 70; recent ebb in, 179; sterilization to counter, 171; unemployment vs., 105–6, 107

ING, 177

injuries, in football and lacrosse, 192

input–output model, 99, 100–101, 102

insurance companies, 184–86

interconnectedness, 8–9, 11–12, 15, 241

internal ratings-based (IRB) method, 196

International Monetary Fund (IMF), 8, 42–44, 101, 225

invariance, 228

investment horizons, 75

Ireland, 27, 42, 44, 47, 165

Italy, 45, 49, 62, 166

It's a Wonderful Life (film), 29–30, 31

James, Kevin, 245

Japan, 47, 48–49, 183, 251; banking crisis in, 65, 152–53, 186–87

JP Morgan: during Covid-19 pandemic, 236; in London Whale scandal, 130–31, 146; Morgan Stanley split from, 148; solvency of, 59, 176, 177; Value-at-Risk developed by, 80–81, 195, 196, 197

Kaizen, 193, 195, 225

Kaku, Michio, 208

Keating, Charles, 38

Kerviel, Jérôme, 143
Keynes, John Maynard, 94, 96–99, 101, 112–13, 125, 158, 236
King, Mervyn, 20
Klingebiel, Daniela, 46
Knight, Frank, 94, 95, 97, 99, 101
Kohn, Meir, 56
K-shaped crises, 8
Kurzweil, Ray, 209

Laeven, Luc, 9
Leeson, Nick, 217–18
Lehman Brothers, 47, 71, 78, 175, 226
Leland, Hayne, 118–19
Lenat, Douglas, 215
Lenin, Vladimir, 209
Leontief, Wassily, 99, 100, 102
leverage, 15, 58, 116
leverage ratio, 59, 136, 176
Lewis, Michael, 20, 127, 217
LIBOR, 23–24, 159
linear programming, 99–100
liquidity, 30, 31, 112, 164, 241; during crisis of 2008, 32, 149, 170, 17832, 149, 170, 178; difficulty of measuring, 244
Little Britain (television program), 208
Lloyds Bank, 174
loan-to-value ratio, 180, 183
London, 12–14, 15, 35, 55, 79
London School of Economics, 20
Longerstacy, Jacques, 81
Long Term Capital Management (LTCM) crisis (1998), 9, 122–23, 124–25
Lucas, Robert, 107, 236
Luxembourg, 36, 37, 62, 64

MA (riskometer), 172
machine learning, 207
Macrae, Robert, 21, 144, 173, 183, 212
macroprudential regulation, 98, 169, 174, 177–78, 184, 226, 246; artificial intelligence ill-suited to, 212, 216,

219; in less democratic countries, 183; winners and losers under, 182
Maginot Line, 157
Magnus, George, 153
Malaysia, 183
Malkiel, Burton, 125–26
Mandelbrot, Benoit B., 256n4 (chapter 5)
Manias, Panics, and Crises (Aliber), 153
margarine-and-divorce fallacy, 89–90
margin buying, 116–18, 179
margin calls, 117, 124
Markowitz, Harry, 193–95, 197
mark-to-market feedback, 14
Martin, William McChesney, Jr., 149–50
Marx, Karl, 58–59
McNamara, Robert, 100
mean–variance model, 194–95
Mencken, H. L., 89
Mendeleev, Dmitri, 139
Merton, Robert C., 122
Mexico, 69, 149
microprudential regulation, 191; by artificial intelligence, 211, 216, 218–19, 222; Basel Accords aimed at, 173, 174, 177
The Milkmaid (Vermeer), 8
Millennium Bridge, 109–12, 114, 116, 117
Minority Report (film), 168
Minsky, Hyman, 3, 94, 102, 103–4
Minsky effect, 69–70, 104, 186, 193, 216
Mises, Ludwig von, 96
model risk, 91–92
Moldova, 34
momentum investing, 124
A Monetary History of the United States (Friedman and Schwartz), 32
Monetary National Income Analogue Computer (MONIAC), 106
monetary policy, 20, 105, 158, 179, 181
money market funds, 69
monoculture, 190
Monte Carlo experiments, 90–91

Moore, Gordon, 208
Moore's law, 205, 208
moral hazard, 22, 37, 151, 162, 163, 233, 235–37
Morgan, John Pierpont, 148, 241
Morgan Stanley, 148
MSCI Inc., 197
Murray, Bill, 26
The Mystery of Capital (Soto), 28

Netherlands, 36, 84–85, 153, 177
network effects, 12
New York City, 15
Nifty Fifty stocks, 153, 154
Nixon, Richard M., 157
Nomura, 124
normal distribution, 82, 84
Northern Rock, 20, 39–41, 80, 226
Norway, 47, 183
The Number That Killed Us (Triana), 81

Occupy Wall Street, 27
offshore banking, 42–44
online banking, 42, 214
The Open Society and Its Enemies (Popper), 203
options, 133–34
Organisation for Economic Cooperation and Development (OECD), 66
Orlik, Thomas, 153
ossification, 202, 226
Overend & Gurney (O&G), 150–51

Panama disease, 190
Panopticon, 3, 53–55, 71, 216
Pareto, Vilfredo, 85
Pascal, Blaise, 74, 225
PayPal, 238
Peltzman, Sam, 192
pensions, pension funds, 58–59, 76, 199, 228–29, 231, 245
Petrov, Stanislav, 2
Phillips, Bill, 105–7

Phillips curve, 106
Ponzi financing, 102–3
Popper, Karl, 203–4
portfolio insurance, 118
Portfolio Selection (Markowitz), 194
Portugal, 42, 54
Powell, Jerome, 181, 247
precautionary principle, 112, 241
prices, 95, 102, 114–16, 118
Price Waterhouse, 63
Prince, Chuck, 34–35
principal-agent problem, in financial trading, 143
private equity, 246
procyclicality, 67, 193, *194*, 212; Basel regulations and, 175; financial monoculture linked to, 191, 202, 203, 213, 236, 249; macroprudential regulation and, 179, 181, 186–87; of regulatory laxity, 156
Prudential Regulation Authority (PRA), 64
public transport, 54–55
put options, 113–14, 118–19

quant funds, 137–39
quantitative easing, 15, 45, 238

Rain Man (film), 209
A Random Walk Down Wall Street (Malkiel), 126
Rato, Rodrigo, 23
RBS (Royal Bank of Scotland), 174
RBS-ABN AMRO, 175
real estate, 3, 10, 103, 153, 182–83
reasoned probability, 102
Rebel Ideas (Syed), 227
recession, 31, 141
Reconstruction Finance Corporation, 41
Reform Act (1832), 28
RegTech, 211
Regulation Q, 69
regulation vs. supervision, 52–53

regulatory capture, 161
relative value trading, 123
religion, 55
reserve requirements, 30, 33
Richelieu, Armand Jean du Plessis, duc de, 22
risk: aggregating, 244–45; aversion to, 57, 160, 161, 252; difficulty of measuring, 3, 4, 57, 72–77, 82–85, 92, 126, 127, 129, 179, 186, 196, 231, 241, 244; endogenous, 3–4, 67, 68, 109–27, 214, 225, 228, 241–42; exogenous, 3–4, 68, 113, 114, 195, 214, 226, 228, 252; fat-tail, 82–85, 231; growth linked to, 17, 21, 25; incentives for, 56; latency of, 76–77; manipulable measurements of, 108, 127, 133–36, 143, 146; perceived vs. actual, 121; systemic, 2, 8–10, 16, 18, 20, 55, 177–78, 184; uncertainty vs., 95–96, 195
"Risk, Uncertainty and Financial Stability" (Goodhart), 107–8
risk competition, 192
RiskMetrics, 197, 211
risk theater, 169, 172, 175, 185, 188
risk-weighted assets, 59
Robinhood trading platform, 115
Rodgers, Kevin, 159
Roosevelt, Franklin D., 38, 149
Rothschild, Nathan Meyer, 126, 249
Royal Bank of Canada (RBC), 177
Rubinstein, Mark, 118–19
Rumsfeld, Donald, 100
Russel, Stuart, 207
Russia, 42–43, 124, 183

Sanrio Company, 68
Santander, 165
savings-and-loan (S&L) crisis (1980s), 10, 37–38
Schlosser, Eric, 130
Schneier, Bruce, 169
Scholes, Myron, 122–23

Schumpeter, Joseph, 163
Schwartz, Anna, 32, 148–49
scientific socialism, 203–4
secular decline, 231, *232*
Securities and Exchange Commission (SEC), 217
securitization, 20, 80
self-driving cars, 209–10, 217, 219
sell-on-loss rules, 119
September 11 attacks, 227
Seven Years' War, 6–7, 120
Shackle, George Lennox Sharman, 101–2, 107
shadow banking, 8, 236
Sharpe, William F., 121
Sharpe ratio, 121
Shin, Hyun Song, 66, 113, 121
shipping, 150
significance testing, 79
silos, 230
Singapore, 36, 42, 183, 248–49
Skalweit, Stephan, 6
Smith, Adam, 58, 126
Socialism (Engels), 203
Soto, Hernando de, 28
South Korea, 37, 225
sovereign debt crisis (2010s), 16, 42–44
sovereign wealth funds, 231, 245, 248
Soviet Union, 2, 69, 89, 97, 99, 188, 209
Spain, 22, 23, 153, 165, 177; bank overexpansion in, 42; corporate finance in, 237, 251; traffic enforcement in, 54
Spanish flu pandemic (1918), 190
speculative financing, 102
speed limits, 29
spurious correlation, 89
stagflation, 157, 179, 236
Stalin, Joseph, 209
Stamp, Josiah, 101
Standard & Poor 500 index, 77, 83, 88–89, 119, 123, 131
sterilization, 171
Stewart, James, 29–30

Stumpf, John, 57
subjective probability, 102
successful general's syndrome, 157, 158
supermarket sales, 207
supervision vs. regulation, 52–53
supply and demand, 118
Sweden, 26, 47, 48, 49
Switzerland, 11, 49, 170–73, 177
Syed, Matthew, 227
systematically important financial institutions (SIFIs), 161, 175–76
systemic risk, 2, 8–10, 16, 18, 20, 55, 177–78, 184

tail risk, 82, 92, 134, 190, 228–29, 231, 243
Taipei 101 building, 67–68
taxation, 44, 180
technological singularity, 209
Tesobonos, 69
t-GARCH (riskometer), 172–73, 201
Thailand, 36, 37, 183
Tolstedt, Carrie, 57
"too big to fail" problem, 25, 34
Tourre, Fabrice, 23
Toyota, 193
traffic laws, 29, 52, 54
traffic-light rule, in risk measurement, 134
tranches, 140–42
transfer of responsibilities, 202
Triana, Pablo, 81
Truman, Harry S, 73, 130
Trump, Donald, 15, 184
Tucker, Paul, 181
Tukey, John W., 78
tulip mania, 153
Turing test, 209
Turkey, 69, 182
2001 (film), 222
Typhoon Soudelor, 68

Uber, 169
UBS, 4, 133, 134, 146, 176, 218
Unelected Power (Tucker), 181

unemployment, 33, 105, 107
United Kingdom, 9, 49; corporate finance in, 150, 251; deposit insurance in, 41–42; financial sector in, 36–37; monetary policy in, 182; Northern Rock failure in, 20, 39–41, 80, 226
U-shaped crises, 8
usury, 55
Uthemann, Andreas, 212

Valencia, Fabián, 9
Valenzuela, Marcela, 104, 245
Value-at-Risk, 75, 91, 134, 142, 143, 243; in Basel regulations, 76, 81; manipulability of, 130–33; misapplication of, 76, 133, 145; JP Morgan's development of, 80–81, 195, 196, 197; as volatility alternative, 81
Varley, John, 23
Vayanos, Dimitri, 21
Venezuela, 15, 34, 183
Vermeer, Johannes, 8
Vietnam War, 100
Viniar, David, 138
volatility, 2, 14, 75, 83–84, 134; clustering of, 86; crises linked to, 104–5; diversity vs., 190; fat-tail risk inversely related to, 231
Volatility Index (VIX), 123–25
Volcker, Paul, 70
Voltaire, 225
Volvo Cars, 5, 169–70, 175, 227, 235,
V-shaped crises, 8

Walker, Andrew, 166
Walmart, 207
Washington Consensus, 60–61, 170
The Wealth Effect (Chwieroth and Walter), 166
The Wealth of Nations (Smith), 58
Weatherstone Dennis, 80
Wellington, Arthur Wellesley, Duke of, 27

Wells Fargo scandal, 57
Why Aren't They Shouting? (Rodgers),
   159
Why Xi's China Is in Jeopardy (Magnus),
   153
Wirecard, 62, 220
World Bank, 46
WorldCom, 225
World War I, 157

Xiaochuan, Zhou, 103–4

Yankelovitch, Daniel, 100
Yellen, Janet, 104
yield curve, 70

Zer, Ilknur, 104, 245
Zhang Heng, 73
Zhou, Chen, 90, 134
Zigrand, Jean-Pierre, 21, 121
Zimbabwe, 183
zombie banks, 48–50
zoning, 180